REMEMBERING THE PRESENT

To my parents,
E. Jacqueline and Joseph Cassaniti

REMEMBERING THE PRESENT

Mindfulness in Buddhist Asia

J. L. CASSANITI

CORNELL UNIVERSITY PRESS
ITHACA AND LONDON

First published 2018 by Cornell University Press

Printed in the United States of America

Library of Congress Cataloging-in-Publication Data

Names: Cassaniti, Julia, author.
Title: Remembering the present : mindfulness in Buddhist Asia /
    J. L. Cassaniti.
Description: Ithaca : Cornell University Press, 2018. I Includes
    bibliographical references and index.
Identifiers: LCCN 2017052060 (print) I LCCN 2017054552 (ebook) I
    ISBN 9781501714177 (pdf) I ISBN 9781501714160 (epub/mobi) I
    ISBN 9781501707995 I ISBN 9781501707995 (cloth : alk. paper) I
    ISBN 9781501709173 (pbk. : alk. paper)
Subjects: LCSH: Buddhism—Thailand—Chiang Mai—Customs and
    practices. I Buddhism—Sri Lanka—Kandy—Customs and practices. I
    Buddhism—Burma—Mandalay—Customs and practices. I
    Mindfulness (Psychology)—Thailand—Chiang Mai. I Mindfulness
    (Psychology)—Sri Lanka—Kandy. I Mindfulness (Psychology)—
    Burma—Mandalay. I Meditation—Theravada Buddhism.
Classification: LCC BQ4960.T5 (ebook) I LCC BQ4960.T5 C37 2018
    (print) I DDC 294.3/910959—dc23
LC record available at https://lccn.loc.gov/2017052060

CONTENTS

PREFACE

As Jon Kabat-Zinn made famous in his Mindfulness-Based Stress Reduction programs at the University of Massachusetts Medical School, mindfulness can be thought of as "paying attention in a particular way: on purpose, in the present moment, and non-judgmentally" (1994, 4). Different people define mindfulness differently, but this definition and the many scholarly programs on mindfulness that have emerged alongside it offer some sustained key points about the processes and benefits of its practice. Mindfulness, it is suggested, is centrally about the present moment; it helps one to develop positive emotions; it is about empowering the self; it is practiced without moral judgment; and through its practice it helps one to be a better, healthier person. Mindfulness is often understood to draw predominantly from Buddhist thought, and especially from the Theravāda Buddhist, Pali-language term *sati*, but mindfulness in its current form can also be considered modern, scientific, and even a-religious. It is not, people will point out, necessarily a Buddhist concept at all, even if it draws so largely from the Buddhist tradition. Mindfulness is often considered a-contextual, a-cultural, more a universal capacity and disposition than an idea tied to any one time or place.

At the time that a growth of interest and a development of mindfulness as a modern and scientific concept were occurring during the past ten or fifteen years in America, I was carrying out doctoral dissertation research as a graduate student at the University of Chicago on what at first seemed to me to be a fairly different topic: the psychological anthropology of Buddhist practice in Thailand. In my research I came across mindfulness often, in the monasteries and homes of people in the small rural community I was working in the rural far north of the country. There, I realized, mindfulness is not considered to be a trendy or new idea, although in some of its more recent expressions it is considered that in Thailand too. For most people in Thailand, mindfulness is considered less of a stand-alone, a-religious concept and more of an integrated part of a large complex of Buddhist teachings, ones that are followed by more than 95 percent of the people in the country. I came across talk of mindfulness in Thailand first in my own meditation retreats in the country, and later as part of casual conversations with friends reminding themselves and each other to not "lose" one's mindfulness. In Thailand, people consider it to be a kind of mental power and health to be mindful, while lacking mindfulness is seen as unhealthy, and even dangerous. It was only later that I started to notice some of the connections mindfulness has in Thailand that seemed different from those in America. Back in Thailand, while learning about supernatural spiritual experiences across cultures as part of a comparative, collaborative project that I became involved in as a postdoctoral fellow at Stanford University, I found that people talked about mindfulness as connected to ghostly encounters and to powerful social, psychological, and even political meditative achievements. For many people in Thailand, mindfulness is understood to tie in to a kind of mental potency, or power, that is more than just a general capacity to feel happy or healthy. When one loses mindfulness, I was told, the effects of others, even supernatural others, can be felt; and on the other hand, the negative affective influences of these forces can be kept out, and controlled, when one achieves high levels of attainment.

Talk of ghosts does not usually come up in American conversations about mindfulness. Instead, science is seen to sterilize or denude the local folk understandings of what might be considered a nonscientific Buddhist past. The more I heard about mindfulness as I traveled back and forth between research trips in Thailand and the United States, the more it seemed that two parallel, though intertwined, discourses were at play. When I arrived at Washington State University as an assistant professor of psychological and medical anthropology, I decided to investigate what these differences might entail, and the meanings that people made of them in the context of their own cultural models of the person. *Remembering the Present* is the result of that investigation.

Through two years of data collection gathered from over six hundred research participants I found that the ways people understand and practice mindfulness in Southeast Asia do in many senses echo the ways that people in the United States do: in both contexts there is an emphasis on being aware in the present, on cultivating desired feelings, on accessing a kind of power or potency of practice, and on using this in a positive way to improve one's life. Yet within these general similarities I also found some significant differences, ones that I do not think have been fully recognized or explored in current contemporary Western contexts. Among some Western scholars the dominant assumption in mindfulness studies is that science is taking culture out of the picture; but instead of decontextualizing mindfulness, the Western assumptions about mindfulness and its workings and purposes may be recontextualizing it in their own new contexts. For many people in America this new contextualization works well, and there is a robust body of evidence that suggests as much. But while mindfulness is being understood in new ways, other, different, and possibly beneficial meanings can be lost in the reconstruction. People in Thailand, Myanmar (Burma), and Sri Lanka—part of a region I here call Theravāda Asia, the part of the world where Theravāda Buddhism (the "School of the Elders," one of the main branches of Buddhism) is followed by the majority of the people—told me again and again that mindfulness is not only about attending to the present but also about "remembering" it, suggesting different relationships to time; these relationships have to do with issues of affect, or emotion, as mindfulness was described as developing calmness over happiness. People feel that they access a magical, social, and political potency of the practice along with self-empowerment, suggesting a broader engagement with issues of power. I learned again and again that being aware of goodness is especially important in mindfulness, suggesting a central ethical component. And people invoked mindfulness as pointing to an alternate picture of the person, different from what I was used to at home, bringing into question issues of the self.

Attending to these meanings among people who today are practicing mindfulness within wider Buddhist contexts allows us to broaden and clarify current Western understandings that seek to encompass universal (and not only culturally bound) contexts. This in turn allows for not just the improvement of Western mindfulness but also that of mindfulness in the areas in Asia that continue to grapple with ongoing pressures of westernization and modernization. More broadly, attending to the meanings of mindfulness in contemporary Buddhist Asia, and "remembering the present" in them, can help us to better understand how all psychological concepts are made in and through, rather than apart from, the historical, power-laden, social influences of cultural practice.

ACKNOWLEDGMENTS

I would like to take this opportunity to offer thanks to the international team of researchers, informants, and colleagues who helped to create this book. *Remembering the Present* has been possible in large part because of their hard work gathering, translating, transcribing, analyzing, and sharing their thoughts on mindfulness practices in Theravada Asia. I am grateful for them all.

In Thailand, Justin Van Elsberg, a student at Washington State University, teamed up with Santi Leksakun, a student at Chiang Mai University, to assist with the Thai data collection. Additional assistance came from Dr. Somwang Kaewsufong, Thanat Chainaboon, Piyathida (Niw) Chaihung, and Bhikku Ñeyya, all of whom helped to track down texts, informants, and popular sources of mindfulness in the country. A visiting scholar position at Chiang Mai University's Department of Religion and Philosophy provided a physical and intellectual base while in the field. Apikanya (M) McCarty at Cornell University and my Mae Jaeng host cousin Nutsicha (Jaa) Nestor added valuable comments to the Thai section of the manuscript.

In Burma, Ko Soe Htet, a Burmese monk living in Bangkok, put me in touch with research assistants Kine Nyein Aye, Nyein, and Moh, who worked tirelessly to aid in the data collection, transcription, and translation process. Nyein had been a political prisoner before doing a Fulbright program in Portland, Oregon, and helped with the first group of monk interviews at Aungchanga Monastery, along with his friend Moh, a lecturer at the monastery. Kine Nyein Aye, a graduate student at Mandalay University with a passionate interest in Buddhist practice, drove around the city with me day in and day out finding people to interview, and sat with me late into the night translating and transcribing the interviews. Aye Thant and Tom Patton helped with transliteration and Burmese cultural context in the final stages of the writing.

In Sri Lanka, the research benefited from the kindness of friends and friends of friends, including Ven. Bhikkhunī Dr. W. Mawidharma, Dr. Danesh Karunanayake, Dr. Gananath Obeyesekere, Ven. Bhikkhu Chandrasana, Andrew Dicks, Bambi Chapin, Elizabeth Pearce, Sajeeva Samaranayake, Michael Fronczak, Neranjana Gunetilleke, and Barbara Dybwad, all of whom helped put together a team of excellent local researchers and informants, among them Rushma, Sabrina, Karishna, Teranga, Indika Somaratee, and Ken and Visakha Kawasaki. Jeffrey Samuels, Jasmine Obeyesekere Fernando, and Viru Gunawardana offered valuable critical suggestions to the chapter that resulted from this fieldwork.

A wonderful group of research assistants helped to organize and analyze the more than four thousand pages of data that poured in from the field during the two years of data collection and the two years of writing that followed; these include Piyawit Moonkham, Jessica McCauley, Jason Chung, Marissa Appleton, Kristell Pearson, Kelsey Gallegos, Laura Johnson, Lora Prosser, Gina Phiel, Jonny Douglas, Christopher Lanphear, and Justin Van Elsberg, who has offered a particularly significant critical eye throughout the project. A broad cohort of fellow anthropologists, psychologists, and Southeast Asia scholars added additional invaluable help in their reading and critiquing of the many versions of the manuscript as it came into being, especially my PhD adviser from the University of Chicago Richard Shweder, my postdoc adviser from Stanford Tanya Luhrmann, and colleagues and friends Steven Collins, Jocelyn Marrow, Jacob Hickman, Katherine March, Thomas Csordas, Janis Jenkins, Justin McDaniel, Adam Dedman, Felicity Aulino, Nancy Eberhardt, Rebecca Hall,

Jeannette Mageo, Matt Yoxell, Michael Chladek, Rosalyn Hansrisuk, Joel Robbins, Nishant Shahani, Uthen Mahamid, Gaewgarn Fuangtong, Thong-suk Mongkhon, and Stijn Vanderzande, among many others. I feel so lucky to be going on this intellectual journey with each of them.

The organizers and participants of a series of workshops and invited talks at which I have presented parts of the work in this book have strengthened it immeasurably with their different disciplinary and personal reflections. These include Thomas Borchert and Jeffery Samuels at the Buddhism and Ethnography Conference at the University of Vermont; Michael Herzfeld and the Department of Anthropology and Thai Studies Program at Harvard University; John Dunne and the Center for Southeast Asia at the University of Wisconsin, Madison; Steven Collins, Juliane Schober, and the Luce Foundation of the Theravada Civilizations Project; Erik Braun and the East Asia and Contemplative Sciences Centers at the University of Virginia; Webb Keane, Donald Lopez, and the Departments of Anthropology and Asian Languages and Civilizations at the University of Michigan, Ann Arbor; Jacob Hickman and the Anthropology Colloquium at Brigham Young University; Michel Desjardins and the Psychology Department at the University of Saskatchewan; Jared Lindahl, Willoughby Britton, Daniel Stuart, the Robert H. N. Ho Family Foundation for Buddhist Studies, and the American Council for Learned Societies at the Conference on Body, Emotion, and Trauma: Contemplative Practice across Cultures at Brown University; Craig Reynolds at the Thirteenth International Conference on Thai Studies in Chang Mai, Thailand; Tanya Luhrmann and the Culture and Mind Program at Stanford University; and the Cultural Anthropology with a Hint of Psychological Anthropology Reading Writing Group at Washington State University.

The Fulbright Foundation, Washington State University, and the National Science Foundation have contributed invaluable funding to this project, and a visiting fellow position at Cornell University's Southeast Asia Program (SEAP) in Ithaca, New York, aided in the final stages of writing, especially through the contributions of Thak Chaloemtiarana, Tamara Loos, Thamora Fischel, Arnika Fuhrmann, Erick White, Kamala Tiyavanich, and the Robert H. Treman-y spirit of the Kahin Center. Jim Lance, Ange Romeo-Hall, and everyone at the Cornell University Press have been fantastic to work with throughout the process, from initial idea to editorial overviews to the book's cover design and promotion. Beyond these many supports, this work has benefited most from the confidence and encouragement of my parents Jackie and Joe, and my sister and brother Jocelyn and Jarret Cassaniti.

Finally, I would like to offer special enduring thanks to the many, many people in South and Southeast Asia who have been willing to share their personal thoughts, feelings, and experiences of mindfulness with me. From an elderly female monastic in Sri Lanka, who took the time, even after she had already spent the day answering my questions, to introduce me to a newborn elephant living at her school grounds, to the head psychiatrist at the crowded government hospital in Burma who popped in between his busy rounds with patients to sit and talk thoughtfully about mental health, the fieldwork for this research project was made up of one extraordinary encounter after another. My goal has been to give voice to these many people; I hope to do justice to their kindness with this book.

Terms

Some Pali-language terms used in reference to mindfulness in Thailand, Sri Lanka, and Myanmar (Burma):[1]

anicca, dukkha, anattā—Impermanence, nonsatisfactoriness, and non-self (together referred to as the three characteristics of existence).

dhamma (dharma in Sanskrit)—Buddhist teachings, truths about the world, mental concepts.

samādhi—Concentration; sometimes used to refer to *samatha*, calming and concentration meditation.

sangha—The monastic order.

sati—Mindfulness (Thai *sati*; Burmese *thati*; Sinhalese *satiya*).

vipassanā—Insight and awareness meditation.

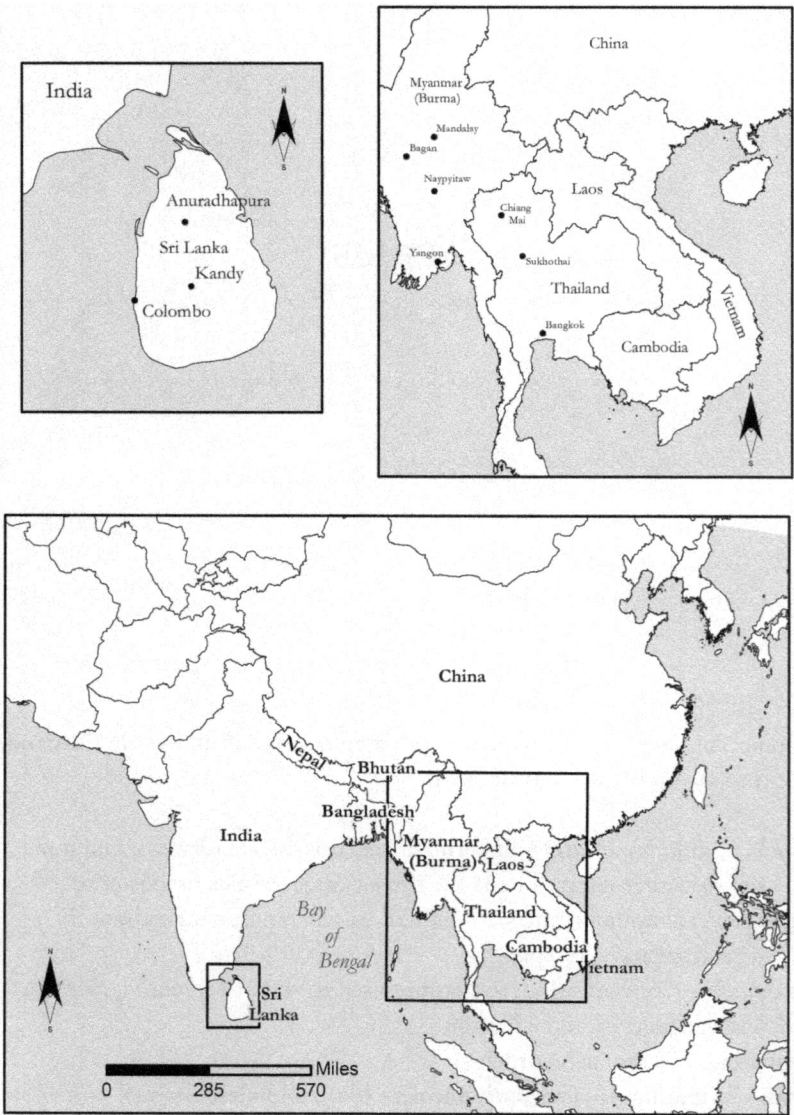

Figure 1. Study region: Sri Lanka, Thailand, and Myanmar (Burma)

Remembering the Present

INTRODUCTION

Entering a Landscape of Mindfulness

Sen appeared from the shadows of the inpatient ward of the Suan Prung Psychiatric Hospital in Chiang Mai, Thailand, where he was waiting out yet another round of electroconvulsive therapy. It was Sen's third stay at the hospital,[1] for what had turned into a prolonged, oscillating state of alcoholism-induced psychosis. Each visit had lasted a few months of the year, for each of the previous three years. For three years he had gone through a cycle of drinking, hospitalization, recovery, and then starting to drink again. Apart from his recovery after the first visit, when he came to the hospital so sick the doctors said he wouldn't live through it, he didn't seem to be improving much at all. I had stopped by to see Sen during a break from my work doing research on Buddhism and psychology in Chiang Mai, after writing about his long road to alcohol addiction and his (partial) recovery in *Living Buddhism: Mind, Self, and Emotion in a Thai Community* (2015).

The doctors called out to Sen behind the bars of the hospital ward, letting him know he had a visitor. When he came out, I saw that his skin was an almost ghostly white, peeling from the long stay and from the soap that he was allergic to. He had a vacant look, the hospital robes hanging loosely from his increasingly skeletal frame, but he was chatty, and seemed glad to see me. As we sat eating the chocolate snacks he liked, which I had sneaked in, Sen looked around and said to me in Thai, "Thi ni pen thi samrap khon thi mai mi sati"—This is the place for people who don't have mindfulness.[2]

"What do you mean?" I asked. I was surprised to hear Sen mention *sati*, or "mindfulness," to explain the reason for his being at the hospital. Sati suddenly seemed to be everywhere. The Thai-language, Pali-based Buddhist term is part of the religious language of Theravāda Buddhism and can be found as far back as in the earliest recorded teachings of the Buddha. In recent years it has become especially popular as a psychological, almost colloquial concept in Southeast Asia and around the world. Sati's Sanskrit-language equivalent, *smṛti*, is also sometimes translated as "mindfulness" in English, as are a handful of other Pali words (e.g., *sampajañña*), but sati is the most central Buddhist conceptual term to have influenced "mindfulness," an idea that Jon Kabat-Zinn and others helped to spread from their own encounters with Buddhist thought. The overlap between the terms "sati" and "mindfulness" is not perfect—and untangling some of the meanings of the Buddhist root concept is an important part of this book—but today's English term "mindfulness" draws in very large part from this Pali term. It is known wherever Theravāda Buddhism is practiced. As with Latin in many European religious settings, Pali is read and chanted formally throughout the region of Thailand, Burma, Cambodia, Laos, and Sri Lanka (which I collectively refer to as "Theravāda Asia") as the formal language of religious knowledge. Pali has also influenced hundreds if not thousands of colloquial language terms in the region. The mindfulness of "sati" as a Pali-derived, locally contextualized term provides a uniquely powerful window into the ways that social ideas and personal mental phenomena are connected in practice.

In recent years mindfulness has become a hugely prominent idea in the United States, where it is increasingly becoming integrated into clinical therapeutic techniques for mental health, investigated in neuroscientific research, and championed in spiritual and secular settings from Buddhist monasteries to primary school classrooms.[3] Often at the introductory and concluding sections of American scientific journal articles on mindfulness its Buddhist influence is referenced explicitly or implicitly in passing, but it is rarely elaborated on. Even when the Buddhist roots of the idea are discussed, they are usually referenced by indexing a kind of distant Buddhist past that mindfulness was thought to be originally tied to but has since unraveled away from.

And yet rather than existing in the past, or in someplace only of the imagination, mindfulness is very much present in contemporary Buddhist cultural contexts. Along with more extreme meditative austerities followed in the search for nirvana (in Pali *nippan*, the soteriological goal of the religion), mindfulness is found in the omnipresent monasteries of Buddhist Asia; it is a subject of training in public schools; and it is seen regularly on TV in public-service messages and commercials, in political campaigns, and in popular songs. Mindfulness is raised regularly in everyday, casual speech to refer to mental training and psychological well-being.

From a Psychiatric Hospital to the Thai Monastery

"Well, it's what's wrong with me," Sen said, as we sat on the bench at the psychiatric hospital in Chiang Mai. "I don't have any sati. My mind is blurry. I don't remember where I am." He had mentioned this in the past to explain how he felt when his mind felt lost, but this time he was telling me that it wasn't just him.

"Sati is to *yom*, to accept," I recalled a Buddhist nun at a monastery outside of town telling me, "and if you cut your sati then you don't know anything. If you cut your sati, it means you're crazy." Others had said the same: "I was so worried at one point," a villager in Sen's hometown of Mae Jaeng told me, as she related a difficult period in her life; "I was scared, it was like I lost my sati. If you lose your sati it means you're crazy." "I used to practice without a teacher," an old man told me about his own meditation practice, "and I'd get distracted. To practice sati, we need a good teacher—otherwise we'll lose our mind."

The connection between mindfulness and mental health is part of popular culture in Thailand. Even the singer Carabao, one of the most famous musicians in the country, made a well-known song called "Baa"—"Crazy"—about a man in a mental hospital. The central refrain repeats:

"I'm crazy, but it doesn't mean I'm a bad person, it's just that my mindfulness is no good!"

"So if this place is for people without sati," I asked Sen, "and if you're in here because you don't have any, well, are the doctors teaching you how to get it?"

"No," he answered. "They just give me medicine, I don't even know what kind. Sometimes the psychologist comes in and talks to me, and wants me to talk to her, but not much. I can't totally remember. . . ." Sen's memory was particularly poor that day—in the previous few weeks he had been put through a series of rounds of electric shocks, after all—but he had told me at other times too about the therapies he underwent at the hospital, from shock therapy to talk therapy to a skills-based learning project whittling wood into little dolls. Given the centrality of mindfulness and Buddhism to Sen's own understanding of why he was there, it struck me as rather conspicuously absent from the more common treatment regimens that were trying to help him deal with his problems.

The absence of mindfulness as part of a therapeutic intervention for Sen felt puzzling to me not only because of its central place in the religion that he and almost everyone else I knew in Thailand followed, but also because of its meteoric global rise in popular consciousness and medical research. Wouldn't this Buddhist idea be helpful for someone like Sen, I thought, especially when it has been gaining so much scientific backing as a useful tool for mental health? Even more puzzling was that I knew some of the doctors and other staff members at the hospital, and not only did they all follow Buddhism, but some of them were even working actively on mindfulness as part of their training, using the kind of American scientific programs that were beginning to become as popular in Thailand as they are in America.

A nurse named Ta at Sen's hospital, I had heard, was even leading a six-week mindfulness-based stress-reduction workshop for the residents and other members of the staff. As she sat in her office a few days later in one of the front buildings of the hospital, her hair cut short and her white lab coat spotless, she told me about the program.

Ta described the seminar, talking about sati as practicing being aware of the present moment in a nonjudgmental way, the bedrock teaching of mindfulness in America. She told me about exercises she had participants keep track of in notebooks at home as they trained themselves to attend to the present, and report back in their weekly sessions. "This is all so interesting," I said to Ta after a while, "but I can see your notes for it are all full of measures and instructions translated from Kabat-Zinn's English American program into Thai . . . and we know that mindfulness comes from Buddhism . . . and here we are in a Buddhist country. So what are some of the more local, religious ways of practicing mindfulness here that you integrate into your seminar?"

"Oh no," she corrected me, "mindfulness isn't about culture or even religion. Sure it comes from Buddhism, but it's something anyone can practice of any religion. It's more of a science really. It's not necessary to think of it as Buddhist to benefit from it."

I shrugged, and we talked for a while more. After I thanked her for her time, she got up to walk me out to the main gate of the hospital. As we were walking she asked why I was interested in mindfulness. I told her I was intrigued by the idea of it, and its potential to help people, and also that as a cultural anthropologist I was curious about the ways that mindfulness was understood in a Buddhist context like Thailand. I told her I was a little surprised to hear that mindfulness wasn't seen as particularly Buddhist, even in a Buddhist country.

"Oh no!" she said, laughing and correcting me again. "Actually it's *totally* a Buddhist concept! Only I don't teach it that way in the hospital because we do the program from America, and they don't teach it that way. We get our funds from there, so we follow their way . . . and, well, look at me, I'm a nurse in a hospital. If I show up teaching about mindfulness with my local clothes on, prayer beads in hand, people will think I'm crazy!"

"Crazy?" I said, laughing. "Even in a mental hospital they'd call you crazy?" She nodded, smiling, and went on:

"Everyone would start arguing about their own lineage teachings of mindfulness, their teacher's teaching, saying 'this is the right way to understand it,' 'no, this is,' and it would get complicated and we wouldn't be productive. It's simpler this way. We lose some of the meanings of the ideas, but it's easier this way."

I asked Ta about some of these meanings that were lost in the translation of the American (or "scientific") representations, and she sat down and talked for another hour about mindfulness—we were sitting at the canteen at the entrance of the hospital grounds at this point—not about its scientific methodology but about feelings of ghostly energies, abilities gained through mindfulness, even supernatural abilities like flying, and about different meditation techniques and attainments, and the purposes and ideas connected to her own conceptions and experiences. The tropical sun was beating down on the pavement just inches from our shady spot, the heat reflecting off the pavement and hitting us, rendering useless the fan on the counter. She told me about her own Buddhist lineage teacher, a woman named Mae Ying, a powerful laywoman who had taught her about the psychological power of sati: "If you practice mindfulness you can get whatever you want," Ta said, "a new house, peace . . . even super-powers, if you want. If you have a lot of mindfulness you can keep away ghosts, you can keep away the negative effects of other people." She told me about the interpersonal sociality of mindfulness, of politeness and etiquette, and about the style of mindfulness meditation she especially liked, a local technique called *yup no phong no* that emphasized super-slow walking, and said that with mindfulness developed by this means you have a kind of strength, even superhuman, that you can use to keep away negative feelings. I scribbled notes as fast as I could as she went on, having turned off the voice recorder at the end of our formal interview in the office inside. At the end she told me about some of the politics of the hospital, the way different doctors did or did not want to incorporate mindfulness into their practices there, and the ways they saw it as either acceptably "scientific" or else too "local."

Finally, she told me she had to get back to work, and as I watched her walk back into the air-conditioned office building, my head was swimming with her stories, stories that she hadn't thought to share with me in her formal interview but that suggested a whole world of mindfulness that was only tangentially connected to the hospital program. It seemed that, at least officially, she was willing to foreground an American-filtered version of mindfulness, rather than focus on the one that was more personally and affectively charged for her. I thought about how these other, more meaningful connections she suggested about mindfulness might stand to help my friend Sen—and not just Sen but others, too, even Americans, to lead healthier and more fulfilled lives.

Just what does mindfulness offer, I wondered, in an overwhelmingly Buddhist country like Thailand? I have read Buddhist *suttas* (teachings based on the words of the Buddha, called *sutras* in Sanskrit) on mindfulness, and commentaries on these suttas and commentaries on those commentaries. The suttas and the many commentaries drawn from them have been crafted in time that spans from the Buddha's own life over two thousand years ago to doctoral dissertation projects that were being written as I talked to Ta, and continue to be produced as I write this book. Mindfulness can be found throughout them.

Yet the ways that people practice mindfulness in cultural environments where Buddhism is prominent aren't usually thought of as part of the modern mindfulness tradition. They should be, however, because mindfulness is not simply an objective, acultural, unchanging concept. It is also part of how people in Buddhist countries grow up today, part of the often unspoken, assumed fabric of regular life. In these areas mindfulness is deeply felt in social worlds, as part of the "webs of significance" that Geertz (1983) pointed to over thirty years ago as representing the enmeshed structures of meaning that we live by and through. These webs are complex and increasingly global, spanning geographic regions and periods of time, but while abstract in their structural makeup, they are also personally felt and embodied in individual lives. In order for mindfulness to accommodate individuals through the lenses of particular lives, these experiences need to be explored, and their variation needs to be understood. What does mindfulness look like for people in these contexts? And how might understanding mindfulness as practiced in the lives of people in places like Thailand tell us something about how we can all live well within—and not apart from—the complexities of our own lives?

As I left the hospital that day after talking with Ta, I realized that the questions I had about mindfulness are more than just academic. Abstract ideas like mindfulness may be interesting in themselves as concepts to think with, isolated in labs or meditation rooms removed from the messiness of personal and cultural experience, but a better understanding of the concept in its local articulations has even more potential to help people— even if such understandings might at first seem complicated or, as Ta had said, "crazy."

At first, though, I didn't want to do a project on mindfulness. I didn't want to do the project even after I heard my friend Sen and so many others point to it as a source of well-being, or heard about it from interviews on religious experience in the Thai countryside, or from seeing magazines

8   *Introduction*

about it in the checkout lane of my American co-op grocery store or in psychology journals, or in the everyday kinds of passing comments about it in Thailand and the United States. The topic seemed too "hip" somehow, too "New Agey" in some way, more a fad popular with a certain kind of liberal middle-class American whiteness than with relatively shadowed, less-privileged others in the regions it was taken from. It didn't seem to be what serious scholars of Buddhism in Asia were interested in, who shunned it as much in reaction to its popularity in America as to the implicitness and integrated quality it took on in Buddhist cultural communities in Asia. I knew what an American Thai-studies anthropologist friend was talking about when I told him at a conference in Kyoto about the possibility of my new research on the topic: "Oh God," he said, "I hate mindfulness!" I was taken aback by the abruptness and extremeness of my friend's reaction, but I knew what he meant. Of all the complicated ideas in Buddhist thought and practice moving around social space, of all the ways that Buddhist ideas are connected to other ideas, mindfulness has been especially extracted and isolated as special, while at the same time, one might suggest, it leaves out other equally important ideas and becomes distorted in the process. But as I continued to ignore mindfulness in my main research on Buddhism and psychology in Thailand, I started to come across it more and more wherever I went.

An American graduate student I met at Wat Suan Dok monastery in Chiang Mai one afternoon finally made the decision to study mindfulness for me. The student was in town teaching monks how to lead mindfulness-based therapies, as part of her doctoral research in a neuropsychiatry department back home. I was aghast that she would be telling monks how to practice mindfulness, and I told her so.

"Wouldn't you want to, like, *learn* from them?" I asked.

"Well, I'm trying to create change and help people," she said in reply. "Learning from them is what anthropologists like you would do!"

I was surprised by her answer, because it seemed to me that she was saying she knew more than they did about mindfulness, and about how it could help people. It seemed to me that the monks I knew were aware of much more with regard to mindfulness than she probably suspected. When so much scientific research takes place in Western countries, the claims to scientific validity and the claims of an authority rooted in cultural, political, and economic power can overlap and become conflated.

Yet as I was thinking about the encounter over dinner with friends in Mae Jaeng that evening, I realized that the student had her own, well-informed perspectives and intentions, having learned about new therapeutic methods that combine American clinical psychological ideas with those of Buddhist teachings. She wanted to share these methods with people in Thailand, who could then combine them with their own evolving ideas about mind and health. And I realized that she was right about me, too: learning about mindfulness from people for whom it is a central and well-engrained concept, after all, *is* something that an anthropologist like me would do! To think like an anthropologist is to listen first and judge later. To pay attention to the perspective of the monks and others living within Buddhist contexts I would have to talk with them, hear from them, try to experience what they experience, and record their thoughts—not as objective "truths" about mindfulness but as sources of knowledge that might in turn help inform people in America and elsewhere who are interested in the concept as part of a larger understanding of cultural and psychological experience in the world.

Places, People, and a Research Plan

To find out about mindfulness, I wanted to seek out conversations with a wide range of people in the region and learn about mindfulness in a multiplicity of social environments. I would aim for a balance of different perspectives, from learned monks to countryside villagers to local health care professionals. Most of the work would necessarily take place in Thailand, as Thailand has been a social center of Theravāda Buddhist practice for hundreds of years and is where I have spent fifteen years studying the language and making contacts. I would be able to gather the richest data there, from monks, meditation retreats, and social and health care centers. For comparison, I decided to go to Burma and Sri Lanka too, where Buddhism is also practiced by the majority of the population, and where people would have intriguing perspectives to complement those from the main field site in Thailand. People in Thailand (as elsewhere) point to Burma as the place where the practice of Buddhism is especially integrated into everyday life, and where modern forms of meditation developed. People in

Thailand and Burma (as elsewhere) point to Sri Lanka as a place where the knowledge of Buddhism is especially strong, in light of its historical connections as the birthplace of Theravāda Buddhism. The regional comparisons would permit the tracing of some of the regional movements of ideas about mindfulness around the Indian Ocean, in a region that the scholar Anne Blackburn has referred to historically as "Pāli-Land" (2010). It would show variation as well as continuities, so that practices in Thailand would not become potentially glossed as representative of a general "East." Thailand, Burma, and Sri Lanka make up a layered religious and cultural space where Pali-language-based Theravāda Buddhism thrives today and where mindfulness in its Pali root of *sati* is a common part of everyday life.

In relating the practices of mindfulness in only Thailand, Burma, and Sri Lanka, however, I do not mean to suggest that Theravāda Buddhism is the only kind of Buddhism, or that these three countries are the only places in Southeast Asian where Theravāda Buddhism is practiced. People in Laos and Cambodia are predominantly Theravādan as well, along with followers around the world, and politically Sri Lanka is not a part of the region called Southeast Asia. Cambodia and Laos also have much to offer a study on mindfulness, as do Tibet, China, Korea, Japan, and other places across Asia where mindfulness is practiced in Buddhist contexts outside the Theravāda world. The majority of Buddhist scholarship on mindfulness, however, draws from early Buddhist textual accounts that are most closely aligned with the Theravāda school, and from *sati* as the central term through which mindfulness is translated into English (Rhys Davids 1881; Wilson 2013, 15). For practical reasons of time and other resources I limited the focus of the present research to the study of sati in Thailand, Burma, and Sri Lanka, but future ethnographic and textual research on mindfulness in Cambodia and Laos, as well as across Asia and in other cultural contexts (Buddhist and otherwise), would be a very fruitful addition to the findings of this book.

I chose the northern provincial capital of Chiang Mai to gather the Thai data, and the cities of Kandy in Sri Lanka and Mandalay in Burma for the regional comparisons. Each of these three cities is connected to international communities and movements of knowledge, but each is also not so central and unrepresentative of the rest of its country as the respective metropolitan capitals of Bangkok, Colombo, and Yangon (once known as Rangoon, though now replaced as the national capital by Nay-pyidaw) would be. I already knew Chiang Mai well from my years of research there, and Kandy and Mandalay are similar to Chiang Mai in many ways, not only in size but also in their cultural history as old capitals of nation-states and in their "coolness" factors, hip with both nationals and foreigners, so they would serve as good parallel comparisons. In addition to learning from people in the cities, I would also collect information from people in the nearby countryside, to see similarities and differences in urban and rural settings.

Along with gathering data from relatively similar kinds of social environments in each of the three countries, I wanted to be systematic too in speaking with similar groups of people in each place, so that the results would reflect a comparable mix of perspectives. I would start out with ordained monastics, but I didn't want to learn about mindfulness only from them. Scholar monks, meditative monks, and Buddhist studies scholars would know the most about mindfulness in many ways, connected as they are to the textual and meditative teachings of the religion that spawned the movement, and to the hierarchically oriented relationships with the sangha, the broader community of Buddhist followers. Philosophical textual analyses that I could read at home could offer sophisticated accounts of mindfulness in the Buddhist suttas and commentaries, and many people would talk about them in their discussions.[4] But I was interested not only in patterns of religious and textual authority but also in how regular people living in cultures so heavily influenced by Buddhist teachings thought and felt about mindfulness. The ways that a child in a Thai countryside village learns about mindfulness from a teacher at school, or a monk does in a remote monastery in Myanmar, or a psychiatrist in a hospital in Sri Lanka, are all connected explicitly or implicitly to ancient texts, transformed and reinterpreted and constructed over time as they are to reflect the interests of people living today. Scholars often look to the elites and virtuosos of a religion for guidance, but I had learned from previous work (Cassaniti 2015c, 2006) that while such people may have more-refined thoughts on the subject than non-elites tend to have, non-elite Buddhists are especially well positioned to inform us about the way that the religion's ideas can be practically put into use in the context of non-ordained social life.

Methodology: Five Groups, Three Countries, Six Hundred People

In the end I chose to gather data from five groups in each of the three countries: (1) a group of monks at a local center of Buddhist learning (usually a monastery), (2) a second group of monks at a different monastic center (to get a sense of the similarity and difference of monastic teachings on mindfulness and not depend on just one lineage), (3) a group of students at the local university (who weren't explicitly studying Buddhism), (4) a group of psychiatric hospital staff members working in the local psychiatric treatment facility in each location, and (5) a group of rural villagers (including some rural monks) living for the most part outside the main city center. For each group, ten people in each location were interviewed at length, and written questionnaires were gathered from at least thirty more.

TABLE 1. Sites of each sample group in each location

Research sites	Chiang Mai, Thailand	Kandy, Sri Lanka	Mandalay, Burma
Monks group #1	Suan Dok Monastery	SIBA (Sri Lanka International Buddhist Academy)	Aungchanga Monastery
Monks group #2	Chedi Luang Monastery	Chandrasana's Kandy monasteries*	Intensity Language Institute for Monks*
University students	Chiang Mai University	The University of Peradeniya	Mandalay University
Psychiatric hospital staff	Suan Prung Psychiatric Hospital	Kandy Hospital's psychiatric ward*	Government psychiatric hospital and Aye Mya Nadi private mental health clinic
Villagers	Mae Jaeng	Kandy surroundings	Yekyi village in Patheingyi township

* Surveys from monks group #2 in Burma were collected from the Maha Gandharaong Monastery in addition to the Intensity Language Institute (because of too few respondents at Intensity to make up the thirty); four of the monks group #2 interviews in Sri Lanka were gathered from scholar monks at Colombo University. For the hospital site in Sri Lanka, surveys were collected from general psychiatric staff in addition to mental health specialists (owing to too few respondents in the target group); surveys were similarly supplemented in Mandalay at a private general hospital.

A semi-structured interview protocol was designed to be fairly open-ended topically, but also to be systematic for the purposes of comparison. The questions invited respondents to discuss the meanings, everyday experiences, religious and cultural associations, and purposes of mindfulness in their own lives. I had spent the previous summer conducting preliminary research for the project as a visiting fellow in the Department of Religion and Philosophy at Chiang Mai University, gathering ideas with the help of Dr. Somwang Kaewsufong and Justin Van Elsberg, an American student who had come along to the field. At that time we had spoken with a broad range of people about mindfulness, and from their discussions thought about what kinds of questions would yield the kind of insights into mindfulness and its meanings that would be useful to put into conversation with Buddhist thought, social life, and psychological science. After beginning with general demographic data, we asked the fourteen questions below:

MINDFULNESS INTERVIEW QUESTIONS

1. In your view what is mindfulness (sati)? How would you define it?
2. Do you remember how/where you first learned about mindfulness?
3. What did your parents teach you about mindfulness? What did your teachers teach?
4. Can you tell us about a specific time or a situation when you didn't have mindfulness? Why did you not in that situation?
5. Can you tell us about a specific time or a situation when you had more mindfulness than usual? Why did you in that situation?
6. Do you feel that mindfulness is related to supernatural powers or local spirit practices? If so, how?
7. Do you know what non-self (*anattā*) is? Do you think that mindfulness is connected/related to ideas about non-self? How?
8. How does one gain mindfulness? What is the goal of having it?
9. Do you think people of other religions can practice sati?
10. Do you think that doctors (e.g., psychologists) should teach about mindfulness in their work? How?
11. Has the idea of mindfulness changed over time, or has it stayed the same? How so?

12. Do you think people from all places will have the same ideas about mindfulness?
13. How do you feel about people in America learning about mindfulness? Are there aspects of Buddhism that you think people in America might want to learn about to understand mindfulness better?
14. Do you have any other thoughts or questions for us about this project?

For each group of people the same questions were asked, translated into the three different dominant languages of the region. Along with the particular groups of people interviewed, the issue of language is important, because asking questions in English and gathering data from only those who could speak it would impose and privilege English categories of thought. I wanted the interviews to take place in the local languages of each area, to gather thoughts framed in people's own terms. The interviews would be recorded, transcribed in the language they were spoken in, then translated and transcribed into English; the questionnaires would also be handed out in the local languages, asking people questions with options they could choose from or write in. This would entail much more work than doing the interviews in English or translating them in situ at the time of the interview, but it would also enable more locally meaningful discussions on mindfulness than a preconceived English-language concept would allow. My research assistants and I conducted these interviews in Thailand, and I trained research assistants to help me carry out and then go over each interview in Burma and Sri Lanka.

With these places, people, and research questions in mind, we set out on a journey to learn about the mindfulness practices of people living in the countries of Theravāda Asia. The following chapters are the account of what we found during this journey over the course of that year, and during four periods of less-structured ethnographic research in the four years before and afterward. In the end, over six thousand pages of interview and questionnaire material were collected, along with over one thousand pages more of observations and experiences recorded in field notes. In addition to the informal conversations, formal interviews, and questionnaires, I also practiced the kinds of teachings I had been learning about for more firsthand knowledge, taking part in meditation retreats in order to place the ideas being offered even further into the context of what it feels like to live them.

In telling the story of mindfulness in practice, the first-person narratives of people living in the region are put to the fore, through select representative accounts that illustrate how mindfulness is made meaningful in individual lives. I refer to third-person accounts almost exclusively when they are brought up by people in the field. It has been tempting to include much more of these third-person sources, as so much has been written on mindfulness, and because people often told me I would learn a lot from reading them. Canonical texts are brought up when they are referred to by my interlocutors, but in the end I have chosen to let the contemporary experience of my informants speak, with their own words and practices making up the core of *Remembering the Present*. The specific textual teachings referred to about mindfulness are thus relegated to the background. The people and their personal interpretations are the stars of this book.

Results: The TAPES of Mindfulness

Most of the findings of *Remembering the Present* are drawn out through the richly personal, socially meaningful, and culturally contextual narrative stories that make up the following chapters. Beyond them, though, I found mindfulness in Theravāda Asia to be tied to some general shared ideas about the mind, and about our culturally embedded relationship to the world. The ideas about mindfulness in Theravāda Asia suggest ontological and therapeutic orientations to mental processes that appear to be quite different from those suggested by contemporary globalized psychological research. Along with the larger cultural contextual findings about the role of mindfulness in mental life, I encountered five domains of mindfulness across Theravāda Asia that, in their articulation, contrast with how mindfulness is often understood in the United States and in other "Western" contexts.[5] I call these domains the "TAPES" of mindfulness. What I refer to as the TAPES of mindfulness are associations to mental processes that we may have when we think about the concept, assumptions about how the mind works and what a good life looks like. These TAPES of mindfulness run through our heads as orienting guides for engaging with the world around us. They can be thought of as mnemonic scripts and cognitive schemas (Strauss and Quinn 1997;

D'Andrade 2001) that work as the mental "mix tapes" (or in today's parlance, playlists) of ideas that we cycle through and play back for ourselves as we encounter everyday experience. They are the stories we run through our minds, looped and played over and over again to develop through subtly changing and reinforcing iterations of practice (Seligman and Kirmayer 2008). Different cultural contexts have different, varied versions of these "mix tapes" of associations of mindfulness about ways of living and thinking and being in the world. Broadly, the TAPES of mindfulness refer to

- T—Temporality
- A—Affect
- P—Power
- E—Ethics
- S—Selfhood

While these are not the only associations that mindfulness has to mental processes, they are especially central and powerfully influential in understanding how mindfulness is practiced globally today. In many of the mindfulness programs currently popular in North America, Europe, and other regions that can be thought of under the umbrella term of the "West," these TAPES share some general characteristics—characteristics that are often assumed to be universal. Drawing from the popular definition of mindfulness as "paying attention to something in a particular way: on purpose, in the present moment, and non-judgmentally" (Kabat-Zinn 1994, 4), as well as from empirical data I gathered from 125 Americans in the Pacific Northwest, and from the published scholarship of many others (e.g., Brown and Ryan 2003; Praissman 2008; Grossman et al. 2004), the dominant associations of the TAPES of mindfulness in the West suggest

- T—Temporality: The importance of attention to the "now" as a present moment of awareness in time
- A—Affect: The development of positive feelings of happiness and contentment
- P—Power: A method for one's self-empowerment and self-care
- E—Ethics: A nonjudgmental, nonmoralistic orientation to immediate action
- S—Selfhood: The realization of who you are, and can be

Each of these qualities in the TAPES of mindfulness points to certain assumptions about the way our minds can and should look. They are assumptions that are often taken to be universal, a-cultural, and a-religious, transcending time and space. They are powerful, and powerfully motivating, factors in the global mindfulness movement. And yet I found that each is quite local and variable in culture.

In an important sense these associations are part of the ways that mindfulness plays out not just in the "West" but in Southeast Asia also. Yet along with what could be considered some generally similar orientations, I found a different set of dominant associations for each of them. These differences point to what can be thought of as the Theravāda Asian associations in the TAPES of mindfulness:

TABLE 2. Theravāda Asian associations in the TAPES of mindfulness

The "TAPES" of mindfulness in culture	American (or "Western") mindfulness	Theravāda Asian (or "Eastern") mindfulness
Temporality	*The "now" as a present moment of awareness in time*	*The past as implicated in attending to change over time* • Mindfulness speaks to a connection between the past and the present, one that emphasizes the role of memory in present-moment awareness, and which may point to cultural variations in conceptualizations of the passing of time.
Affect	*The development of positive feelings of happiness and contentment*	*Calm, non-"emotional" feelings developed and aspired to through affective nonattachment* • Mindfulness reveals a local model of the construction of feelings in which attitudes become implicated in the personal response to sensation through an awareness of change, with ideal affective states that revolve around calmness and nonattachment.
Power	*A method for one's self-empowerment and self-care*	*Influence and control over one's own and others' experiences through religious and social potency* • Mindfulness is understood to connect to psychological power accessed and leveraged for the purpose of not only one's own mental health but also for social influence, including supernatural, political, and medical sway, along with local and global movements of authoritative voices about the role of cultural concepts in scientific practices.

(Continued)

TABLE 2. *(Continued)*

The "TAPES" of mindfulness in culture	American (or "Western") mindfulness	Theravāda Asian (or "Eastern") mindfulness
Ethics	*Nonjudgmental, nonmoralistic orientation to immediate action*	*Moral action as deeply inscribed within its development, practice, and effects* • Mindfulness suggests moral goodness as a foundational component for its development, a vital part in one's experience of it, and a direct effect of its practice.
Selfhood	*The realization of who you are, and can be*	*The realization of a non-stable, permeable, de-centered self* • Mindfulness suggests there to be no core person at the center of one's experiences, but rather an always transient, interpersonally connected self, evoking a model of mind that is impermanent, interpersonal, and susceptible to wandering off and coming back again.

The following chapters demonstrate how these Theravāda Asian TAPES, of temporality, affect, power, ethics, and selfhood, play out for people in the region in ways that are different from how they are usually understood in the United States.

There is a good deal of variation in these TAPES of mindfulness within and not just outside Theravāda Asia, and uncovering the variation is one of the goals of this book. And while there are general trends of the TAPES in the region, they are not in binary opposition to separate, "Western" ones. Cultural contexts do not exist in isolation from each other: there is a good deal of overlap, movement, and blurred boundaries between the "Western" and "Eastern" perspectives. Attending to these historico-cultural trajectories is to suggest less that mindfulness is static in time and space, and more that mindfulness is situated in a complex global map of power-laden movements of knowledge, and of epistemological suppositions about what that knowledge looks like.

Through the examination of these TAPES in mindfulness in Theravāda Asia we can better understand the complex role that culture plays in mindfulness's meanings, practices, and purposes. This knowledge can help us better understand not only mindfulness itself but also the wider mechanisms at work in the complex co-construction of mental processes and social context. It suggests how we can more fully develop the potential of mindfulness, and other cultural concepts like it, for the benefit of pluralistic global (and not monistically globalized) health. What we can learn from studying mindfulness in Southeast Asia is that the way one thinks about the mind matters. I found that people who follow Buddhism in Southeast Asia see the mind as an intentional agent that, through training, changes what it encounters. Maybe we can all benefit from that.

Part I

Thailand

1

Monks' Mindfulness

Phra Thēp: Yoking the Buffalo to the Post

I had seen Phra Thēp in Mae Jaeng before, as he walked slowly by in front of my friend Sen's family home near the main intersection of town. I didn't know where he was lodging, or anything about him, but from his sparse belongings and slightly dirtier and darker robes than the bright orange ones worn at the local monastery I could tell that he was a *thudong* monastic, a wandering forest monk who travels the country by foot and is often the solitary temporary resident of remote countryside monasteries. Instead of being seen as lowly or unsophisticated for their poor and itinerant lifestyle, *thudong* monks are highly admired in Thailand. There is a shared sense that one doesn't necessarily need book learning to deeply experience Buddhist teachings; instead, an itinerant lifestyle is itself a source of social capital in contemporary Thai culture. *Thudong* monks are often seen as even more admirable than those monks who are more engaged in the "corruptible" relations of social life. In *Forest Recollections: Wandering Monks in Twentieth-Century Thailand*, Kamala Tiyavanich (1997) describes the modern emergence of this ascetic social category, suggesting that the current position of reverence that *thudong* monks in Thailand hold is due largely to a rapidly modernizing contemporary society, one in which people yearn for what they imagine as a traditional Buddhist past to belong to. Rather than dying out, or being a cultural holdover of an older era, the movement is steady and growing. *Thudong* monks can be seen passing through rural towns like Mae Jaeng fairly regularly, a satchel over their shoulders, an orange umbrella in hand, with a slow, mindful gait, walking by homes and businesses in worn sandals or with no shoes at all.

A rural monastic *thudong* monk like the one I saw in front of Sen's house, I thought, living outside the formal national education system of Thailand, seemed like a good place to start my journey into lived mindfulness. Such a monk might be able to offer some personal and perhaps less formulaic accounts of mindfulness than a more mainstream monk might offer in the larger, more institutionally embedded cities.

I was staying with Sen's family at the time, visiting old friends and informants while Sen was at the psychiatric hospital. Sen's younger brother Noi was staring at the computer as usual the afternoon I decided to track down a forest monk. Noi was listening to music and switching between video games and emoji-filled chats with his friends on Facebook, when I asked him to help.

"Noi," I said, "if you're not doing anything, come interview some monks about mindfulness with me." Noi had graduated from high school a few months earlier and was waiting for his visa to get approved before moving to Sydney to work and study, as part of his parents' attempt to help him avoid the lifestyle that had befallen his brother Sen. As his symbolic older sister, I wanted to offer him a few more religious experiences before he left, as I imagined he might have a hard time seeking out a Thai Buddhist monastic community in his new country.

"Mindfulness? Mindfulness is just, like, obvious," he said, as we got on one of the family's old motorcycles and drove out toward the hills on the edge of town to find a *thudong* monk. "It's just instinct," he went on, though he elaborated only a little. He had long learned to begrudgingly humor me, the curious foreigner who had started staying at his house years before. "It's just, like, something you have, the thing to remember, to be good."

At nineteen years old, Noi had already been a novice Buddhist monk twice: once for a few days when he was very young, to honor a relative's death, and once for a few months when he was eleven, at a kind of Buddhist "summer camp" during vacation, with ninety-nine other classmates from school. Noi wasn't particularly interested in Buddhism any more than the next person, but he went to the neighborhood monastery like everyone else to make merit and practice the teachings when his parents told him to. He had learned about mindfulness at the monastery and in school, and nodded when I asked if he knew about it, but smiled sheepishly and shook his head when I asked if he remembered any of the books he had read about it during his short ordination.

I turned our motorcycle up a dirt path at the edge of a rice field, where the valley meets the hills, and slowly wound us up the road, wobbling around the stones and gullies formed by the rivulets of the rainy season, until we got to the top. We parked our bike and hesitantly approached the small cluster of structures that made up the monastery. The place was silent, and the base of the monastery's stupa was covered in hundreds of small pieces of mirrored glass, distorting our faces as we walked past. At first we thought the monastery was empty; there was no one around the stupa or the meditation hall, only a few dogs sleeping in the shade. But we heard the sounds of a transistor radio coming out of a little cabin-like building (*kuti*) to the side of the structures, and a minute later an old monk appeared at the door, blinking in the sunlight. It was Phra Thēp.

The monk looked a little befuddled as we approached, no doubt wondering what a foreigner and a local teenager from down in the valley would want with him.

"We're here to ask you some questions about mindfulness," I offered hesitantly, as we raised our hands palms together near our foreheads to greet him in the formal *wai*, a sign of respect in the country, and lowered our heads. "Might you be willing to speak with us for a bit?" The monk motioned for us to sit down at the table.

"Oh, mindfulness is very well known," he said. "And it's very interesting. It reflects the direct teaching of the Buddha. Meditation begins with mindfulness. It's the nature of humankind." He paused to offer us water

and put his glasses on in an unhurried way, and told us about his experience with sati.

Phra Thēp was sixty years old. He had been a monk for the past seven
of those years.

"It was so busy," he said, explaining why he left his job as a taxi driver
in Bangkok to ordain and move to the countryside. "I started going to a
monastery in Nontaburi near where I lived, and the master there taught
me about meditation. I'd always been interested in Buddhism, so I went
there more and more. I grew tired of driving the taxi. And then my parents
died. I'm the youngest child, and now only one sibling is left. I started
thinking how I wouldn't live forever, and I decided to change my life. It's
peaceful here. Quiet."

Like Noi and Phra Thēp, virtually all Buddhist males in Thailand
ordain as a monk at some point in their lives. This was not Phra Thēp's
first time being ordained, either, though it was his longest. Most monks
in Thailand undergo temporary ordination, which means that the time
during which they retain their monk status may last anywhere from a few
hours to a lifetime (unlike in, for instance, Sri Lanka, where the ideal if
not always the practice is for monks to ordain for life). Most ordain for
a few months or a few years and then disrobe to reenter lay social life,
having gone through what is considered a kind of "morality injection" of
Buddhist teachings, although some stay on for much longer. The reasons
for ordination are many; actively working to be the aspirational embodiment of the Buddha's teaching is only the most general of them. Many
novice monks ordain as children to access less-expensive schooling than
in the institutional public system or, as in the case of Phra Thēp, ordain
when older, after living in the world as adults and becoming disillusioned
with it. Only two of the Buddhist men of the many hundreds I've met in
Thailand have never been monks. One of the two was an old man covered in traditional protective tattoos whom I came across in a rural area
in the far north of the country, who had walked over to Mae Jaeng from
Burma when he was young and never obtained a national identity card.
The other was Sen—and even Sen, I found out later from his mother, had
been ordained for a few days as a child. The prevalence of ordination for
virtually all males means that almost a full half of the people in the Kingdom of Thailand have spent time as Buddhist monks. Virtually everyone
among the country's 95 percent Buddhist population visits these monks

at the more than thirty thousand monasteries in the country to practice the Buddhist religion. For a small country of approximately sixty million people, this is a very high number of monasteries.[1] Even sitting with Phra Thēp at the mountaintop, I could see dozens of monasteries sparkling in the valley below us.

Phra Thēp did not remember his parents teaching him much about mindfulness, but he knew it was always around when he was growing up. "Especially at the monastery that I went to near my home when I was younger," he told us; "I learned about it there. And, of course, I learned about it from driving the taxi! It's so crowded and chaotic driving around, and it's easy to lose mindfulness, but it's so dangerous not to have it, especially when you're driving! That's why people always say to themselves before they start the engine, 'Remember to have mindfulness!'"

The monastery above Mae Jaeng was a far cry from that earlier life, Phra Thēp said. "When I was driving around everywhere in traffic it was easy for my mind to get lost, but you have to focus!" He wasn't as interested in talking about that part of his life with us, though. He was more interested in talking about his life now as a monk, and mindfulness as part of it.

"But what is mindfulness, exactly?" I asked, speaking in Thai and using, as he did, the Pali word *sati*. I wanted a definition for mindfulness, but when I asked for one, I couldn't use the word "mindfulness" directly, of course, because like virtually everyone else I interviewed in Thailand, Phra Thēp didn't know English. "How would you define it? What does it mean to have it?"

"Oh," Phra Thēp answered without hesitation, "It's *raluk dai*—to be able to recollect." Recollection suggests an intriguing link to memory, or remembering, that isn't usually brought up in English-language definitions of the term. *Raluk dai* can also be translated as "to bring to mind." He added another short definition, too: "And it's to know the body and mind." Here he used the words "*ru tua.*" The word *ru* is fairly straightforward: it means "to know." Translating *tua* is much more complicated: it refers to one's corporeal body, and also to a kind of mental sense of personhood. To *ru tua* means to be conscious of one's being in space.

Raluk dai and *ru tua* are the most common descriptions of mindfulness in Thailand. They were regularly offered, and not just by monks but by over two-thirds of all 150 people I gathered data from in the country.[2]

Before repeating *raluk dai* and *ru tua* a second time, Phra Thēp added one more word, speaking in a cadence as if memorized from a chant: "*sati-sampajañña*," he said, combining *sati* with the Pali word *sampajañña*, or "awareness."

"Sati is like this robe here," he explained. He motioned to the faded orange cloth wrapped around his body. "Sometimes the cloth sways. The mind is like that. Mindfulness keeps the mind together. It's the same for a baby rocking in a cradle. If you rock the cradle too much, the baby cries.

"Or, imagine taking a photo," he went on: "If our hands are shaking, the photo won't be clear. But if we have sati, our hands will be calm, and we'll have a nice picture." He told us that mindfulness is what saves us from having something that is commonly called a "monkey mind." "Our minds are like that of a monkey," he said, "because we think of this, we think of that. Sati is the thing that pulls the mind back. It recollects the mind."[3]

Recollection implies the involvement of memory, but it is not only (or always) the past that is being pulled back, or re-collected. It is seen as a kind of drawing in, a bringing "back" or "remembering" the present, one that can incorporate memory but isn't squarely of it.

Phra Thēp's analogies helped me relate to the experiences that he had that sometimes seemed so different from those of other, ordinary laypeople. I was all too familiar with the feeling of sitting down at my computer to work, only to find myself mindlessly moving from checking Facebook to reading an article a friend had posted there to checking out a pop culture reference in the article and then somehow going to get a snack—it was only when I remembered or "recalled" my mind back from the distraction that I would return to work, as if I were forcefully pulling my mind back to a post. This work of recollection, for Phra Thēp, was what he did almost all the time while he was living at the monastery up on the hill. He practiced bringing back the mind.

As a monk, Phra Thēp followed a fairly strict code of conduct about how to behave, and what to do and not do in following this project of mindfulness. Among the many codes of moral behavior that he followed, he adhered to the 10 precepts that are the best known among the 227 practices laid out in the extensive texts of the *vinaya*, the monastic standards for comportment that he and all (Theravādan) monks follow. These precepts and many others require Phra Thēp and all other monks in Thailand and elsewhere to refrain from, among other things,

1. Killing
2. Stealing
3. Engaging in sexual behavior
4. Lying
5. Taking intoxicants
6. Taking food at inappropriate times
7. Dancing, singing, or attending entertainment programs
8. Wearing perfume, cosmetics, or other decorative accessories
9. Sitting on high chairs or sleeping on soft, luxurious beds
10. Accepting money

While fully ordained monks must follow many more directives beyond these, novice monks follow these ten in particular, and lay members of the public often try to follow especially the first five of them, changing the refraining from all sexual behavior to only sexual *mis*behavior, and with other less strict interpretations. At times of heightened religious practice, including the yearly three-month rainy season, laypeople take on more or follow the five more strictly. The precepts, though emblematic of the monkhood as a whole, are interpreted in different ways by different people at different times following different Buddhist traditions. I have often seen monks handle money, and have come across novices listening to pop music, both of which in some interpretations of the codes are forbidden. But while there is some degree of flexibility in practice in all of them, they are standard in principle.

"It's really at the level of the precepts that I make my mindfulness," Phra Thēp tells Noi and me as we sit at the table at the monastery above Mae Jaeng. "The precepts are like discipline. They are the method for making me mentally healthy. Keeping the precepts allows for concentration to arise, and from there wisdom follows. It's like a chain. It's like three friends together who don't separate: the precepts, concentration, and wisdom." In raising these three "friends" of Buddhism—moral behavior, concentration, and wisdom—Phra Thēp was referring in broad terms to the Eightfold Path, the principal practical track set out by the Buddha for people to follow on their way to the enlightenment of *nippan*, nirvana.

Morality, concentration, and wisdom are well known in Thailand as making up the components of the Eightfold Path, a guide for mental development that is the fourth of what is known throughout the Buddhist world as the Four Noble Truths, the main teachings of the Buddha.[4] The eight points on the Eightfold Path indicate different aspects of this focus on morality, concentration, and wisdom, and the seventh of them is *sammā sati*, or "right mindfulness." "Really we have to use all the teachings to think carefully, and develop wisdom," Phra Thēp says. "But really it begins with the precepts."

The precepts are the basis for allowing mindfulness to develop, he tells us. But he also relates how he reminded himself of mindfulness and actively worked to develop it not necessarily only during some special "morality" time, but through the regular activities he takes part in in the many moments between waking up and falling asleep: "It's just what I do every day," he says simply.

Phra Thēp's daily schedule, like that of most monks, is fairly routine. He rises each day at 4:30 a.m.—a typical hour for monks—and performs the *tham wat chao*, "making the monastery in the morning," for a period of somewhere between a few minutes and an hour, meditating and chanting in Pali, and cleaning the monastery grounds. Almost all monks in the country, not only the forest monks like Phra Thēp, take part in this and perform it again in the evening as *tham wat yen*. A young monk I once spoke with in Chiang Mai repeated an only slightly modified version of Phra Thēp's description of a typical monastic routine, speaking of the rigidity as well as the flexibility of the practice: "Around every morning we'll wake up at four thirty and start to chant, and then practice meditation for at least thirty minutes . . . and the evening session normally will be longer, for an hour, because we have more time, but it also depends on each monk, as they might have to do other errands."

After the *tham wat chao* it's time to get prepared for the day: as the sun is rising, most monks walk around the neighborhood by their monastery for the ritual alms round (called *binthabat* in Thai, *piṇḍapāta* in Pali), to gather the morning meal from laypeople, who come out of their house and kneel on the ground, the monks offering them blessings in the form of Pali chants as people place rice and other items in their bowls. My host family in Mae Jaeng had brought me with them many times in the early, misty mornings to make these offerings, where we heard terms like *anicca* (impermanence) and *sati* in the chants. As a *thudong* monk, Phra Thēp goes on the formal alms round less often than the relatively more stationary monks in town. When he doesn't walk through the village, a boy from the Mae Jaeng valley comes up to bring him food. After the ritual of the morning meal, Phra Thēp, like other monks, rests and engages in studying, meditation, cleaning the grounds, or leaving the monastery to perform ceremonies for people in the community. Mindfulness is part of all this. The second, and final, meal takes place at 11:30 each morning: monks in Thailand take the sixth precept (of refraining from eating at inappropriate times) to mean eating no solid food after noon. The monastery that Phra Thēp was staying in is especially quiet during the day, because of its remoteness from the villages in the valley, but most monasteries are also quiet, especially during the heat of the midday, when even the cats and dogs that people leave behind because they know the monks will look after them take a nap. Sometimes in the mornings and afternoons laypeople come to the monasteries and kneel before the monks, offering them monetary donations, toiletries and other supplies in a ritualized activity of making merit. This is thought to help them practice the dhamma and gain positive karma, all within a religious system that emphasizes the creation and inevitable results of ethical intentionality thought to be gathered over many lifetimes. In the more remote monasteries in the hills there are often no visitors at all. Phra Thēp, like almost all other monastics of the Theravāda Buddhist world, goes to sleep soon after the sun sets, around 8 or 9 p.m.

In saying that practicing mindfulness is in essence what he does every day, Phra Thēp is referring to the common ideal of all these activities a monk participates in, all of which are thought of as meditation. I ask Phra Thēp to be more specific about how he practices mindfulness in these activities, and he tells us it is part of when he wakes up early to chant and sit in meditation, and when he is eating at sunrise, and walking in the village to find his food. It's when he is having his midday meal, and repairing materials at the monastery or reading, and when he chants and meditates again before going to bed. "When I'm sitting doing meditation and chanting before I sleep, it's a time I have a lot of sati. Or when I do meditation before I eat, or in the really early morning. When I practice mindfulness in this way, I can stabilize myself."

"But how?" I ask. "How do you do that?" Meditation is a peaceful process, but it is also a notoriously difficult one, full of strife and struggle, especially in early training but even too in later practice. What Phra Thēp was saying sounded simple, but I knew that it wasn't.

"Well, for example, I'll focus on the point between my eyebrows," he explains: "That way, even if there are noises outside, I'm not bothered. With a mind stable with sati I'm not interested in those sounds." He pauses and continues, laughing, "Though if there's a really big noise outside, my mind will go out and search for it—and that's called losing sati!"

"What about when you're not sitting?" I ask. "How do you practice it then?" "Well, like in walking meditation," he says. "And also just in regular walking. Like, let's say I'm down in the valley"—he motions to the roofs and fields of Mae Jaeng below us. "If I'm near town, I'll go on *binthabat* in the mornings, and when I'm walking, I need to have mindfulness. When I walk, I say to myself, '*phut-tho, phut-tho*,' breathing in and out to keep my mind with me. Because sometimes when I'm walking, my

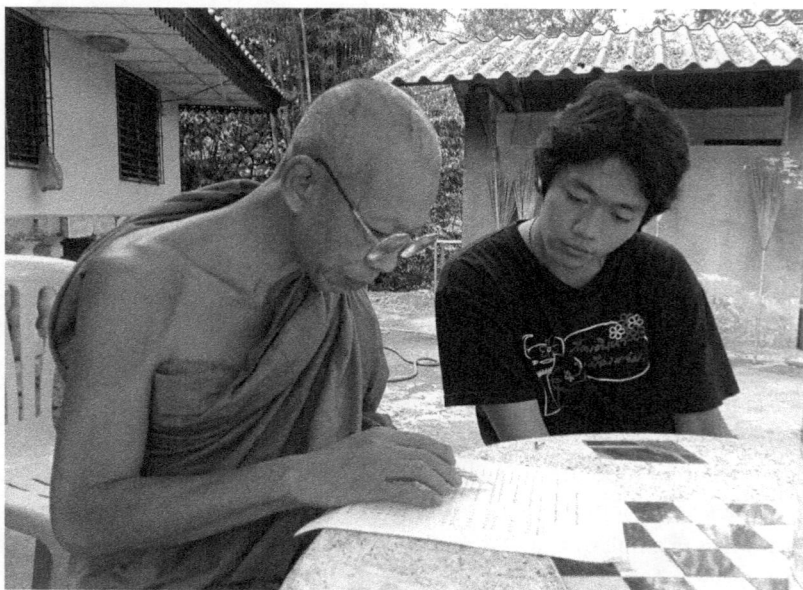

Figure 2. A monk discusses mindfulness at a remote hilltop monastery in Northern Thailand. Photo by J. L. Cassaniti.

mind is lost. I'll be thinking about something else, but I can pull it back again and start again. So many times I've lost my sati! But I can rein it in this way."

As he speaks, I can feel the mood slow down at our table, the breeze at the hilltop spot and the shade from the trees above us keeping us cool. Noi is listening quietly and asking Phra Thēp to elaborate or clarify from time to time as he talks, motioning for me to write down something or spell something a certain way.

Phra Thēp's preferred practice, of *phut-tho* meditation, is to slowly say the Buddha's name through the inhalation and exhalation of the breath, quietly saying or thinking *"phut"* on the inhale and *"tho"* on the exhale. It is a very typical style of meditation, used by many people, including my host mother Mae Daeng in the valley. People say that it draws from textual teachings, but when I ask them to tell me just which ones it draws from, they tell me it's just basic knowledge. Its everyday iteration incorporates an ease of practice that many monks and laypeople like. A variety of techniques and styles of meditation are used in Thailand to develop mindfulness (many of which are discussed in chapter 2), but for the most part monks will practice meditation according to their own preferences and predilections. "There is no rule on what styles of meditation to use," one told me. "Some might feel more comfortable with a *phut-tho* style and gain more sati that way than other styles. For all of these methods, the most important thing is not about the style. It's about how you can control your mind." The techniques are Phra Thēp's and others' way of anchoring "the buffalo to the post," as he had put it, to not get lost in the mind, and to stay in touch with perceived, objective reality.

"So, did you learn all this about mindfulness by yourself?" I ask Phra Thēp, after he had explained more about the different styles of meditation he followed.

"Mostly I learned from my meditation teacher in Nonthaburi," he replies, "and from the Tipiṭaka, but mostly from my teachers." In mentioning the Tipiṭaka, he was referring to the corpus of Buddhist teachings in general, a compilation of what has been called the "canon" of the religion.[5] Teachings on mindfulness can be found throughout this thousand-page text, but like most of the teachings in the canon, they are offered in different forms with different interpretations in different monastic lineages. The lengthy version of the Tipiṭaka considered authoritative in

Thailand can be found in its full-volume form on the almost out-of-reach top shelves of bookstores and monastic and university libraries throughout the country, along with a wide range of excerpts and exegeses with them. While some monks (and increasingly, non-monks) read the Tipiṭaka in Pali or Thai versions, most encounter parts and interpretations of it in the form of dhamma sermons, as well as many vernacular texts, both old and new.

Phra Thēp describes to Noi and me how he makes his own path through the monastic system. He would stay at this small, solitary monastery at the top of the hill in Mae Jaeng, he tells us, for the rest of the rainy season retreat, a traditional three-month period where even wandering monks normally reside in just one location, before moving on. I thought of him spending his days at this remote spot, with no noise but the wind and the animals around him, and imagined how different it must be from his previous life in the big city.

Before Noi and I left to go back down the hill to Mae Jaeng, Phra Thēp said to us, while talking about where and how he was able to practice mindfulness well, "I like it here, where it's quiet. Usually when I'm in a quiet place I can have a lot of sati. When it's really quiet, without any noises to bother me, it's easy to practice. But actually," he said, pausing before he went on, "actually those who have been practicing well can have sati no matter where they are, and the noises will never bother them. They won't be attached to any thought—they'll feel *choei-choei* [a Thai word loosely translated as "unaffected"], they'll have *upekkhā* [a Pali word for "equanimity"]. But for me I like it here, because it's peaceful."

After Phra Thēp had spoken to us for a little more than an hour, and then filled out the short mindfulness measure we had brought along, Noi and I said our thanks and good-byes. As we made our way back to our motorcycle, I turned to watch the monk walk toward the small building he had come out of. He paused to pick up a few things outside the door in the same unhurried manner in which he had first approached us, and disappeared inside.

Back down in the valley Noi and I pulled up to our house and sat at the benches outside for a few minutes, looking out at the street. The one dusty intersection in town seemed busier and more bustling than when we had left it that morning. Trucks rumbled by, bound for the remote hills with their supplies, and a few tourists from Bangkok and abroad paused in their nice cars and dusty loaded motorcycles to stock up at the market before continuing on their way. The cool breeze of the hilltop monastery seemed far away. Noi went back inside and sat back down to his video games and internet friends, many of whom were also sitting at their computers less than a block away, and I went over the notes from the meeting with Phra Thēp. Practicing mindfulness might be a natural and easy thing to do in some ways, but in others, as the monk had told us, it takes time and work. I was impressed with Phra Thēp, because even as a monk ordained for years, talking to a visitor who had entered into his space without warning or invitation, he was patient, humble, modest, and honest. As did so many other monks, Phra Thēp balanced his role as a representative of the religion with his own personal experiences. He talked about his preference for the quiet area while also saying that he was walking a path where later it wouldn't matter at all if it was quiet or loud. He may have had more dramatic experiences in his earlier life as a taxi driver, but he didn't find them important to tell us about; the important thing was the practice at hand.

The ways that Phra Thēp related to mindfulness seemed both simple and complex. In focusing on the center of his forehead, or breathing in and out while saying the Buddha's name, his practices appeared simple in some sense, but they were also deeply complicated, in the sense that they didn't seem easy to do, especially when, as he said, noises and everyday business intrude and disrupt the mind. As part of his larger society, Phra Thēp and others like him need to engage with people for food and shelter, if nothing else. But most of his everyday life was spent away from the entanglements of people, and he liked it that way. In early Buddhist accounts, mindfulness and meditation were considered especially appropriate for people who could find the time to leave society and practice them at length; but for most people, including monks living in today's dense social reality, mindfulness is increasingly understood to help mental cultivation for both soteriological, religious ends and for the quite practical, utilitarian end of getting by in society. Although Phra Thēp referred to specific teachings and teachers a little less than did other, more institutionally entrenched monks I would encounter, in many ways he represents a general picture of what mindfulness means for monastics today: a guide and a skill used to follow the path of the Buddha.

Phra Chan's *Navakovada*: Basic Thai
Buddhist Teachings on Mindfulness

The social relevance of mindfulness is even more apparent in the lives of the majority of novices and monks who live in monasteries located in the centers of towns, rather than far off from them. While relatively rural and underpopulated, the Mae Jaeng valley is full of these monasteries, scattered around the rice fields that supply the town's fifteen hundred or so people with its staple food. Two of these valley monasteries serve as monastic schools, where the hundreds of novices from the other, non-school monasteries make their way in packed pickup trucks each morning, to learn about Buddhism before heading back to their home monastery in the evening.

Most of those in Thailand who continue as monks for a longer time than a few months, or who ordain as adults, start out as novices (children or youths who ordain between the ages of seven and twenty) and participate in the country's monastic system of education. This system keeps those who are ordained busy. The monastic education system runs parallel to the country's more secular national school program; it is less

Figure 3. Most monks in Thailand are responsible for performing rituals in the community, along with their more scholarly and meditative pursuits. Here a group of young monks leads a procession at a Poy Luang festival in Mae Chaem to celebrate the completion of a new monastery building. Photo by J. L. Cassaniti.

expensive than the government schools (which are free but require a token amount of money for uniforms, books, and other expenses, which for some is unaffordable) and offers a heartier dose of religious training (such as Pali-language study and dhamma study). In many ways, however, it resembles the national secular system of education. Monastic schools offer courses on topics from social studies to English to computer science, allowing novices to enter into lay society with the tools necessary to do so, when and if they choose that path. Many monks who continue as ordained members of the sangha past their early teenage years continue to live in their local monasteries without going to school any longer, but some continue on to monastic boarding high schools in the cities if they want and if they pass a series of exams. A still smaller percentage of these continue on to monastic universities, which offer Buddhist BA, MA, and PhD degrees. The teachers at the small, local monastic schools in Mae Jaeng, as elsewhere, are monks or lay instructors, many coming from the local area but others arriving from other parts of the country, or even farther abroad. I had volunteered as an English teacher at Wat Pa Daet, one of these monastic schools in Mae Jaeng, while I was living in the community a few years earlier.

A few days after the meeting with Phra Thēp, I stopped in at that school to learn more about the mindfulness of these relatively more socially integrated monks. As I approached the monastic grounds, I could hear the teenage novice monks chanting the Pali-language lines of their lessons in the outdoor classroom. Beyond the sound of the chants it was quiet and peaceful, the workers in their fields nearby taking a break from the midday sun to gather in the sun shelters and share snacks. A young monk I recognized as a teacher came out of the central office building to meet me when the sound of my motorcycle announced my arrival. His head shaven and his orange robes bright in the sun, he introduced himself as Phra Chan, and though I didn't know him personally, and he didn't know me, he motioned me into an open-air pavilion to sit down. "I can go get the head monk to talk to you," he said first, about to go inside one of the buildings on the side of the grounds, but I told him that wouldn't be necessary, and that I just wanted to ask him a few questions about what the novices learn at the school.

After performing the standard ritual ceremony of *wai*-ing the monk, as I had with Phra Thēp, I asked Phra Chan what kinds of things he taught the novices about mindfulness at his monastery. He retrieved a small book from a back room of the monastery and showed it to me. *Navakovada*, it read in Thai on the cover, and he explained that it was a short summary of all the Buddhist teachings, which he uses to instruct the novices. It can serve as a guide to the many larger iterations of textual knowledge of Buddhism, including those about mindfulness.

"All the novices have to memorize this book," he told me. "They're tested on it in an oral exam." The full text of the *Navakovada* was about fifty pages long, organized into a short-list format summarizing the central lessons of Buddhism thought. The *Navakovada* was written by the brother of Thailand's King Rama IV in the 1800s; today it is part of the monastic education system that most all novice monks in Thailand go through. It is popular with some laypeople, too, and represents some of the religion's "basic" ideas, summarizing the Pali canonical texts through a Thai inflection. The standardizing of monastic learning in Thailand is a relatively recent phenomenon (Tiyavanich 1997). During the early twentieth century, Thailand's kings instituted a series of reforms that served to streamline and nationalize the Buddhist sangha (see Schedneck 2015; Cook 2010; Almond 1988; Winichakul 1994; Tambiah 1984), though there is still significant variation in how monks at different monasteries ordain, live, and learn about Buddhism (McDaniel 2008). Even with the variation in teachings popular at different monasteries, attending to the education curricula of monks in any one monastery can tell us a lot about what and how Buddhism is practiced, as well as what monks know and teach about mindfulness throughout the country.

Phra Chan opened to the first page and showed it to me, as if asking me to step into the mental space of a young Thai monk. The very first word on the very first page of the *Navakovada* read: "Sati."

"Sati is to be able to recall," the writing proclaimed, in the first section on the first page, under the heading of "Dhamma-s of Very Great Assistance." The other "Dhamma-s of Very Great Assistance" was *sampajañña*—awareness—which had been mentioned by Phra Thēp too in his definition of *sati*.[6] The section was short: there were only two "dhamma-s of very great assistance" listed: mindfulness and awareness.

"Sati" appeared a few pages later, too, and again a few pages after that. It was most prominent in a section called the "Sati Paṭṭhāna Si" in

Thai, drawing from the Pali Satipaṭṭhāna Sutta, the "Four Foundations of Mindfulness."[7] This list, and the text it draws from, are based on the most important and most well-cited sutta on mindfulness in the entire Buddhist canon. People in Buddhist communities around the world are familiar with its teachings in various forms, whether distilled into short interpretive lessons or elaborated in multivolume books. The main teaching of the sutta is to pay attention to four different aspects of the body and mind as a practical guide to develop mindfulness. In the *Navakovada* that Phra Chan was showing me, these four "aspects" or "foundations" of mindfulness were listed in their Pali form using Thai script, followed by short Thai translations next to each of them.

The Four Foundations of Mindfulness are also considered the foundation of modern Theravāda *vipassanā* meditation movements around the world. The purpose of these arisings, or foundations, Phra Chan explained, is to instruct practitioners to meditate on the transience of each of these components. The text of this section in the *Navakovada* is a short summary that in its more "canonical" version is also quite short, at about seven pages long (or fifteen minutes of oral recitation, the more traditional medium of knowledge transfer), though there are pages and pages and even books that comment on it.

I would come across references to the Satipaṭṭhāna Sutta in its slightly different versions and guises again and again during the course of my research, with meanings and interpretations and variations in its practice offering telling clues about mindfulness in the context it had been developing in since the origination of formal Buddhism. The Satipaṭṭhāna Sutta has come to be considered the most important guide for developing mindfulness by Theravāda Buddhists everywhere, and even for meditation as a whole. Crosby and Khur-Yearn (2010) have called the Satipaṭṭhāna Sutta "the *locus classicus* for instructions on how to perform meditation in the Pali canon of Theravāda Buddhism." In his introduction to the text, Soma Thera (1941) describes it as the method "for reaching that *summum bonum* of the Buddhas," with enlightenment being the clear goal.[8] As it is elsewhere, the sutta is very well known in Thailand: forty-four of the sixty-six monks that I gathered data from in Thailand mentioned the Satipaṭṭhāna Sutta by name as being an especially good text from which to learn about mindfulness. Many of them had learned about the Satipaṭṭhāna Sutta for the first time through the *Navakovada* that

Phra Chan was showing me now. The practices of mindfulness through an attention to body, feelings, mind, and dhamma are indelibly important. As listed in the *Navakovada*, they are

- *kāya-upaṭṭhāna*: the way of the body;
- *vedanā-anupaṭṭhāna*: the way of feelings or sensations;
- *citta-upaṭṭhāna*: the way of heart or mind; and
- *dhammā-upaṭṭhāna*: the way of mental formations or truths about the world.[9]

Phra Chan turned to another page in the *Navakovada* and we encountered sati again, this time in a section called the "Anussati," or "Activities of Which One Should Be Mindful." The *Navakovada* explains what the *anussati* mean. *Anu-sati khu arom kuam raluk sip prakan*, it reads in Thai: "The *anussati* are feelings to recall through the following ten points." As with the Four Foundations of Mindfulness, the section on the *anussati* listed each Pali term and then offered a few words in Thai to explain each:

- *buddhānussati*: "mindfulness of the virtues of the Buddha"
- *dhammānussati*: "mindfulness of the virtues of the dhamma [the Buddha's teaching]"
- *saṅghānussati*: "mindfulness of the virtues of the sangha [the Buddhist community]"
- *sīlānussati*: "mindfulness of one's own *sīla* [moral action]"
- *cāgānussati*: "mindfulness of *dāna* [donations] one has given out"
- *devatānussati*: "mindfulness of virtues that make people become *devas* [angels/gods]"
- *maraṇānussati*: "mindfulness of death and how it is bound to come to oneself"
- *kāyagatāsati*: "mindfulness of everywhere in the body so that one sees that it is ugly"
- *ānāpānasati*: "mindfulness of the breath going in and out"[10]
- *upasamānussati*: "mindfulness of the supreme virtue of *nibbāna* in which there is the quenching of the *kilesa* [defilements] and the mass of *dukkha*"

This teaching, though not as famous as the Satipaṭṭhāna, is also a well-known list in the Theravāda world of points considered important to attend to and think about in the development of mindfulness. Like the Satipaṭṭhāna, the list of *anussati* can be found in variations in many different Buddhist texts; the *Navakovada* lists the famous text the *Visuddhimagga* (I:197) as its source. The different factors of the *anussati* are also found in other teachings about mindfulness; *ānāpānasati*, for instance, appears in some versions of the Satipaṭṭhāna, and is also the central topic of a sutta of its own. Even in the short text of the *Navakovada*, perspectives about sati start to circle around on each other and reinforce themselves in the logic of the teachings even as they also take on complex meanings of their own.

These Satipaṭṭhāna and *anussati* are the two textual references on sati encountered most often in Thailand, but in looking through the short *Navakovada*, Phra Chan and I find a few additional references to the concept. Mindfulness is also part of

- the *bojjhaṅga*, or "Factors of Enlightenment," where it is the first of seven factors, defined as "being able to recollect the mind";[11]
- the *nāthakaranadhamma*, or "dhammas for help and protection," where it is the ninth of ten helpful and protective dhammas, described as "being able to remember what one has done and what words one has spoken, even a long time ago";[12]
- the *makmiong paet*, or the "Buddhist Eightfold Path" (the fourth of the Four Noble Truths), where *sammā sati* or "right mindfulness" is the seventh of eight points on the path, and is described as "being able to recollect within the Four Foundations of Mindfulness."[13]

Although monks in Thailand do not always refer to one particular text, many of the practices that they engage in are drawn from the references pointed to in the *Navakovada*. While the *Navakovada* is straightforward and lends itself to memorization without too much effort, its teachings are rich and interrelated, often becoming more complex rather than less complex the closer one gets to their meanings. In some ways it is from taking a step back that they become clearer, even as the details and patterned complexity within them appear lost. In referring to the way he would focus on his forehead, Phra Thēp was practicing, in a sense, the mindfulness of the body, part of the *kaya-passana* as related in the Satipaṭṭhāna Sutta; in his attention to the breath and the Buddha's name one could say he was following the *ānāpānasati* and *buddhānussati* methods of the *anussati*; and in raising a connection between morality and mindfulness through the "friends" of concentration and wisdom it could be said that he was drawing from the teaching of the Eightfold Path. Phra Thēp didn't refer to each of these directly, but he learned about them and filtered them through his own experiences in and out of the monastery, putting them into practice for himself. The teachings on mindfulness as represented in the *Navakovada* are not the only teachings or the only versions known by people in Thailand; the small booklet offers only short summaries of what are much more elaborate teachings, many of which I would come across often. In summarizing these teachings and making them available to novice monks (and interested laypeople, including the visiting anthropologist) the *Navakovada* points to the central teachings of the religion with which most people throughout the region will have some familiarity. As with English renderings of Buddhist teachings that alter and define terms in their translations and choices of inclusion, the Thai renderings of what are thought to be authoritatively more official Pali-language textual lessons point in large part to shared ideas throughout the Buddhist world; yet they also point to particular attitudes and assumptions about what is important and worth attending to in contemporary Thai society.

"So, do the novices learn a lot about these teachings here?" I asked Phra Chan, after we had finished looking over the booklet's entries.

"Oh no," he said, modestly. "We talk about sati, we go over this stuff, but to learn more they have to go to the Buddhist high schools in Chiang Mai."

I knew from previous research in Mae Jaeng (Cassaniti 2015c, 2006) that for a variety of reasons people say that they and others aren't very familiar with a concept, even when they are. I knew that the novices were familiar with mindfulness, partly from the lessons they had learned based on the *Navakovada* and other schoolbooks and partly from just using it in everyday contexts; but I knew also that Phra Chan was being deferential to an established hierarchy of formal Buddhist knowledge, one from which forest monks like Phra Thēp might be relatively exempt but that many monks in the monastery schools are taught to see themselves as part of. Mindfulness in Thailand, as everywhere, is as social as it is personal.

Phra Chan told me how novice monks study versions of the teachings in the *Navakovada*; he and other monks like him will extrapolate on these teachings in lessons, offering commentaries on the concepts in the contexts of the students' lives. Some monks spend more of their time engaging with the textual sources than others, but all are generally familiar with them. Even those monks and laypeople who can't "recollect" or "bring to mind" the exact phrases or sources will be familiar with many of their central points.

"How many of these novices here go on to these Buddhist high schools in the bigger cities?" I asked. We looked over to the open-air pavilion nearby, where a few dozen young novices were doing their lessons in varying states of attention.

"Maybe five or six [of the approximately twenty-five graduating] this year," he told me. "It's really up to them. And it's not only about them deciding if they want to. They have to take a test to see if they can get in. Next week we're taking them to Chiang Mai to visit the schools and think about whether they want to continue." A week later I saw the pickup trucks packed in the back with novice monks, heading out over the mountains to Chiang Mai, two hours away. While there, they would visit a few of the boarding high schools connected with the monastery, as a kind of monastic-school tour.

After I thanked Phra Chan for his time, he rose and returned his copy of the *Navakovada* to the monastery library and resumed his work in the office. When I got home that afternoon I asked Noi if he remembered learning anything about mindfulness from the *Navakovada*. He nodded vaguely, but as usual he didn't elaborate. The following week I took my motorcycle over the mountain to the big city of Chiang Mai, too, to see what mindfulness looks like there.

Chiang Mai is a sprawling metropolis, the cars packing the streets, and even the many monasteries are crowded with the monks in residence and the people coming in to visit. Even as the city monasteries remain places of relative quiet, the monks are very much immersed in the bustling urban environment. With the help of Santi, a graduate student whom my colleague Somwang Kaewsufong helped me find at Chiang Mai University, and Justin, the American student who had returned to the country following our first preliminary data-gathering trip, I spent the next month seeking out monks at the city's many monasteries. First we would have to decide where to go, as there are hundreds of monasteries in town. For Buddhists in Thailand, the decision of which monastery to frequent, whether for study or just to visit, is complex. Most people, including monks, will not base their decision to visit or study at a particular monastery on broad political divisions. Instead, they usually visit whatever monastery is closer to their home, or sometimes travel across town (or even across the country) for ones whose particular lineage of teaching they find especially interesting. For many the decision is practical: as one monk at a monastery in Chiang Mai put it, when I asked why someone would visit one monastery over another: "It's like why you go to a supermarket," he told me. "Some people go because it's close to the house, some people go for the selection or some other quality."

We decided to focus on two monasteries in particular, Wat Suan Dok and Wat Chedi Luang, the two most central sites of Buddhist learning in Chiang Mai. We interviewed ten monks at each site, and also administered thirty additional questionnaires at each site, asking about mindfulness and the ways that a monk will encounter it. Wat Suan Dok, or "Flower Garden Monastery," occupies a large area on the edge of town near Doi Suthep mountain, while Wat Chedi Luang, or "Grand Stupa Monastery," is in the middle of the city's old town. Some of the novices that graduate from the country's four hundred-plus high-school-level monasteries in the kingdom may enter one of these or another Buddhist university.[14] Both schools have long and complex histories, accumulated over their more than seven hundred years of existence. Today Wat Suan Dok and Wat Chedi Luang are host branch campuses of larger, more nationally connected monastic universities in Bangkok (Mahachulalongkon Ratchawitthayalai University at Wat Mahathat, and Mahamakut Ratchawitthaya University at Wat Bowonniwet, respectively).[15]

Phra Mon: How to Not Hit a Novice on the Head

Phra Mon Winitkhanatorn is a forty-year-old monk who has been ordained for almost all his life. Like most monastics, Phra Mon comes from a small rural village not unlike Mae Jaeng. But unlike Phra Thēp, whose days in Mae Jaeng are filled mostly with the rustling sound of the leaves and little else, Phra Mon's life at Wat Suan Dok is full of activities. He follows a daily lifestyle similar to that of Phra Chan, but within a heightened level of commotion and responsibilities as a teacher at a large monastery. In charge of many of the student monks and the administrative

Figure 4. A monk walks by royal Northern Thai funerary stupas at Wat Suan Dok in Chiang Mai. Amid the bustle of modern life, monasteries in Northern Thailand offer a relatively quiet respite from the city. Photo by J. L. Cassaniti.

running of the school, Phra Mon also deals regularly with laypeople, both when they come to the monastery and when he goes out with other monks to perform religious ceremonies. He has also recently started giving talks on the dhamma to the public, as a kind of monastic version of volunteer lectures. Just before talking with us he had returned from delivering a talk to inmates at the local prison.

Phra Mon has a lot to do, and he tells us how he uses mindfulness to develop a sense of emotional calmness for himself amid it all. "It's not easy," he said, laughing, when asked about his mindfulness practices. "Sometimes the students don't do their work, and I want to hit them on the head!" Hitting novices on the head isn't something one usually imagines when thinking of a Buddhist monk, at least not in my experience in Southeast Asia. But many of the monks we spoke with talked about moments when they felt an urge to lash out in what we might call a moment of anger; and they too spoke of remembering their mindfulness as a way to not actually do so. Only one monk at Phra Mon's monastery didn't talk about wanting to sometimes hit novices on the head, and this one exception was himself a novice monk, who said that the time he especially was lacking in sati was when one of the older monks had hit him on the head!

In many ways the meanings and practices of mindfulness that Phra Mon followed are similar to those of Phra Thēp. He told us that mindfulness is to *raluk dai*—to be able to recall. He elaborated a bit more on his definition and the specifics of what he learned about than Phra Thēp did.

"It's to *ru tua*, to know the body/self. Really, it's the thing that allows us to recollect why things happened in the past, and [why they're happening] in the present. To know the present means to know the reason why things happened in the past. This is mindfulness."

Phra Mon learned about mindfulness first from his parents when he was young. He came from what he called a stricter-than-usual Buddhist family, where he was taught to make merit and practice a minute or two of meditation every day, and later he learned more in the formal setting of the Buddhist monastery. His first technical textual exposure was through the *Navakovada* as a novice, and later in class in high school. He cited as an example one of the most commonly used readers for the high school levels of dhamma training, the *Nak Tham' Chan Tri: Nangsue Buranakan Phanmai* (Ministry of Education 2003), or "Integrated book of dhamma: level three" (out of five levels), where there is a section dedicated to the Satipaṭṭhāna Sutta, as well as a section on the Ānāpānasati Sutta, a sutta on the mindfulness of breath, which was raised only briefly as one of the *anussati* in the *Navakovada* but which refers to a meditation technique very well known in Thailand. The teachings in this text are more elaborate in their descriptions than in the *Navakovada*, though they draw from the same canonical sources. The *Nak Tham* textbooks that Phra Mon used as a student are in all Buddhist high schools in the country; he was now using them to teach with. "At the high school level," I was told by one monk, "we basically adopt the policy from the Thai Ministry of Education . . . it's a 'must' to have this kind of curriculum." Along with its mention in the texts, sati also comes up in formal settings in monastic school through quizzes, called *krathu tham*, and when students have to discuss it in their exams.

"We learn about sati in the high school system, as in the Satipaṭṭhāna Sutta, the Ānāpānasati Sutta, but still only briefly," Phra Mon explained. "If a monk wants to study more, because of general interest or to pass further levels of education, he'll learn more about sati in other Buddhist texts, like the *Visuddhimagga* [the "Path of Purification," the famous fifth-century commentary from Sri Lanka] and the *Abhidhamma* [the third of the three *piṭaka*, or baskets, of the Tipiṭaka canon, a collection of teachings about psychology]. Teachings from these texts are found in more advanced levels of textbooks, such as at the *Prayok Tham* fourth and fifth levels." Most will read these texts in Thai, with just the titles in Pali, but some will study the Pali more seriously and will learn to read, recite, and comment on the Pali text.

Phra Mon knows a good deal about the textual teachings of mindfulness that monks learn about in school partly because he had gone through the school system himself, and partly because as a teacher who used the texts in class, he was less likely to forget the specifics of them than others who went through the same system. "Really though there are so many books about meditation and how to train in mindfulness," he tells us, when asked for more details on influential works. "I learned from them, and from meetings with my teacher, and also from supplementary texts I could pick up from other places for free." He was speaking of the pamphlets given out on the dhamma at monasteries, and texts in libraries, and even short teachings found at the counters of the ubiquitous 7–11 stores around the country. The general sense that teachings of mindfulness are found everywhere was shared by other monks, too: "I learned from the Satipaṭṭhāna," one said, when asked for specific references, "and, um, in the *Abhidhamma*, and in, well, general basic dhamma books." Another reported plainly: "Mindfulness is in every dhamma book." And although it is agreed that one can study the details in depth, the dhamma isn't something that is considered to be available only at elite levels. Phra Mon was unusual in having read more dhamma texts than most others, but his point about the availability of these texts is true: from free pamphlets at the country's many monasteries to the popular books at the counters of countless convenience stores, dhamma books are everywhere.

For Phra Mon and other monks in Thailand, mindfulness is found partly through these books and from their teachers, but it is especially found through its everyday practice, and not just from others. A large part of these experiences is about affect: the development and training of feeling. Almost everything Phra Mon says about mindfulness, beyond his definitions of it as embodied recollection and his references to important texts, has to do with mindfulness as a tool for affectively and effectively mastering the mind. This hints at how affect interacts with the ability to recollect the mind, or "tie it to a post," as Phra Thēp had put it. "My parents told me to be careful and aware of what I'm doing," he tells us, "so I don't forget things, and that when I'm feeling stressed or angry I should have sati. They said that I should be able to control myself—which is like what the Buddha said."

It hasn't always been easy for him to follow this advice, however. "This is very personal," he says, pausing, "but a long time ago, when I didn't have much sati, I had a lot of anger and hate. But with practice, the more I meditated, the more the anger seemed to lessen. I still have trouble with anger," he continued, perhaps a bit more honestly than other monks typically would. "Though it's hard to give you an example, because I'm a monk." It wasn't clear if he meant that since he was a monk he didn't have much experience with anger anymore, or that it wasn't something that was wise for a monk to talk about.

"When I feel violent anger, that's when I've lost my mindfulness. And there was one period where I would get angry so often. When I would teach the novice monks here at the monastery, and I wanted the novices to understand what I was teaching them, but they wouldn't understand, and I would feel angry. I had high expectations of them, because I wanted them to pass their exams. But they wouldn't pay attention, and I would get so angry sometimes it would get so bad and I would want to slap them on the head!"

Phra Mon explains that the wish he felt at times to hit novices was mostly about expectation. It was about attaching to an idea and feeling angry when it didn't work out.

"It's a problem for people who have high expectations," he says. "People who expect too much from others. When I don't get what I want, I lose my balance, and the anger is greater than the sati, and the sati goes away." Here he was referencing, as Phra Thēp and Phra Chan had, mindfulness as a kind of basic quality of being, similar to mental stability or innate instinct, in the way Noi had pointed out but hadn't elaborated on. Mindfulness is something that one has, Phra Mon explains, a kind of feeling of informed consciousness that one can access in times of confusion or need, and it is something that can be overridden with other feelings caused from attachments.

"The Buddhist teaching says that where there is a feeling there is one's heart, and where there is a heart there is a mind. The meditation training of the monk is to train the mind, to train in mindfulness. Sometimes when I forget what I'm doing, like when I'm reading and I hear something and I get distracted, or when I get angry, this is called being without sati. That means that the mind is unstable."

"I'm better now, though," he adds, wrapping up his discussion of his problems with anger: "The more I meditate, the more the anger seems to lessen. So it's not that often something like that happens now."

I thought of Phra Thēp's robes blowing lightly in the wind. In Phra Mon's case, though, he was talking about the rustling quality of the many people and situations he found himself in every day. For Phra Mon, one of the goals, the practical benefits, of mindfulness was to decrease the feelings that can cause one to lose emotional control.

"But how do you practice?" I ask him, as I had asked Phra Thēp and was asking so many others. "I mean, how do you get better at mindfulness?"

"When I practice meditation, then mindfulness forms," he says, and mentions the two main types of meditation practiced in Thailand, *vipassanā*, "insight meditation," and *samatha*, "concentration meditation," and then offers,

> How do I practice [meditation]? To make it simple, things that happen in front of me are the things I can sense from my five senses. What we can see, what we can smell, what we can taste, hear, touch, the things that happen to us, and these senses go to our heart, our mind, and if we understand what these senses represent, our heart and mind will process them. The result of that can be one of three things: we'll feel good about it, we'll feel bad about it, or we'll feel unaffected, so-so [*choei-choei*] about it.

He would practice feeling neutral about these things, through recognizing what they are, and seeing them as impermanent.

"Every monk has to practice sati. For example, we chant every morning and every evening, and that trains our minds. Once we learn about sati from a text, from a teaching, it becomes part of our lives. Then we can use it in our daily lives, and it becomes part of us. When mindfulness has formed I can use it to feel calm."

Phra Mon describes his practice as a kind of snowballing or spiraling process: the more mindfulness one has, he was saying, the calmer one feels, and so the more mindful one can be; remembering to be mindful helps one in turn to be calm and develop mindfulness. When asked to explain more about how this works, Phra Mon tells us about impermanence, using the Pali teaching of *anicca* to refer to constant change. "The Buddha said that we have to be aware all the time. That everything in the world comes into being, remains there, and then goes out. All the time. Like this iPad you're using to record this interview"—he points to the device on the table in front of us—"It's not permanent, it's not ours really. So don't be stressed if you lose it. If we understand these concepts, we'll be able to understand that our life is always changing." He adds, "This is useful, especially if we're sad or upset." He gives one more example: "Like, if a relative passes away. If we understand with sati that everything changes, that everything is impermanent, we'll be less sad." I thought of another monk I knew well, who had told me the same thing after his father died: "When my father passed away, yes, I was sad," he had told me, "but from my practice as a monk I wasn't as sad as my brother and sisters." It wasn't a coldhearted indifference that Phra Mon was referring to, but a cultivated attitude of what in Thai is called "*tham jai*," a process of "making the heart" (often translated as "acceptance") and coming to terms with events through a recognition of the inevitability of change.

Before we ended the interview we asked if mindfulness is connected to spiritual, even supernatural, powers, and Phra Mon told us, "Well, when you have a lot of mindfulness you never fear the negative energy of others," which was a kind of indirect reference to local understandings of ghostly forces. He mentioned politics in a similarly oblique way. Politics was a charged topic that was beginning to be particularly taboo in the country. "Mindfulness," he said, "keeps someone who is angry at the government from using violence in protest."

As Phra Mon spoke, other monks and novices and laypeople were circulating around him. It was the later mid-morning by this point, and the monks would have to gather to eat soon before noon, but Phra Mon was focused on the discussion. His focus wasn't just a put-upon presentation of self or an obliviousness to what was going on around him, though an awareness of comportment, as part of the training of monks and an ability to not become easily distracted, were without doubt a part of this focus. Phra Mon spoke honestly about his struggles. He talked about how, over time, instead of wanting to hit the novices on the head when they weren't paying attention, he began to feel calm and clearheaded. He thought about the abstract concepts he learned in his textbooks and in the dhamma talks given by the head abbot of the monastery, which he had listened to with others, but it was through putting them in practice, rather than seeing them as abstract, in seeing moments of failure and success, that he worked on mastering his emotions. "After meditating a lot," he told us, in conclusion to his long discussion, "mindfulness became intertwined in my work with people." He described how he had recently started going to the local prison to give talks to the inmates, and his experience at the session he had just come from.

"In the prison I have to have a lot of mindfulness. Especially when I first went there, because it's a very different place from what my life is usually like." Now, he said, he had started to realize that mindfulness can help him not only to be calm and to decrease anger, but also to be kind to others. "Seeing those people in prison has made me realize that I have to bring more dhamma, *mettā karunā* [loving kindness, or friendliness] into my life. Sati helps me to be more alert, more calm, and more kind." Phra Mon was suggesting not just that he had learned to "control" his emotions or "manage" them; he had also learned to experience affective situations differently. After speaking for a while more, we thanked the monk for his time, and after he filled out a short mindfulness scale we had brought with us[16] and asked a few questions of his own about the project, he got up and went to join the others for the midday meal.

I thought about tracking Phra Mon down again after that day, and tracking down Phra Chan and Phra Thēp, too, to find out more about the particular meditative practices and personal details of their lives. Yet while the particulars of individual experiences matter, the feelings that these monks expressed and the lessons they shared about mindfulness were especially useful as being representative of many others like them. In relating the individual engagements of Phra Thēp and Phra Mon, I have focused on specific individuals to illustrate the experiences of many, an approach that has become known as a Weberian emphasis in the scholarly analysis of personalities (Kitiarsa 2009; Collins and McDaniel 2010). This method has gained a great deal of traction in Asian studies in recent years, as exemplified by a series of short case narratives of various individuals in *Figures of Southeast Asian Modernity* (Barker et al. 2013)—including my own focusing on my Mae Jaeng host sister "Goy" (Cassaniti 2013).

I have followed this approach here to show how the lessons of mindfulness are put into play in always particular, but also representative, lives. Many monks are comfortable with and even proud of

Figure 5. One of the many monks living and studying at Wat Suan Dok in Chiang Mai. Some lay visitors sit near the altar, making offerings, chanting, and spending a few moments in meditation. Photo by J. L. Cassaniti.

their names, accomplishments, and titles. They think about the complicated struggles involved in altering and developing their consciousness in following a Buddhist path, struggles that are often more difficult than either Phra Thēp or Phra Mon let on. Yet most monks, like these two, aspire to transcend such worldly associations, in this life or another. Part of that project is to practice detaching from self-centered reflection. As the interviews continued and the monks left after each interview, fading into the crowd of others with their shaved heads and virtually identical robes, they became part of the large group that make up the community of those dedicating themselves for a period of their lives to the religion.

The TAPES of Monks

The things I learned from Phra Thēp, Phra Mon, and other monks in Thailand help to reveal the practice of mindfulness in social life; other findings point to particular assumptions about how the mind works within these social worlds. Monks' experiences show that mindfulness isn't exclusively either a state that one "has" or that one "does" as a process of becoming: rather, it is practiced and reinforced in reciprocal iterations of expression and development, of being and becoming. Monks' experiences also show that while religious texts are relevant as guides, the ways that mindfulness is put into practice for them are much more personal. They draw from formal contexts only through their application into affectively laden situations, from the interpretation of a sound outside a quiet monastery on a hill to the challenge of crowds of people in monasteries or even prisons. The monks' experiences show that apart from, or in addition to, the abstract spaces of intellectual engagement, or even the silent domain of meditative sitting, one can rehearse mindfulness in everyday social contexts. As part of the long process of walking the path toward the liberation of nirvana, monks consider mindfulness as offering what could be thought of as a "side benefit," too, in "getting by" in everyday life (as one monk put it), by helping them to recall their mind and be emotionally centered.

Beyond these general findings, the monks taught me more nuanced connotations about the connections of mindfulness to other aspects of psychological experience, especially as these connections apply to what I have called the TAPES of Temporality, Affect, Power, Ethics, and Selfhood. While all five of these TAPES were touched on, three of them were especially relevant in practice.

T—Temporality

Monks understand mindfulness in large part through the relationship of their minds and bodies to time. Mindfulness is very much about being aware in the present, as demonstrated through their definitions of the concept as the ability to *ru tua,* or "to be conscious of one's being in space," and in being able to *raluk,* or recall, the mind back to the present from wherever it may have wandered off. These two definitions, the most common not just to monks but to everyone in Thailand, suggest a kind of returning, or remembering, of the immediate now, to "tie the buffalo to the post," as Phra Thēp and many others said. The present moment is undoubtedly central to what most monks think about when they think about mindfulness. But mindfulness for them is also, significantly, connected to the past, and to making use of past experiences to understand present ones through drawing the mind away from where it may have wandered off in time as well as in mental space.

If you recall something to mind, the monks told me, you have remembered it, even if that means "remembering" where you are. "Let's say you interviewed me here, and then later I saw you again somewhere," one monk told me; "I would use mindfulness to remember who you are." "I used mindfulness to remember to come to this interview!" said another. For some this "remembering" quality of mindfulness is not just for remembering the present, either. It can also be about remembering the past more explicitly; and even the future. The ways that temporality is implicated in mindfulness vary for different people and, I would come to learn, in different locations in Theravāda Asia. But for most it is not simply or only about bare attention to the present moment. One monk even told me that not only was mindfulness useful in helping people remember past events, but "they can even remember past lives!" "But it's very hard," he went on: "Mindfulness is about the present moment, but it's not just that."

A—Affect

Along with its engagements with temporality, for Thai monks mindfulness is also closely connected to affect. This is especially so in the project of training emotional processes to construct feelings of calmness. For Phra Thēp, Phra Mon, and virtually all the eighty Thai monks who took part in the project, mindfulness is used as a method for crafting an orientation to emotion that helps to decrease anger and develop particular attitudes about emotional reaction. Far from the increased calmness when mindfulness is taken to be just about emotion "management," used to regulate the social expression of feelings after one automatically feels them, mindfulness for these monks was used much more to develop immediate affective experiences in line with desired religious goals. Not only is one able, through mindfulness, to control feelings of being angry or upset, but one is also less likely to have robust or problematic emotions in the first place when a difficult situation arises. This was true for Phra Mon at Wat Suan Dok and others there and at Wat Chedi Luang who learned how to not feel like hitting delinquent novices on the head in anger, and it was true for Phra Thēp, too, in the peaceful quietness he developed at the mountain monastery above Mae Jaeng. For them, and for the other monks, the practice of mindfulness and the experience of calm affective dispositions work through self-reinforcement: the more mindfulness one has, the calmer and less reactive one becomes, and the calmer and less reactive one becomes, the more one is able to practice mindfulness.

Part of what affect looks like for Thai monks is related to these ideal affective states of calmness, but within this is another layer of meaning about the process of affective construction itself: rather than being calm as a way to be "happy" in a robust or riled sense of joyous well-being, Buddhist perspectives on emotional calmness are much more about an ideal "equanimity," a concept that in its formal Buddhist framing is tied to an attitude about reacting to sensations. While calmness is seen as a good feeling to have, the monks pointed to a sense of ideal affect in which the goal is less about feeling good rather than bad, and more about not being attached to affective states of either positive or negative feelings. I would learn more about this process in my own meditation training in Thai monasteries and from

others in the country and the region; in the discussions with monks
it was only hinted at, a kind of behind-the-scenes attitude about how
emotionality works.

E—Ethics

These considerations of temporality and affect, along with other orientations to mindfulness (such as power and selfhood, which are introduced in the chapters below), are considered to be part of a larger
ethical project. Mindfulness for these Thai monks is seen to be "good"
to do, in a general moral sense of spiritual and psychological cultivation, and also one that requires goodness to do. This ethical component in the general moral sense of mindfulness was raised as part of
an assumption that mindfulness is helpful in living a good life, both
in the present and as part of the development of a future moral path
toward enlightenment. This "goodness" takes on many forms: it is pre-
sumed to be "good," in a moral sense, to be aware of the passage of
time, to develop affective calmness, and to generally "tie the buffalo to
the post" and bring the mind back to the present. The moral reading
of mindfulness as creating positive outcomes is one aspect of its ethical
component, but there are more. Mindfulness is seen to not just create
morally valued subjective dispositions, but also to be created by them.
This was evident explicitly when Phra Thēp discussed the components
of moral practice. It is at the level of the precepts, of moral action, that
Phra Thēp develops his mindfulness: in acting morally, concentration
and wisdom arise, he said, as three friends linked in a chain. As with
affect, the moral component of mindfulness is considered cyclically self-
reinforcing: by doing good one is able to practice mindfulness more easily, and by practicing mindfulness one is able to do good. The role of
morality in mindfulness wasn't drawn out explicitly by every monk, but
it was very much a part of the development and purpose of the practice,
one that would come to be elaborated more in the experiences of others across the region.

Beyond indexing social practices and these three TAPES of psychological experience, a final point that monks brought up often in their discussions is that in order to develop mindfulness, it is good to meditate. Even
while everyday contexts of living help them to develop mindfulness, most

monks referred to meditation, either directly or indirectly, as important, even crucial. And as one said, summing up his thoughts on the subject: "To understand meditation you have to practice it yourself."

Meditation, of course, is easier said than done. Different monks discussed different techniques of meditation and talked about their preferences for one over the other. Some monks talked about their own personal experiences with meditation, saying that when they first started meditating it was uncomfortable and difficult to sit, but then it got easier. Yet few went into much detail. "I knew from talking with others that it could be uncomfortable," one old monk who did discuss his feelings in meditation said of his early experiences: "My body hurt so badly when I first ordained, and I felt heat inside and my mind couldn't stay still, and I got sleepy"—but he went on to say that eventually the practice lent itself to a feeling of ease and calmness. Another monk, in his mid-twenties, even said he felt a kind of joy when he meditated, a state considered to be the first level of meditative absorption in the path of meditative practice: "When my body starts to hurt from sitting too long, I think, "It's pain, it's just pain," and I try not to attach my mind to that pain, and then I feel at peace . . . and then I feel free, cooler, light, floating. If you're asking me to talk about the feeling I have when I'm meditating, before it was very difficult, but now my emotion is still, it's free from attachment. It's a kind of quiet joy."

These personal, felt descriptions of meditation are fascinating, but they are relatively rare. Monks in Thailand don't often talk about the personal, felt side of religion and meditation, perhaps because doing so is considered to be discussing struggles that they are working to overcome, and dwelling in them means to be attached to them and to the corporeal, individual self, which is seen as antithetical to the process. I have come across only a few of these more personal accounts.

One of the questions Phra Mon asked us about the project at the end of his interview was about practice.

"Do you practice meditation?" he asked. "To really understand mindfulness you have to practice it."

"I don't meditate much," Santi had replied, sheepishly looking up from where he had been busily taking notes. As a graduate student of religion and philosophy working on European traditions, and spending his days and nights at the coffee shops and bars of Chiang Mai's fashionable neighborhoods, Santi had agreed to help me with the project only because his adviser had asked him to. He didn't think monks would have much to teach him, he had told me, even though like most others in his country he was raised Buddhist and visited the monastery from time to time. It was only after the project had ended that he wrote to me to say he was thinking about the interviews and realizing the relevance of these monks' insights.

"I meditate a little bit," Justin added after Santi, "but not much."

"Well, if you meditate before you go to sleep each night," Phra Mon said, trying to offer a practical and doable suggestion, "it will help you sleep well. If you do that, you won't dream when you sleep. And if you do dream, you'll have a good dream."

"I have nightmares almost every night," Santi told him.

"And that's because you don't practice," Phra Mon replied.

"To know about mindfulness," the monks told me and Santi and Justin again and again in the interviews we were conducting and the question-naires we were collecting and the conversations we were having around town, "well, it's quite difficult at the beginning, but you have to meditate."

2

The Feeling of Mindfulness in Meditation

A man at a restaurant in Chiang Mai was drinking beer and talking adamantly with his friends. It was the summer of 2014, just after the country's military coup, and the restaurant was right next to a controversial, left-leaning bookstore, so I thought the man might be talking about politics. Instead, he was talking about mindfulness.

"With mindfulness . . ." I heard him say, as he spoke between bites of grilled pork from the barbecue in front of him, ". . . with mindfulness you can know everything. You can become enlightened. When people practice the dhamma, most of the time when they die they're reborn, or reborn better if they practice a lot; but when you practice mindfulness you can be reborn in the heavens. You can get to where you can achieve nirvana. . . ."

The man continued, telling his friends about the benefits of mindfulness practice, the techniques for gaining it, what it is and what it can do, from nirvana to being reborn as a *thewada*, a kind of "angel" or celestial deity. His friends were engaged, listening, and asking questions, though they weren't quite as enthusiastic as he was. I was sitting nearby, reading a book and listening in on the discussion. After a while, I decided to go over and say hello.

"I couldn't help but overhear you talking about mindfulness," I said, hesitating as I approached the group, "and I'm interested in mindfulness. May I join you?"

"Sure—he's really into mindfulness!" one of his friends said, laughing. She gestured for me to sit down, and the man went on to tell me about his recent experience with meditation.

The man's name was Kay. He looked to be about forty years old and was from a small town outside Chiang Mai. "I just got out of a meditation retreat," he explained, gesturing to some woods nearby at the base of the city's mountain. "It was great."

From his appearance, which was a bit red from the beer starting to have its effect, as well as his demeanor and his almost extreme gesturing and intensity, I wouldn't have guessed that Kay had just been meditating for days, if not months. But often after people sit in meditation for extended periods, especially if they are not used to doing so, the response right afterward is just this: a kind of exuberance or even physical and mental release from the extreme discipline they had just put their bodies and minds through in the retreat, coupled with a feeling that the experience was good, and the wish to share what they had learned with others.

"It's all really about the Satipaṭṭhāna," Kay went on, "the way to practice mindfulness. That's what we did at the retreat. . . . Sati is so important. It helps keep you from feeling disoriented, distracted by things."

"What monastery did you go to for the retreat?" I asked.

"I was at Wat Rampoeng," he replied, pointing to the forested area a few kilometers to our left.

"Why did you pick there to go to?" I asked. "I mean, there are so many monasteries in town, and some have meditation retreats for laypeople, too."

"There are a lot of monasteries, that's true," he answered, "but Wat Rampoeng is a great place to *practice*, to practice the dhamma, to practice sati." Wat Rampoeng is one of the most popular meditation centers for lay practitioners in Northern Thailand. It was made famous under the leadership of its head monk Ajan Tong, who after a study trip to Burma years earlier developed a style of meditation based on the teachings of the Burmese master Mahāsī Sayādaw. Ajan Tong now presides over a second, "franchised" monastery in the town of Chom Thong about fifty kilometers from Chiang Mai on the way to Mae Jaeng, but the lineage of Wat

Rampoeng remains his, and the style taught there is, as with most of the mindfulness meditation styles in Thailand, firmly rooted in the Burmese-inflected modern *vipassanā* tradition.

I had heard of Wat Rampoeng by this point from interviews and word of mouth, and from scholarly books on modern Buddhist meditation. Along the way I had picked up the meditation booklet handed out at Wat Rampoeng, which offers instructions on how to practice. On the first page is a description of mindfulness and its central role in meditation:

> The Four Foundations of Mindfulness are the heart of the Buddha's teaching. The Lord Buddha repeatedly taught them to his disciples from the time of his enlightenment until his ceasing. As he stated strongly and clearly in the Mahasatipaṭṭhāna Sutta: "Look, you who find the cycle of rebirth harmful, the Four Foundations of Mindfulness are the only way to the purification of all sorrows and lamentations, the end of all suffering and grief, and the attainment of Nibbāna [nirvana]."

Figure 6. *Vipassanā Kammaṭṭhāna* (*Insight Meditation and the Technique [of] Practice*): the meditation instruction manual for retreats at Wat Rampoeng just outside the city of Chiang Mai, in its English (*left*) and Thai versions. The manuals explain mindfulness training as the main meditative technique of the monastery. Image reprinted with permission, courtesy of Wat Rampoeng.

The booklet then lists in turn the Four Foundations of Mindfulness of the Satipaṭṭhāna Sutta, with a short discussion of how to practice each of them:

1. *Kāya*: Mindfulness of the Body is to contemplate bodily action and sensations. This includes, for example, acknowledging or being conscious of the lifting, stepping, and placing of the feet during walking meditation, and acknowledging the rising and falling of the abdomen in sitting meditation.

2. *Vedanā*: Mindfulness of One's Feelings is to contemplate the happiness/suffering/neutrality of your experience. That is, to acknowledge happiness, to know how happy one is, or to acknowledge misery, and to know how miserable one is, or to acknowledge the neutral feeling which is neither happiness nor misery.

3. *Citta*: Mindfulness of the Mind (Thought) is to contemplate one's thoughts or to be conscious of the passion, anger, delusion, sloth, distraction, peace, etc. in the thought. While in meditation our minds may think of the past or the future. We then take that thought as the momentary focus of the meditation by acknowledging "thinking-thinking-thinking" before returning our focus to the breath or the feet.

4. *Dhammā*: Mindfulness of Objects of the Mind is to contemplate mental recognition and other volitional activities. Recognition is to know something when perceiving it. Volitional activities happen when we think about or comment on something. While we think, we must be mindful of thinking. When we are desirous, angry, slothful, restless, or doubtful as a result of thinking or external stimulation, we must be mindful too.[1]

"Mindfulness helps you see what arises," Kay said, "that all there is is *anicca, dukkha, anattā* [impermanence, nonsatisfactoriness, non-self]." As Kay and I talked about his experience at the retreat, and about sati in general, he reiterated how important mindfulness was, and how cool and special. After a while I excused myself, not wanting to interrupt him for too long. After he gave me his phone number and offered to talk more, I left the restaurant. As I was leaving I heard him continue recalling his stories of mindfulness and meditation to his friends over dinner.

Many people I know in Thailand will mention their experiences meditating in passing, as something they did to practice mindfulness.

They do not, however, usually elaborate on what exactly it was that they did in meditating, or what it felt like. When they do describe some of their personal impressions, as they did in interviews when I directly asked them to, they would say something along the general lines of liking it and benefiting from it, and that, as one man told me in a way similar to the few monks who had discussed it, "When I first started meditating it was uncomfortable and not easy, but then I got better at it, and now I find it peaceful." People talk in generalities about particular emphases of meditation they like, such as the *phut-tho* breathing style that is Phra Thēp's preference, or Phra Mon's general allusion to *vipassanā* (insight) and *samatha* (concentration) in describing his meditation, or Kay's general *satipaṭṭhāna* (way of mindfulness) style from Wat Rampoeng, but they usually do not go into details about what it actually feels like to meditate. Maybe this is because most people in Thailand grow up in an environment in which meditation and mindfulness are taken as natural and known, and so it didn't seem like something that would be novel to comment on at length. People may also not talk about their experience meditating because they feel that talking about one's own experiences is to express a kind of hubris in focusing on one's self excessively. They may also feel that part of the purpose and training of meditation is to decrease discursive thought and speech. Yet even with these shared tendencies away from narrative elaboration, understanding what mindfulness is like in meditation, and not just in social lives, is important, because it is through meditation that people train to develop and improve mindfulness, and it is through meditation that many of the lessons of mindfulness can be shared with others.

Not everyone in Thailand meditates at length, and not everyone goes to meditation retreats to do so. Many do, though, and also gain practice in meditation in less intensive moments at their local monasteries. Those who meditate are not just monks and the elderly, who make up the two groups in popular Thai consciousness that are thought to have more spiritual interests and more time available to pursue them. Meditation in practice is also common for nonordained, working people, both rich and poor, old and young, and increasingly as part of the larger trend of what has come to be called the "laicization" of Buddhism over time

(McMahan and Braun 2017; Cook 2010). While the specific places where people go to meditate can be traced to local historical and socio-economic factors that play out in their lives, across social groups most people in Thailand meditate in some way or another. They do this by becoming ordained for a period of time, by attending meditation retreats, by spending a few minutes every evening performing meditative chants before sleeping, by spending a few minutes once a week at the monastery sitting in meditation, chanting, and making merit by offering monks everyday goods, or listening to a monk give a sermon. Many people do all these things, grouping them under the umbrella term of *patibat tham*, literally "to practice the dhamma." Part of practicing the dhamma is meditation, which plays a necessary role in gaining firsthand experience of the religion.

Meditation is hard. The work and cognitive/bodily effort that it takes is important to consider when thinking about mindfulness, especially in an age of shortcuts and social-media short attention spans. People throughout history, of course, have tried to find shortcuts to meditative progress, spurring among other things the popularity of the *vipassanā*, insight style of meditation as a "quicker" technique than the *samatha* concentration style, as well as the popularity of charismatic and "magical" teachers around the world. But even with these techniques to "speed up" the process, it is a generally agreed upon fact that mindfulness isn't an automatic skill. Scholars who don't try to actually practice meditation may find it easier to generalize about it in vague terms, or to even see it as a relatively unimportant part of social life in contemporary Buddhist societies. Yet disciplining the mind and body through iterations of practice takes work, and has real effects wherever one is in other areas of life.

Scholarship on the subject of religious embodiment, and especially on how particular teachings come to be embodied in the rituals of religion, suggests that specific bodily and sensory forms of training give rise to culturally varied forms of experience (Csordas 1990, 1997; Mahmood 2005; Hirshkind 2009). This is undoubtedly the case in meditation. This kind of training is part of what Mauss (1934) called "techniques of the body" and Foucault (1988) describes as "technologies of the self": by practicing and repeating certain kinds of ritualized comportment, people who train in meditation strive to shape their subjectivity by their actions. Analysis often collapses particular embodied religious subjectivities and the processes that get one there, however, either because different methods are thought to cause the same result or because one method is seen to always result in one effect. Showing how particular techniques are part of meditation in ways tied to various outcomes helps to disentangle the abstract and particulars of practice. In doing so it demonstrates some of the similarities and diversity of mindfulness.

Choosing How to Meditate

To understand mindfulness, I would have to meditate, but what kind of meditation should I do? Two general kinds of meditation are practiced in contemporary Theravāda Buddhism: *samatha* meditation, which emphasizes concentration, and *vipassanā* meditation, which emphasizes insight. *Samatha* teaches techniques to not let the mind wander away, sometimes employing the use of mantras or visual images to help focus, and *vipassanā* refers to the practice of developing insight, or awareness, with techniques designed to work on becoming acutely aware of the phenomena around one.

In developing mindfulness, should one practice *vipassanā* or *samatha*? The answer seemed to matter in some way: monks and scholars over thousands of years have thought about the strengths and weaknesses of each. Yet the more I asked about the difference, the more I learned that while both these styles are well known and differentiated in Thailand, and some meditative traditions stress one over the other, they are often used interchangeably in the way people talk about practice. In Thai the generic word for "meditation" is to *nang samādhi*, and usually encompasses all kinds of meditation, including *vipassanā* and *samatha* styles. *Samādhi* means one thing in Pali (concentration) and another in Thai: concentration and, more generally, meditation as a whole, of which *vipassanā* can be a part.[2] Only sometimes when differentiating the two will people speak of them by name, and when they do they talk of the *samatha* style as *samādhi*. Of the few monks who spoke of *samādhi* and *vipassanā* as different, one of them told me that "*samādhi* helps more in gaining peace in your mind, and *vipassanā* helps you gain more wisdom."

While both styles are incorporated in most meditation trainings, of the two, *vipassanā* is thought of as the most common style in connection to mindfulness. Just one monk I spoke with, at a small monastery in the hills behind Chiang Mai University, said that he really preferred *samādhi* over *vipassanā*: "*Samādhi* is like a secret trick for everything," he told me. "It's the key to all religions, not just Buddhism. You focus your mind and you feel religious, it's what they do when they teach religion whatever it is, Buddhist or Christian or whatever. You feel *samādhi*, from sitting in meditation to kneeling in prayer at a church service, and you call that feeling religious." Most of those, however, who separated the *samādhi* and *vipassanā* in their discussions said that for those who want to learn meditation to develop especially high levels of mind, and especially those that train in mindfulness, *vipassanā*-style techniques are the most appropriate.

Soma Thera, in his introduction to the Satipaṭṭhāna Sutta, stated this connection between mindfulness and *vipassanā* meditation explicitly: "The Discourse on the Arousing of Mindfulness . . . deal[s] with the method for training for insight (vipassanā) according to the Buddha's teaching. . . . Insight is the understanding of the true nature of things by which a complete transfiguring of mental life takes place." Religious studies scholar Brooke Schedneck found this connection between sati and *vipassanā* to be the case in her ethnographic study on meditative practices in Thailand: "Many vipassanā meditation teachers assert that all instructions and practices necessary for vipassanā meditation are contained in this [Satipaṭṭhāna] sutta" (2015, 27). The well-known contemporary Burmese monk Khruba Bunchum entered a cave in Northern Thailand in 2010 to meditate for three years because "he thought he should practice *vipassanā* meditation if he wanted to gain enlightenment" (Jirattikorn 2016, 387), with mindfulness considered to be part of this process (Jirattikorn, personal communication). The famous meditation teacher S. N. Goenka even went so far as to say: "Vipassanā and [mindfulness as followed in the] Satipaṭṭhāna are the same thing" (*Discourse on Vipassanā*, 1992).

Beyond the general preference for *vipassanā* in mindfulness meditation, many people in Thailand say that different kinds of people will prefer and benefit from different, more specific styles. "I like the *phut-tho* style," Phra Thēp had told me, "because it's easiest for me." Others had offered similar explanations for their own preferred techniques.

There is a classical tradition in the Pali canon (especially elaborated in the *Abhidhamma*) and the *Visuddhimagga* of a kind of "personality psychology" classification that suggests particular meditation techniques for particular kinds of people. While there are variations in interpretations of these, and few people I spoke with adhered to the personality theory explicitly, in general this list suggests the following:

- A greedy temperament will especially benefit from meditating on impurities and foulness of the body (as in the cemetery contemplations and mindfulness of the body of the Satipaṭṭhāna).
- A hating temperament will benefit from meditating on divine abidings (heavenly realms) and the color *kasina-s* (meditation objects).
- An easily deluded temperament will benefit from meditating on mindfulness of breathing (some versions say "an unintelligent" or "a discursive" temperament in place of "easily deluded"). Others divide this further and say that those of an unintelligent temperament should meditate on a wide meditative object, and of a discursive temperament on a small one.
- A faithful or devout temperament will benefit from meditating on the first six recollections (of the *anussati*, as listed in Phra Chan's *Navakovada* as the Buddha, dhamma, sangha, "morality," "generosity," and "deities").
- An intelligent temperament will benefit from meditating on the rest of the ten recollections (of the *anussati*) of "death" and "peace" (some versions also include "perception" and "analysis").[3]

Some versions break this classification down even further:

- Those who are dull-witted with a craving nature will especially benefit from contemplating the body.
- Those who are keen-witted with a craving nature will especially benefit from contemplating feelings.
- Those who are dull-witted with a theorizing nature will especially benefit from contemplating consciousness.
- Those who are keen-witted with a theorizing nature will especially benefit from contemplating the dhamma.

Having studied cognitive and social psychology in college, and as an anthropologist of Buddhist practice and scholar of comparative human development from graduate school, I was excited by these fairly explicit guides. I wanted to follow the instructions of the lists of personality types in choosing a style of meditation ("I have an intelligent temperament!" I thought; "I should meditate on peace, death, perception and analysis! . . . Or am I more the delusional, discursive type, so mindfulness of the breath? Keen-witted and theorizing! Or craving?") The list seemed almost pre-made for the click-bait era of BuzzFeed personality quizzes. Maybe no one would really see themselves as "dull-witted," but a teacher handing out meditation exercises to students might, and assign a meditation technique accordingly. There seemed to be a lot of potential in these personality guides.

Yet while some people I spoke with advocated some kinds of meditation for themselves and others, the fairly esoteric list offered in the texts, I found, was not particularly followed in a prescriptive or guiding sense. "There is no rule on what styles of meditation to use," as the head monk of one monastery in Chiang Mai had put it. "Some might feel more comfortable with, say, the *phut-tho* style and gain more sati that way than with other styles. But for all of these methods, the most important thing is not about the style."

Instead of following explicit guidelines, most people follow the "grocery store" approach that a monk had described while explaining why someone goes to one monastery over another: people practice a particular style because it's taught near where they live, because someone they know recommended it, or because they have heard that it has something that they like. My first meditation retreat came about in that way. So did the next, and the next, and the next. I followed a general trajectory of more internationally friendly and secularly oriented retreats at first and progressively moved to more locally Thai ones, based on my increasing familiarity with the language and culture, though each of the retreats I went on was open to both international and Thai meditators, and (other than the first two) was open to both those who were ordained and those who were not. Along with Pali chants, the language of instruction of the first retreat was English, the middle two used a mix of English and Thai, and the final two were all led in Thai without any English spoken at the monastery at all.

Retreats 1 and 2: Goenka's *Satipaṭṭhāna Vipassanā* Meditation, Scanning for *Saṅkhāra-s*

I signed up for my first-ever ten-day silent meditation retreat while traveling through Dharamsala in Northern India in 2000, exploring the region's ancient and contemporary Buddhist sites. Dharamsala is the center of today's Tibetan community in exile, but the kind of meditation retreat I took part in while there comes from the Theravāda tradition. The retreat was a course started by the Burmese layman S. N. Goenka; meditation courses based on his teaching are now offered in more than 130 meditation centers in over ninety-four countries around the world, including nine in Thailand.[4] The existence of Goenka's lineage at the Tibetan hill town in India speaks to the blending of modern forms of practice in the international community.

Goenka's emphasis on the Satipaṭṭhāna Sutta and a particular interpretation of feelings in it can be traced through a Burmese lineage. It runs through Goenka's teacher Sayagyi U Ba Khin and Sayagyi U Ba Khin's teachers Saya Thet to Ledi Sayadaw. Ledi Sayadaw, who in turn is seen to draw especially from his interpretations of the Satipaṭṭhāna Sutta as developed in the *Visuddhimagga*, created and popularized a system of meditation that has since become world famous and central to the global mindfulness meditation revival.[5] Through his connections to these teachers and ancient teachings, Goenka claims to be connected historically all the way down to the time of the Buddha himself.

Lineages are especially important in Buddhist traditions, because even without a fully recorded chronology they help to imagine a continuous link to the original teachings of the religion. The continuity established by claiming to speak of "what the Buddha really said" combines for its persuasive power with an articulation of the teaching that fits with the needs and understandings of a very different kind of audience from the one that listened to the Buddha twenty-five hundred years ago. An example of this kind of innovative (one might say "creative") interpretation is the way that Goenka defines a *bhikkhu*, which is usually thought of as referring to a monk. In his discourse on the Satipaṭṭhāna Sutta, Goenka says that "in the ordinary language of India a Bhikkhu means a monk, a recluse, but in all of the Buddha's teachings a Bhikkhu means anyone who is practicing the teaching of dhamma. Therefore it means a meditator, whether a householder—man or woman—or a monk or nun." When asked to comment on his fairly liberal interpretation of the Buddhist teachings during an interview, Goenka answered, in part, in a way similar to others who emphasize the need for modern meanings and the continuity of such contextualization from the Buddha's time: "The language is twenty-five centuries old," he said,

> and meanings change. Even if they do not, what the Buddha said with his experience cannot be understood without that experience. . . . Commentaries were written on the Buddha's words, some over 1,000 years after his death, although our research reveals that Vipassanā in its pure form was lost 500 years after his death. Others were written within 500 years, but were lost except in Sri Lanka: they were again translated into Pali, but with the translator's own interpretation. They give a clear picture of Indian society in the Buddha's time: the whole spectrum of its social, political, educational, cultural, religious and philosophical background. . . . Yet while they are very helpful, if their words differ from our experience . . .
> (Goenka 1998, 102)

Goenka is saying here that there is room to interpret the teaching to be more in line with what he sees as the Buddha's real meaning, which may be differently framed in different historical eras. Goenka (with his purported lineage head Ledi Sayadaw) may be the most influential figure in the globalization of this Burmese *vipassanā* meditation tradition (Neubert 2014).

Goenka's method is based on his and his teachers' interpretation of the Satipaṭṭhāna, or "ways of mindfulness," as part of his *vipassanā* program of meditation. He teaches the meditator to attend to feelings, *vedanā*, the second "foundation" or "way" of mindfulness in the Satipaṭṭhāna Sutta. By attending to *vedanā* (sensations/feelings), Goenka says, one also attends to the other foundations, of *rupa* (body), *citta* (minds/emotions), and dhamma ([Buddhist] concepts). Through an emphasis on *vedanā*, the other "foundations" of mindfulness—of the body, feelings, mind, and dhamma—are all implicated, especially that of attention to the body. "The second [of the Satipaṭṭhāna]," Goenka says in his commentary of the Satipaṭṭhāna Sutta, "is *vedanāsu vedanānupassī viharati*: to live witnessing the truth of bodily sensations. . . . The truth is observed within the bodily sensations, by direct experience in the same way. . . . *Vedanā* therefore becomes so important. To explore the *kaya* you have to feel sensations. Similarly in the exploration of *citta* and *dhammā*, everything that arises in the mind manifests as a sensation." Goenka offers a fairly specific interpretation of *vedanā*: he says that his (and his lineage teacher Ledi Sayadaw's) emphasis on and interpretation of *vedanā* ("sensations/feelings," the second of the four Satipaṭṭhāna) as affectively felt on the body are both the most appropriate for a contemporary audience and most faithful to the Buddha's actual meaning: "For instance," he has said of one commentary on the sutta, "one tradition takes vedanā as only mental. It is true that vedanā is a mental aggregate and that vedanānupassanā has to be mental. But in several places the Buddha talks of sukha and dukkha vedanā on the body, as in the Satipaṭṭhāna Sutta" (Goenka 1998, 102). It is through an attention to sensations, he was saying, that one gains in mindfulness.

I wasn't thinking of any of this, though, when I signed up for the retreat. I had to sign a "psychological health" form to be admitted, which itself raises a series of important issues about the possible consequences of meditation (Lindahl et al. 2017), but other than that I jumped into the program without much trepidation over what it would entail. Previously, other than a little bit in college, I had never meditated at all, which I realized by the first day maybe wasn't the smartest idea. We were assigned small dorm-type rooms to the side of the meditation hall to sleep in at night, but we spent most of our waking hours in the large meditation hall, where we were instructed to sit on square mats for an hour at a time for ten hours each day for ten days straight, with only short, five-minute breaks in between. Each morning we woke at 4:30 and sat immediately for an hour, only afterward getting the breakfast that was the main meal of the day; after a few more sessions of sitting we ate again at 11:30 a.m. and then nothing until the next morning.

Instead of learning about lineages and histories, from early morning to night we sat there in silence, without speaking and with barely any sounds at all. As we sat, hour after silent hour, my body ached and my mind was so bored I thought I would get up and run out at any minute. I felt more bored than I even thought was possible. I had wanted some kind of magical peace or insight to descend, but all I got was silence and pain.

"Scan the body," Goenka told us at the end of each hour on a cassette recording played in the meditation hall after a few minutes of Pali chants, "and note the changes on the body. These are *saṅkhāra-s*," he explained, "tiny microscopic sensations that are manifestations of feelings and the negative energy stored under the skin being released, karmic residues coming to the surface. Check each section of your body in parts. Over time you'll be able to scan the whole body as a flow, and you'll feel a kind of current to it."

Hour after hour I tried to feel the sensations on my skin arise and pass away, but my back hurt, and the minutes seemed to tick by in reverse. Before the third day was over I thought of everything I had in my head to think about, from Nintendo game theme songs I'd played as a kid to different versions of conversations I had never had. I started craving the sound of the first syllable of the first Pali chant that would signal the end of another hour. I counted the minutes as they went by, though with eyes closed and no clock in the room anyway I could only guess. I sat there, the discomfort in my legs becoming increasingly hard to bear, and the minutes seemed to slow down and laugh as they embedded themselves, excruciatingly, into the spine of my back. I tried to think about plans I had made for when the course was over, and ideas for projects I had not yet thought through. But the more I thought about wanting the time to pass, the slower it seemed to move. When the sound of the chanting at the end of each hour finally did come I would sigh in relief, knowing the five-minute break before the next hour's sitting was about to start. The minutes seemed to slow down, and I spent hour after hour and day after day scanning my body for these *saṅkhāra-s*, what felt to me like little dust particles fallen onto my skin, and tried to keep the boredom and discomfort at bay.

At night there were short, twenty-minute-long dhamma talks, about a range of teachings distilled and interpreted by Goenka from different suttas and commentaries on them. Most of them drew from famous stories told by the Buddha to illustrate particular points, with Goenka's modernist, secular, and "scientific" spin on the teachings. The tradition of Buddhism as being like a science, and available to secular and not just especially religious recluses, draws from a wide variety of sources over a long period of time. One central influence for the scientific spin on Buddhist thought emerged, at least in Thailand, especially during the period when the Bangkok court was responding to colonial pressure from Western forces, and when Western forces themselves were "discovering" Buddhism in the nineteenth century (Almond 1988). While significantly different in many aspects from some central ideas about scientific approaches (especially those of falsifiability), scholarly work on the popular wish to align Buddhism and science continues in texts like *Buddhism without Beliefs* (Batchelor 1998), *The Scientific Buddha* (Lopez 2012), *Buddha-Abhidhamma: Ultimate Science* (Mon 1995), and *Meditation, Buddhism, and Science* (McMahan and Braun 2017). Goenka's framing of his interpretation of the teaching as both modern and ancient is, as with many kinds of contemporary meditation practices, a key reason for his success. The particulars of Goenka's interpretations in forming the teaching for a particular kind of person might not be more or less of a distortion than some other "true" or "pure" contemporary version existing in some imagined remote location. Each of the interpretations of Buddhist teachings can be said to appeal to its particular audience, but who that audience is, and how the audience becomes universalized as a kind of "every person" through courses like Goenka's, becomes important for the way that certain people can benefit from them. I remember learning about how the Buddha said he had nothing up his sleeve, that the insights he offered were all clearly and empirically observable by each person who practiced them, but what would be seen differently by different people?[6]

The nightly stories were related in evocative, narrative styles, almost like moral fables of events in the life of the Buddha. There was a story about Arigulimala, the man who wore the fingers of people he had killed around his neck before meeting the Buddha and becoming enlightened, and I remember one about a cow, too, but I didn't record these lessons, even though I wanted to. Not only could we not speak for the ten days, but we also couldn't write or read.[7] Each evening after the final sitting of the night I brushed my teeth in silence, surrounded by the hundred other people taking part in the retreat, and got ready for some very welcomed sleep. The absence of a need to interact or make eye contact or speak at all did admittedly feel a little refreshing, but I furtively looked around in the evening for words of any kind written on the buildings of the retreat grounds to occupy my mind, even old graffiti or operating instructions for appliances. It was as if I needed a voice, a connection to the outside world, anything to occupy my mind, sensorily deprived and craving something to read.

I had been told that the third day in these courses is the hardest; if you can make it past that, I heard, you can make it to day ten. The first few days you are agitated, restless, thinking you could leave, but by day three it feels like the commitment is sticking: most people who do decide to leave seem to do so on day three. "It would be great if meditation retreats could just start on the third day," someone once told me. "It takes that long to settle in anyway." I'd heard this before starting the Goenka retreat, so when day three came and went, I figured the uphill battle was over. But it got only a little better. At the end of day six I figured it was just a matter of time before I would make it through to ten, but I never "settled in," and certainly didn't feel I was learning anything during the hours and hours of impatient silence, other than that I had somehow been duped into a kind of mental torture. The seconds that felt like they were ticking by in reverse finally added up to the tenth day, and the course ended. After leaving the center, I and the other international travelers I had joined the course with gathered to discuss our experiences in exuberant conversations, finally freed from the confines of the silence. It felt great to speak and be social again. We talked so much over the next few days, gorging on pizza and beer, the words gushing out after the long days of silence, that our throats got hoarse, and I even lost my voice.

I don't remember learning much during that ten-day course, but I do remember thinking that somehow the trees and air around me when I exited back to the "real world" felt different, more alive, almost like they were moving, like I had taken some drug and could see them more clearly, in greater detail. This lasted a few months, until the feeling faded and I started failing on the promise I had made to myself to meditate regularly, an hour or even a half hour a day. The impression from the retreat seemed to disappear; it was only years later that I realized the words "*anicca, anicca . . . change, change*" at the end of every hour of the meditation sittings at the retreat ended up as the topic of my PhD thesis and my first book. It must have made more of an impression than I had thought.

The feeling from the retreat lingered, and I found myself wanting to do another one. I don't know why I wanted to do another one, really. I don't know if it was the sensation of being alive after I left, or the satisfaction of overcoming a challenge, or just that the time that had seemed so awful to sit through that first time I somehow missed once I was back in the fast-paced world. Maybe it was just the sense of calmness that came from listening to the Pali chants at the end of each hour, or the feeling that

I was putting into practice the learning I had only read or heard about otherwise. I didn't feel like I had learned enough the first time to improve on my own, so I signed up for a second ten-day meditation retreat in the same Goenka tradition two years later, this time in the central Thai town of Phitsanulok as a break from conducting PhD field research in the far north of the country.

The form and content of the second retreat were virtually identical to what they had been in Dharamsala, except for the inclusion of Thai in the short comments after every hour and during the evening dhamma talk. The main meditation hall was still packed with people sitting on square mats in rows facing a plain wall, this time about half Thai and half international meditators, and there was still hour after hour of silence. But I found that it was slightly but significantly easier this time to sit through the hours of not moving a muscle, though my joints still ached and I was still painfully restless in my body and mind. Partly it was easier because I had also started doing little one-hour meditation sittings since the first retreat, even if they weren't as often as planned, either on my own, or more often in groups at an artist colony in Chiang Mai in weekly sittings of the Goenka style. This had familiarized the practice for me.

But mostly it was easier because the after-effects of the first sitting still remained with me; I knew more about what it took to endure the silent sessions. This retreat was also ten days, following a structural convention that is becoming increasingly common in mass meditation movements. One change that made this second ten-day retreat easier was to sit with my back fully straight, like a tree, instead of leaning against a wall as I had tried to do the first time, or slouching over to try to avoid the pain. The other thing that changed from the first retreat to this one was a different relationship I was starting to develop between my mind and the time ticking by. I still wanted the minutes to pass; I still craved the end of the session and wondered when it would come, and why I had signed up again in the first place. I was like someone exercising who knows that exercise is good for them but still hopes it will soon end so they can sit back with some potato chips and watch TV.

The second retreat also felt easier because I had learned more beforehand about Goenka's variety of mindfulness meditation. In his commentary on the Satipaṭṭhāna Sutta, I had read a fairly technical explanation for his predilection for scanning for sensation, and what he sees as the relationship between feeling and the body in the *vedanā-paṭṭhāna*:

> Everything within the framework of the body changes into something unpleasant, so it is nothing but *dukkha* [dissatisfaction, suffering]. The law of nature is such. Yet the tendency of the mind is to get attached and cling to a pleasant experience, and when it is gone you feel miserable. This is not a philosophy but a truth to be experienced by *paṭivedhana*: dividing, dissecting, disintegrating, dissolving you reach the stage of *bhaṅga*, total dissolution. You witness the solidified, material structure, the body, as actually nothing but subatomic particles, *kalāpas*, arising and passing. Similarly the mind and mental contents manifest as very solidified, intensified emotions—anger, fear, or passion—which overpower you. Vipassanā, *paṭivedhana*, helps you. With piercing, penetrating *paññā* [wisdom] you divide, dissect, disintegrate to the stage where this intense [feeling of] emotion is nothing but wavelets. The whole material and mental structures and the mental contents are nothing but wavelets, wavelets, anicca, anicca. (Goenka 1998, 6)

Goenka's attention to sensations as feelings in *vedanā-paṭṭhāna* helped me to understand why I was being instructed to pay attention to the fleeting sensations on my skin a little bit more, as part of his interpretation of the training of mindfulness as the observation of feelings manifested on the skin. The idea was to see these feelings as impermanent and by recognizing their always impermanent nature watch them disintegrate, disrupting a tendency to create them into emotions. This made it easier to make sense of what I was being told to do.

The way to get the time to pass, I began to realize, wasn't as I had originally thought. I had had the idea that to help the minutes move I could use the time productively to think something through: what were the logistics for my upcoming travel plans? How could I combine theorist x with ethnographer y to come up with a new way to think about z? Why had so-and-so said that, and what did it mean? I would use the time to plot and plan and methodically track through ideas, following them in my mind like a mouse in a maze to get to some conclusion. Essentially I thought to use this great opportunity for sitting around seemingly doing nothing for hour after hour to my advantage. It seemed to me that this approach made perfect sense, even as I wasn't particularly proud of it in a room of what I imagined were good blank-minded successful meditators: the time would go by, I would get the benefit of sitting through the retreat, and I would solve practical problems I'd had in my mind, all at the same time. But the problem was it didn't work—the time didn't go faster at all. I would sit and think for what seemed like a long stretch about an issue, happily exiting the daydream when I felt I had reached some kind of conclusion, only to realize that really only three or four minutes had passed. And I hadn't solved anything at all. I had just circled through thoughts like an explorer looking through some interesting (or not interesting) pieces of debris. This frustrated me to no end at first; I knew I wasn't supposed to follow a thought, but just let it go instead, like a cloud or the *saṅkhāra*-s on my skin, but practically speaking, why wouldn't it help the time go by?

It was the realization that I could actually get the time to pass *faster* by dropping a thought the second it popped into my head that helped make the second ten-day session feel smoother, and easier. I still thought through a lot of issues in my head at that retreat, and spent even more time feeling angry at myself afterward for having done so, but I was getting better at following the technique of scanning the body for Goenka's *saṅkhāra*-s and not letting my mind wander away. I would scan the body as instructed, noting sensations on the skin, section of the body by section of the body, and then by the fourth or fifth day experiencing what Goenka said would eventually happen, as the scanning took on a kind of flowing movement, and it felt a little as if an electric current was passing through from head to toe and back again.

In practice, this method helped me to distract myself from the thoughts that kept popping up in my head. I would do as I was supposed to and concentrate on the body for a bit, until my mind wandered away a few minutes (or a few seconds) later, and I would either follow the train of thought for a few minutes more or, increasingly, bring it back to the body once I noticed what was happening.

I also listened more carefully at the second retreat to the words that Goenka spoke at the beginning and end of each hour. Unlike the first retreat, where the words were offered only in English with some Pali terms thrown in, this retreat was in both English and Thai, and I heard the mix of Thai and Pali words say again and again, "*Tong mi sati . . . tong mi ubekkha . . . anicca, anicca*" . . . "You must have mindfulness," the recording intoned, "equanimity . . . everything is changing, changing." During our five-minute breaks between hours, I thought of this emphasis on impermanence. I reflected on the many moments in which I was still susceptible to thinking as a way to pass the time. I found myself concluding my thoughts with the understanding that whatever issue I had been thinking about wouldn't last long and so wasn't worth getting too involved or agitated over. In spite of this, those little comments and Pali chants felt most significant at the time because they thankfully signaled the end of another hour.

At night I brushed my teeth and found it even more refreshing to not look anyone in the eye or pay attention to them at all. A lot of energy, I found, was normally spent on polite society, energy that could be saved to put to other uses. During the retreat I still fell asleep within five minutes of hitting the bed each night, and slept like a rock, even though I was told that as one improves in meditation one needs less and less sleep, and can even be said to meditate all night long.

As with the first session, I wasn't permitted to read anything or write anything down. I still craved letters and sounds, and I wished I could take notes as I went along. Even this craving, however, wasn't as strong as during the first retreat. I would find that this wish to record thoughts and feelings from meditation decreased the more I practiced. This isn't unusual—the anthropological psychologist Michel Pagis studied how meditation participants at a Goenka retreat in Israel who were permitted to keep notes successively decreased their journal writing each day they were there (2009). Along with Pagis's work pointing to the importance of embodiment and its critique of discourse as the only relevant site for anthropological analysis, the recognition that recording and analyzing become less and less desirable also helps to explain why monks so rarely discuss in detail their own personal experiences with practice—it is seen as overly self-centered and fixating, not just for ideological reasons but also in a visceral sense. As each day passed, the motley group of meditators, Thai and international, young people and old, sat together in the meditation hall, hour after silent hour.

On the last few days of the retreat, Goenka talked about *metta-bhāvanā*, or "meditating on loving kindness," and the importance of *dāna*, donation. There was no charge to take part, but meditators could donate some money at the end to support the program.

As I packed up my bags on the last day of the retreat I remember feeling a little surprised and confused at the thought that cars were driving on highways and overpasses in cities around me, that things were going on in the world that I had put far from my mind while sitting in meditation and brushing my teeth in silence and sleeping on the cot in the little room at the center. I cleaned the little dorm area and thought of the trains moving around the country, one of which would take me back to Chiang Mai. Instead of boisterously recalling our experiences with others, I talked quietly with a local Thai woman for a while. We hadn't spoken at all to each other the whole period of the ten days, of course, but we had shared an important experience. She invited me to stay at her house with her family for a few days in Phitsanulok before I had to return north and she had to return to work as an administrator at the local high school. Like most people, she didn't talk a lot about the details of how she felt during the retreat. We both agreed simply that it was difficult but worthwhile.

Days later, as I sat on a train with its noise and people, continuing onward with my field research in Northern Thailand, I felt like I was being pushed back into the mess and noise of the regular world. The retreat now seemed like a protective bubble I had left behind. It had been far from easy, and again, as I had after the first course, I swore I would never put myself in the position of committing to a ten-day silent meditation retreat again. Yet it hadn't been nearly as difficult as the first retreat, and even felt like a powerful experience. I've continued to practice this kind of meditation, when in Thailand, at the artist center outside Chiang Mai; some of the people who live there sit together once a week and turn on Goenka's tape recordings at the beginning and end of each hour. One of my friends there has even become, in my view, a little bit obsessed with it, sometimes going to monthlong retreats at the Goenka centers and even considering moving to the new community being built up around it nearby. He told me how when he was a teenager growing up in a Bangkok slum, he would take methamphetamine for fun, and be disoriented and unfocused. The meditation has helped him to develop a level of intense concentration.

Retreat 3: Buddhadasa Bhikkhu's *Ānāpānasati* Meditation: Mindfulness of the Breath

My host sister Goy in Mae Jaeng was a big fan of Thailand's most well-known scholar monk, Buddhadasa Bhikkhu. Like many educated people in Thailand, she had been to his monastery in the south of Thailand

and had read many of his books. For my third ten-day silent meditation retreat, I went to this monastery at Wat Suan Mokkh in Southern Thailand, about an hour from Thailand's famous tourist beaches, to see what kinds of meditation skills I could gain from such a "modernist" monk. I signed up for a third retreat because even though in some ways the first two had felt like prison, they had also felt a little bit like freedom—a kind of freedom from the "prison" of the regular world.

Wat Suan Mokkh is famous throughout Thailand, largely because of the fame of Buddhadasa Bhikkhu. According to some, Buddhadasa has published the largest amount of writings by a single Thai author.[8] In his interpretation of the Buddhist teachings, Buddhadasa has reformed the religion to offer a more modern, "rational" approach, drawing from a heterogeneous mixture of lineages, including Tibetan and Zen schools of thought. He has appealed especially to middle-class, urban, well-educated Thais (and international meditators), and those who aspire to be such. My host sister Goy falls into this latter group and, despite living in a small, rural town, appreciated his modernist slant. While liked by almost everyone, Buddhadasa appeals especially to this middle-class Thai imaginaire (Collins 1998; Anderson [1983] 2006) more than to international Buddhists (who tend to slightly favor other contemporary teachers like Ajan Cha), and more than to rural, less-educated Thai Buddhists (who tend to follow local monks). As an illustration of how Buddhadasa's interpretations are aimed at a particular kind of modern audience, instead of offering a traditional reading of rebirth to not necessarily mean a past life, present life, and future life in a literal sense, he says that one's past life, present life, and future life refer to the person you were a moment ago, the person you are now, and the person you will be a moment from now (Buddhadasa [1967] 1996). In this way Buddhadasa retains the basic Buddhist tenet of rebirth but makes it relevant for a group of people who may not fully believe in past and future lives. He also advocated getting rid of what he saw as the superstitions of Thai religiosity, to make the dhamma more "scientific" and accessible to a more scientifically oriented population. In this way Buddhadasa, like Goenka, advocates for a Buddhism that fits a particular kind of person—someone for whom science is appealing and ritualized practices are not.

Buddhadasa's style of meditation, like Goenka's, is based on the practice and development of mindfulness through *vipassanā* meditation. He draws from some of the same teachings of the Satipaṭṭhāna Sutta, and has written on different meditation techniques fitting different kinds of people. But instead of Goenka's emphasis on the Satipaṭṭhāna and a particular interpretation of *vedanā* as the second of the Four Foundations of Mindfulness, Buddhadasa emphasizes a technique called *ānāpānasati*: the mindfulness of the breath. "Ānāpānasati is the true foundation for mindfulness," he has said, "consisting of the four foundations of mindfulness and included in '*bodhipakkhiya-dhammā*' the qualities contributing to enlightenment" (2006, 11).

Buddhadasa isn't the only advocate for breathing meditation. *Ānāpānasati* is probably the most popular style of meditation in Thailand, if not in the whole world. It is the style for the "easily deluded" type in the list of meditative personalities. The specifics of practice can vary from person to person and tradition to tradition, but many people in Thailand will say that it is the most basic, simplest technique there is. For the most part, *ānāpānasati* meditation means to pay attention to the breath as air enters and exits the lungs and appears on the exhale at the tip of the mouth and nose. There are a lot of different ways to practice mindfulness of the breath. Some traditions teach one to breathe deeply from the stomach for ten long breaths and then breathe normally. Others teach one to attend to the feeling of exhalation on the upper lip. Some say to count each breath aloud or in the mind; some say to imagine the belly getting larger and smaller with each inhalation; some to just breathe as usual and note it. It was to *ānāpānasati* meditation that Phra Thēp was indirectly referring when he told Noi and me that he would say the name of the Buddha under his breath while walking on his alms rounds, "*phut-tho . . . phut-tho*," as a way to help recall his mind back from wherever it had wandered away to. Others I spoke with also reported especially liking this style. A middle-aged head monk at a monastery near Chiang Mai had said: "I usually apply the *phut-tho* style of doing meditation for myself. . . . There are many ways to learn mindfulness, such as *arahang-sammā* [a perception style] or *yup no phong no* [a walking style], but I am more comfortable with the *phut-tho* way of practice. It reminds me of the Buddha." A young monk at this same monastery followed his teacher's preference for meditation, indexing indirectly the power that comes with monastic authority, "Oh, I use *phut-tho* too, because it is easy to do and easy to understand," he said when asked about his own style, "—and it definitely suits me."

Buddhadasa's approach to mindfulness of the breath is fairly straightforward. He suggests starting out with a slightly rigorous breath and then settling in to notice the feel of the breath on the upper lip as one exhales:

> Sit up straight with all the vertebrae of the spine sitting together snugly. Keep the head up straight, with the eyes looking toward the tip of the nose . . . mindfulness pays attention to the entire path of the breath from the inner end point—the navel or the base of the abdomen—to the outer end point— the tip of the nose or the upper lip. However fine or soft the breath becomes, sati can clearly note it all the time. If it so happens that we cannot note or feel the breath because it is too soft or refined, then breathe more strongly or roughly again, but not as strong or rough as before, just enough to note the breath clearly. (2006, 4–11)

As with the Goenka retreat, there wasn't much spoken instruction or philosophical discussion at the ten-day silent retreat in Suan Mokkh. Instead of talking or listening or reading or writing I sat in a large, filled-to-capacity open-air pavilion hour after hour in silence, back straight, paying attention to my breath.

I found that it was easier to sit for hours and hours at this retreat than at the previous two, partly because I had gotten better at meditation but also partly because the schedule of sittings wasn't as strict. We alternated the sitting sessions with a couple of hourlong sessions of group walking meditation in between, walking slowly in a line around a pond near the monastery building. At night before sleeping on hard slabs of concrete we were able to soak ourselves in the natural hot spring at the edge of the grounds, and in the mornings we could participate in a volunteer-led yoga session. The yoga allowed us to stretch out, but it was subtle: the first person who had volunteered to lead these sessions left the retreat on the third day, finding the teachings too different from what she had expected. She had just come to Thailand after months in India learning a style of yoga that was exuberant and at odds with the much quieter style of yoga promoted at Buddhadasa's center. Instead of the very athletic movements that are part of sun-salutations, one of the positions considered especially good at Suan Mokkh is called "dead man's pose," with the practitioner lying in silence pretending to have passed away.

In the evenings there were a few minutes of dhamma talks, as at Goenka's center. Some of the teachings involved instruction on breathing, like those in the publications based on his public talks. I remember especially a discussion of the Buddhist theory of dependent origination, with a Tibetan image of the wheel of life used as a visual prop to explain how people become attached to their cravings and create the sense of self that perpetuates continuous dissatisfaction. "Let's say a bee stings you," a monk said during the dhamma talk one evening, "and the bee sting feels unpleasant. . . . You wish for that feeling to go away; you become attached to that wish, and that brings suffering."[9]

Buddhadasa has said in one of the talks that have been recorded and published that he especially likes the teaching of the Ānāpānasati Sutta as a guide for meditative training partly because it is the most common and popular style of meditation in Thailand. Yet unlike the Satipaṭṭhāna Sutta, of which most people have some passing familiarity, few have read the Ānāpānasati Sutta in summary or in full. This may be because Ānāpānasati is considered to be a part of the first of the *paṭṭhāna* or "way" of mindfulness in the Satipaṭṭhāna Sutta, in the *kaya-paṭṭhāna* mindfulness of the body.[10] But Buddhadasa finds that the Satipaṭṭhāna Sutta inadequately addresses mindfulness: "The perfect form of 'Satipaṭṭhāna'" he has said, "can be found in the short sutra or discourse known as the 'Ānāpānasati-sutta,' while the great foundation of mindfulness or 'Maha-Satipaṭṭhāna' does not deal with it sufficiently. . . . Only a little on Ānāpānasati is mentioned in the Mahasatipaṭṭhāna sutra. Even though the latter bears the name of 'Maha,' which means 'big' or 'great,' it mentions little about Ānāpānasati, and touches mainly on other matters" (2006, 24–25).

The Ānāpānasati Sutta is fairly short. It is only about five pages long (about ten minutes of oral recitation). "Now, how is mindfulness of in- and-out breathing developed and pursued, so as to be of great fruit, of great benefit?" the Buddha is said to have begun the teaching, to a group of disciples sitting around him. He answers this in three short sections, titled "Mindfulness of in and out breathing," "The four frames of reference," and "The seven factors of awakening." The practical discussion of mindfulness of in-and-out breathing starts with a monk being instructed to sit in the shade of a tree or an empty building, crossing his legs, sitting with his back straight, and "setting mindfulness to the fore." Then,

> always mindful, he breathes in; mindful he breathes out. Breathing in long, he discerns, "I am breathing in long," or breathing out long, he discerns, "I am breathing out long." Or breathing in short, he discerns, "I am breathing in short"; or breathing out short, he discerns, "I am breathing out short." He trains himself, "I will breathe in sensitive to the entire body." He trains himself, "I will be breathe out sensitive to the entire body." . . . In this way the meditator is then told to breathe in and breathe out in a fairly natural way, sensitive to, steadying, releasing, calming, and otherwise focusing on a series of seven different factors in turn, including the physical body: rapture; pleasure; mental thoughts; impermanence; dispassion; cessation; and relinquishment.

This sutta, like most of the Buddhist suttas, is repetitive and simple, yet in another sense is also elaborate and complex. It is designed to promote memorization and internalization, focusing the mind in the practice of paying attention to one of our body's normally unconscious but vital behaviors.

As the days of the retreat went by I felt more accepting of each day as it came. For the most part my body still ached, and the time still went by too slowly, and I found myself wanting deeply for the time to hurry up again so I could move on, like so many other meditators at the monastery, and get to the vacation I had planned at the nearby beach. But I also found myself starting to enjoy the sense of peace that I felt from sitting. My back didn't hurt anymore, and the hours seemed to flow by, not necessarily faster but smoother.

I used the lessons I learned at the earlier retreats and the other sittings I had done, reminding myself when I started going down the path of thinking through a thought to just drop it and move my attention back, this time to the breath's inhale and exhale. As I tried to pay attention to my breath, I also practiced dismissing a thought right when it entered my head, instead of letting it run around and stunt the time. I also changed in another way that helped the hours pass quickly, and that in turn helped make the experience more pleasant and more peaceful. Since I had decided that I really truly should try not to solve any intellectual problems while meditating, I would bring my mind back (or "recollect" the mind) to being aware of where I was, but I still felt a nagging sense of dissatisfaction at myself when I caught my thoughts wandering away—why, I wondered, couldn't I just focus the stupid mind on the stupid body, or the stupid breath? Why did I have to always start thinking down some random stupid trail of thought? I had told myself it was because I was an academic scholar, and thinking through an idea was what I was *supposed* to do by profession—to think analytically and work through a problem mentally. That may be the case, but it wasn't the way of meditation, and I had chosen to value both ways of doing things. It had felt frustrating, but sitting there at Buddhadasa's retreat I started to change my attitude to these wandering thoughts, and not only not follow them as they led down a trail in my mind but also avoid getting upset when I caught my mind wandering. When a thought appeared and started to develop I would watch my mind start to go down a path and then, like the tying of the yoke that Phra Thēp had described, bring it back again and continue on attending to mindfulness of my breath. Once I did this the hours passed faster and also, increasingly, were more pleasant. I wasn't attached to the feeling of how I should be meditating, but instead just sat there, aware that I was meditating in whatever way I could.

I don't know if it was Buddhadasa's monastery that helped me not feel dissatisfied at thinking while I was supposed to be focusing on the breath, or if it was just that I had been practicing meditation in general more often. In his teaching on *ānāpānasati*, Buddhadasa says that when one loses mindfulness it is due to the mind wandering—he doesn't say why this happens, but by explaining that it does and that it's common he seems to suggest that it's not something to get too upset about, and that rather the "lack of success is due to the inability of sati to stay with the breathing the whole time. . . . You don't know when it lost track. You don't know when the mind ran off to home, work, or play. You don't know until it's already gone. And you don't know when it went, how, why, or whatever. Once you are aware of what happened, catch the breathing again, gently bringing it back to the breathing, and train until successful to this level" (2006, 9). It was this "gentleness" that had started to sink in.

At night we soaked our sore bodies in the hot spring at the edge of the woods in silence, and afterward I fell asleep like a rock, but even the concrete slab we had to sleep on didn't seem all that bad. The retreat went well, but on that concrete slab one night, without a blanket or a pillow or a sheet, after another day of silence, I realized that taking the Buddha's teaching to its limit was something that in practice would look utterly different from the casual, "what-can-it-do-for-my-regular-life" kind of attitude that I and the others there and the readers of this book may be interested in. I realized that it required a very different outlook and orientation to the world from what I had been used to, a sea change to the way that I saw myself and thought about ideas, and especially to the way I saw myself and my ideas as relevant in a larger world out there around me. The Buddha's teaching didn't help "me" be a better "me": to really pursue them would require dropping all of that as an illusion. I knew that the changes I had glimpsed then weren't the ones that I did or maybe ever would want to actually pursue fully; and I knew that even without them I could still benefit from the practice, a lot. But it was a strange, almost eerie feeling to be aware of it, like touching a truly different way of living.

The ten days of the retreat passed fairly quickly. I don't even remember talking with anyone afterward, just packing up my few things, thanking the monks, and leaving for the train station again. I was slowly becoming a more proficient meditator, and was benefiting more from meditation. Sitting in meditation, I learned, wasn't like entering a kind of trance, and it wasn't even a kind of "flow" experience where I lost my sense of time and space. And it wasn't a chance to think through the problems of the day. It was a lot of things, but one of them, to put it simply, was that it was a process of becoming mindful.

Retreat 4: Wat Tham Thong's *Yup No Phong No* Walking Meditation

I continued to meditate after Buddhadasa's retreat. I sat for a few minutes in the mornings, or a few hours or days at some of the other monasteries around Northern Thailand. It was a few years later that I signed up for my next relatively lengthy retreat after Buddhadasa's monastery. It was at a monastery outside Chiang Mai called Wat Tham Thong, which taught a walking style of meditation called *yup no phong no*. The monastery is not particularly famous; it is hidden in the hills, its presence advertised with just a sign with an arrow on the main road. I wouldn't have even known it existed, but my host mother in Mae Jaeng went there every year, and while I was living there she invited me to go with her.

My host mother Mae Daeng, her twin Mae Ou, their sister Mae Lah, and a half dozen other relatives and friends and I all piled into the back of our family pickup truck, and we headed out over the mountains from Mae Jaeng to Hot, a district near the Burmese border. I asked Mae Daeng what it was like at the monastery, and she just smiled in her typical way and said, "It's nice. It's fun." When we arrived at Wat Tham Thong, a *mae chi* (female monastic) greeted us and showed us around. People wearing white outfits or monks in orange robes were scattered around the grounds—those in white, like Mae Daeng and me, were laypeople who had come as lay renouncers for a short period; and those with shaved heads, like the woman who greeted us, were female renunciates.

The name of Wat Tham Thong (the Monastery of the Golden Cave) comes from its cave on the monastery grounds, deep in the woods at the base of a mountain. There are walking paths leading up to it from the main monastery hall, with monks' meditation *kutis* and a mountain creek lining the way. In the cave itself is a reclining Buddha image carved into the stone. Unlike the other retreats I had been on, this one wasn't strictly a silent one, but as at all monasteries and especially meditation monasteries, there is an expectation of near silence: one speaks only when there something significant to say, which is almost never. After the tour the *mae chi* showed us each a little hut we would be able to use for the duration of our stay. After putting down my toiletries and few extra sets of white clothes, I went to talk with the nun who had shown us around and learn about what to do at the monastery. As the only foreigner that I could see at Wat Tham Thong, and to focus especially on my meditation practice, I asked the *mae chi* if it would be all right if I didn't talk at all. To help with this and avoid my being asked questions by others, she gave me a sign on a string to wear around my neck for the duration of the retreat: *pit waja*, it said, a technical term that meant I wasn't speaking or engaging with others. No one commented on this to me, either during or after the retreat; it was seen as a fairly common thing to do.

While I knew she was nearby, I didn't see Mae Daeng or any of the others again for the rest of the week, because I wasn't really looking at other people. I knew she and the others were close, but they were virtually absent. I imagined them whispering to each other at times in the evenings or while making the midday meal, but other than that they would be doing the same things as I would: following a fairly flexible plan of meditating for periods of time throughout the day.

To begin the meditation retreat I met with the head monk and paid my respects to him, bowing three times with my forehead to the ground. He explained a little bit about the schedule at the monastery: the wake-up bell would ring at 4:30 in the morning, and other than a group session of chanting at 8:30, meditators were free to practice at their own pace and at their own style throughout the day. It was expected that everyone would help sweep the monastery grounds and prepare the midday meal, the only meal we would have. He gave me some paper printouts explaining the meditation technique that he advised at the monastery. It showed outline drawings of a person in a series of standing poses: slowly picking up the heel of the foot, slowly picking up the palm of the foot, slowly raising the foot, shifting the weight of the body forward, slowly putting down the palm of the foot, slowly putting down the heel of the foot, shifting the weight onto that foot, and slowly picking up the heel of the other foot.

"Follow this," he instructed, "and say '*yup no*' on the rising foot, and '*phong no*' on the falling one, following your breath as you move." As with the *phut-tho* breathing technique, part of the practice was to inhale and exhale the words quietly while breathing in and out. He advised me to alternate sitting meditation with this slow style of walking, which could be done faster or slower according to my preference. He said I could do so anywhere on the temple grounds: in my own hut, in the meditation hall, in the woods, or the cave. The meeting lasted about twenty minutes and was the only instruction I received the whole week. When I had left the monastery a week later, I learned that Wat Tham Thong is a branch of Wat Mathathat, a famous monastery in Bangkok. The style of meditation, according to its website, was "*vipassanā* meditation in the tradition of Mahāsī Sayādaw," one of the most important and influential contemporary meditation advocates in his home country of Burma and quite possibly around the world. But the main lesson of the monk was to practice this *yup no phong no* style of walking.

Each morning when the morning bell (or, as I preferred, the "middle-of-the-night bell") rang, I got up in a disgruntled daze and did an hour of meditation in my hut in the dark, and then got ready for the day. As the sun was starting to come out and the grounds were still misty, we all made our way to the main meditation hall. After the group chanting I sat in the meditation hall, or practiced the walking meditation for an hour, alternating each time and aiming for seven sessions each day.

I had learned a little bit about the practice of walking meditation from the Buddhadasa retreat and other centers, and from interviews with monks and laypeople about their own experiences, and I liked it. Some people find walking meditation the easiest and pleasantest kind of meditation. More people I knew liked the *ānāpānasati* style (which some said was also part of walking practices), but a few noted how much they liked this technique—as a respite from the soreness of sitting or because, they said, it helps one to more easily focus. Many of the interviews I was doing tended to see this preference as relating in some way to personality, albeit not exactly in line with the complex personality charts found in some Pali texts. Different people had told me about this relation to personality during our interviews. A woman at the psychiatric hospital in Chiang Mai had said that she liked the *yup no phong no* style "because it fits my temperament so easily. I can gain concentration so easily, and am able to stay for a long time in that state." A monk who also preferred this method had noted that "the style has more of a system to manage thoughts; it's like a system for me to separate my senses and recalling. It provides a clear method to cover all thought processes while I am mediating and gain more sati—and definitely I can sit longer after practicing and get more *samādhi*." And it was thought by many that walking meditation helps one to think of meditation as part of all activity in everyday life, not just in the still silence of sitting. The sweeping of the monastery grounds, which I did along the path leading to the cave in the woods for an hour each afternoon, was also considered a kind of training in this form of meditation.

I sat on a mat in the nearly empty meditation hall by the main building for an hour at a time, as others throughout the grounds were also doing in their own individual ways. I had turned on a fan in the hall and angled it toward me, and after an hour was up I walked across the room for another hour, in the super-slow walking style in which I had been instructed. It was hot out, and the hours were long. I played a game to see how slowly I could actually take to walk across a room; usually it would take four lengths of the twelve-foot space of the room before the hour was up, but once I walked just one length in the whole of the sixty minutes.

Each afternoon I went to the cave for an hour, when the space was cool even compared to the shade of the woods, and sat by the Buddha statue, spending a few minutes sweeping after the hour was up. I spent an hour sweeping the leaves from the path along the creek. The few others around me were doing a similar routine, at their own pace. I was surprised at how easy it was to not make contact with them. I found that I could get by without speaking to anyone, and for the most part I found that I didn't want to, though I was glad they were there. The clothes we wore were cool and easy to move in, and I liked the less formal structure than in the meditation retreats where the bells and chants marked the beginnings and ends of group sessions, though I knew in my mind they were good for just starting out. Some hours seemed to last longer than others, and sometimes it felt a bit boring to sit, but it was also pleasant and peaceful. I felt powerful and calm at the same time, sitting in a space or lifting a foot and slowly, with an increasingly balanced control, move forward to place it back on the ground. There was almost a feeling of joy, the "joyful satisfaction" that a few monks had mentioned feeling in meditation. I found that I almost reveled in it, which itself is a feeling I knew I shouldn't get attached to. It was difficult, but more than the feeling of difficulty was a kind of confidence I had gained from experience in knowing that I would benefit later from the time spent at the monastery.

At night I was exhausted, falling asleep as soon as my head hit the pillow—I still haven't been able to get over that feeling of physical and mental taxation yet in my meditation practice, though it has lessened. But in the mornings I was ready for a new day, even as I was grumbling and in a daze as the bell rang in the early morning, or rather at 4:30 in the middle of the night.

Everything went well at Wat Tham Thong, though there were a few things that I didn't understand, or that I understood but didn't agree with. One of the things I understood but didn't agree with was the gender arrangement for the midday meal. Unlike the meals at the Goenka center or Wat Suan Mokkh, where volunteers of both genders contributed to the making of the food, at Wat Tham Thong the women would prepare the meal and then present it as a group to the monks, who would offer their blessings to the bowing women. I didn't mind silently peeling vegetables and putting them into pots in the cooking area to the side of the main hall, but I seethed like the good feminist I saw myself to be when the rest of the women and I, who had spent over an hour doing all the cooking, had to present it to the monks and pay respect to them while they chanted over us and the food before "magnanimously" eating the fruit of our labor. Someday, I thought, I might come to accept this, as people around me seemed to be doing in following what was said to be the Buddhist teaching of accepting the way things are, but I also hoped that through the actions of myself and other men and women things would change before I got to that point.

I understood the gender inequality even if I didn't like it, but another practice I met with at Wat Tham Thong I didn't understand at all. Sometimes early in the mornings or in the later afternoons I would pass by a building in the woods between my *kuti* and the meditation hall, and I would hear the sounds of people screaming inside. It mostly sounded like older women screaming or crying, sometimes accompanied by other old women chanting, and I would walk past in a hurry, scared and curious, but since I wasn't talking, there was no one I could ask what was going on. I put the building and my curiosity about it out of my mind, and concentrated on the task of meditating, an hour at a time walking, then sitting, then slowly walking again.

Almost as it had begun the week ended, and on the last day of the retreat we did a final walking group meditation outside in a big circle in the yard before we all departed the monastery. The sun was so hot, and the line of the white-robed ascetics I was inching along with were all so closely packed, that I briefly fainted, kneeling for a moment to keep from being dizzy. A few people stopped walking and brought me water and a cool cloth and sat down with me in the shade for a couple of minutes before we resumed. I was embarrassed at first, but they were friendly and kind, and after a few minutes I just continued on as before. Afterward I packed up the things in the hut I had stayed in, found my host mother Mae Daeng, we thanked the head monk, and we left.

As Mae Daeng and her friends and family and a few other meditators all piled in the back of the pickup truck that would take us to the main town bus station to drop off the people who were going farther afield, we chatted casually and happily. I asked them if they knew what the screaming in the building in the woods was all about. "It's a ritual," a young woman with a Bangkok accent to her Thai said, "*poet kam*—it's done to open up your karma." "What?!" I answered—I had never heard of something like that. "It's kind of unusual," she went on, "but the idea is that sometimes you have some negative karma stocked up that you can't get rid of, and the ritual opens up that karmic store and lets it out. Like, let's say you're haunted by the ghost of a war colonel; the ritual lets that ghost free. It's very intense."

"Is this ritual common in Thai monasteries?" I asked, still perplexed. "No," she answered. "It's something well known here, but I haven't heard of it anywhere else."[11] One of her friends chimed in: "I have—there's another monastery that does this, in Bangkok."

At the town center of Hot they and the others bound for Chiang Mai and beyond got out of the truck, and Mae Daeng and the rest of us spent the remainder of the trip back over the mountain to Mae Jaeng laughing casually and snacking on the food we had picked up in town. The wind blew in the back of the truck in the mountains, welcoming us back as we shared a relaxed feeling of closeness. I asked Mae Daeng how the retreat had gone for her: "Good!" she said, but like so many others didn't elaborate. She didn't speak much about it, but I could tell that she liked the experience, and knew she would be back the following year.

The retreat at Wat Tham Thong was different from the others I had done thus far. It didn't emphasize mindfulness explicitly but was part of the implicit training, and through its lineage of the Burmese monk Mahāsī Sayādaw it held mindfulness as a central part of its practice. The retreat had been intense but also relaxing. It had taught me more respect for the meditation retreats of regular people in the countryside of Thailand that are part of their routines. And unlike the intensely structured "meditation injection" provided by the ten-day courses like Goenka's and Buddhadasa's, which made the divide of inside and outside the monastery relatively firm, the less structured, more personally organized schedule at Wat Tham Thong helped to make the boundary between the monastery and the outside world less absolute, more porous. I didn't have as intense an impression of the non-retreat world as a place different from the confines of the retreat after I left, maybe because I continued to live with the people whom I had gone on the retreat with, but the effects seemed to transfer more seamlessly to regular life. When I went to the neighborhood monastery with Mae Daeng a few days later, to make merit, we felt pretty much the same as we always did when we went, but maybe just a little bit more peaceful.

Months later I was asking Mae Daeng about what it feels like when she meditates, as part of a project on spiritual curiosity I was conducting with Tanya Luhrmann at Stanford University, and she told me about an experience she had at Tham Thong:

"When I meditate for a long time I feel like my body becomes lighter," Mae Daeng told me. "At Tham Thong my mind is calm. I was meditating and saying '*phut-tho . . . phut-tho*,' and I remember one day I felt like I couldn't feel my body, and my mind was out of my body, and I could see it. That was a little unusual, but usually it's just calm, and light. Wat Tham Thong is the place for spiritual freedom, to learn about the dhamma." In a later conversation she elaborated, talking about spirits of the person, locally referred to as *khwan*: "The ceremony you asked about there at the end, the 'opening one's karma,' you can't have weak *khwan*. It's only done when one has a lot of mindfulness. You can see past lives." It was a way of talking about the meditative experience that was different from what are often considered the more scientific or rational teachings of Goenka and Buddhadasa. It wasn't that Wat Tham Thong wasn't a place to learn about mindfulness; it's a particular kind of feeling of mindfulness that is created there, one that includes spirits, including the spirits of the self. It spoke to an argument about embodiment, and the ways that ideas become trained through physical practice.

I talked to Mae Daeng's sister Mae Lah a year later, as part of the formal interviews I was conducting for the mindfulness project. When I asked her where she learned about mindfulness, she told me, "I learned the basics from school, from my family—every family teaches about this—and from daily life . . . and when I go to sit in *vipassanā* meditation, at Wat Tham Thong." I asked about the screaming of the opening up of the karma, and she laughed and said, "I only half believe." I asked if mindfulness was part of it, and she said it was: "You have to be really strong in mindfulness to do that kind of thing."

I had my own expectations going into the retreat, and I met them through my own engagement with the experience. Other than feeling that things were just a little bit uncannily beautiful while sweeping the path in the woods by the cave, and the strange sounds of weeping in the woods as karma was thought to be released, I found Wat Tham Thong to be as rational as the rest of the retreats, but with perhaps a slightly different take on what that looked like. I had learned how to embody a new style of meditation, and progressed in my own practice.

Retreat 5: Wat Mae Long's Unstructured Meditation

My fifth and most recent meditation retreat was during a seven-day period at a rural monastery called Wat Mae Long. It wasn't a special monastery, at least not more special than other monasteries, and it wasn't a formal meditation retreat with an official start and stop date. I just went to it and stayed for a while to meditate. I wanted to see what it was like at the majority of meditation monasteries that don't conduct formal periods of retreats.

I had started to incorporate my own preferred styles into my meditation at Wat Tham Thong, using a kind of combination of breathing focus and body scanning to complement the walking meditation, and at Wat Mae Long the program was even more unstructured. I hadn't heard anything about the monastery from anyone, and had come across it just by accident while traveling on a mountainous off-the-beaten-path road along the river from Mae Jaeng to Chiang Mai. The other meditation centers I had gone to were famous, either internationally, nationally, or locally, and I wanted to see what a more "typical" and less well known meditation monastery would be like. I had passed the monastery a year earlier, seeing the spire of the main hall peeking out from over the tops of the trees in the mountain woods, and had stopped in to see what it was like. The head monk and two renunciates had come out to greet me. It seemed quiet and cool, and they said that I would be welcome to visit and stay to meditate there.

I showed up and, after saying hello, asked permission to meditate. The head monk, Phra Luang Po Odom, repeated the welcome to stay at the monastery and told me that the schedule followed there was simple. There was the 4:30 wake-up bell and an hour of group chanting and meditation right after it (as part of the *tham wat chao* and *tham wat yen* done in almost all monasteries in the country), preparation of the food and the ritual of chanting and eating the meal at 11:30, and another hour of group chanting and meditation at 4:40. Beyond that there was unstructured time for meditation.

Of course, no monastery is truly "typical"; Wat Mae Long has its own history and traditions, though I never fully learned what all of them were. It looked typical in its layout: spread out at the top of a hill in the woods, cool and silent and peaceful, the small huts called *kutis* laid out in the forest with walking paths leading up to the main meditation hall with its cool floor and Buddha images at the front, and golden serpents lining the staircase up to the hall. Closer to the *kutis* was a second hall that held a large kitchen in the back and a meeting hall, where laypeople could come in and greet the monastics. There was almost no one there; I saw two women ascetics and the monk, and a pickup truck was parked in the otherwise empty lot. The owners were walking back from the meeting hall.

The one thing that immediately set Wat Mae Long apart from other monasteries I had seen, though, was the color of the female renunciates' robes: instead of the usual white robes of the *mae chi*, the two women at the monastery wore the dark orange-brown robes that I associated with wandering *thudong* forest monks like Phra Thēp, or nuns of the Santi Asok sect. Were these *bhikkhunī*, I wondered, the Buddhist line of female renunciates who weren't officially sanctioned by the Thai sangha, that some people were working on reviving? I didn't ask, because I didn't want to pry. I figured I would ask at the end of my stay; for now I was there to meditate.

Beyond these two female monastics there was the male monastic, and that was it. Usually there was another elderly female monastic, I was told, who normally stayed in the *kuti* I had just been shown to, but she was in Chiang Mai to see a doctor. One of the female monastics suggested I stay with her at her *kuti*, but I asked if I could stay in my own space, still not able to shake what I considered an American need for privacy. The two women showed me to the *kuti* the elderly woman stayed in, a small space with a back porch looking out at the woods, and said I would be welcome to stay there. Other than the very minimal, quiet exchanges during the following week on how to cut the vegetables or follow the chants at the midday meal, I didn't speak to any of the three of them or anyone else for the next seven days.

I spent the week in silence, enjoying the relatively relaxed meditation schedule, and creating my own program aiming at seven hours of sitting a day. I altered an hour sitting in the coolness of the main monastery building with an hour of walking slowly in the woods, an hour walking very slowly in the space of the meeting hall with an hour sweeping the steps of leaves, and an hour in my *kuti* on the back porch. I found the combination of techniques to work well. When the sun was setting and a cool breeze went through the woods and the sounds of the birds and geckos were all around it was especially nice to sit on the back porch for an hour, meditating on my breath or scanning my body for sensation. After the sun set the insects appeared, and I would go inside to do a final hour of walking across the room of the *kuti* before falling fast asleep.

The other three at the monastery mostly followed their own, similar routines, though they also did more work in the running of the center, making phone calls for orders of materials or meeting with a layperson or two who would stop by to make merit. A little before noon each day the four of us would congregate in the meeting hall, the head monk sitting on a raised platform at the front of the room, and we would say a short chant from a chanting book and then slowly and silently eat from the full alms bowls that had been prepared that morning. The mood was a feeling of peacefulness and camaraderie, even if we barely spoke. Laypeople donated food, some coming from as far away as Bangkok, and sometimes one of the monastics would go into the town twenty minutes away in the back of a *songthaew* pickup-truck taxi to get supplies. The monastery wasn't rich, but it also wasn't poor. In the mornings and evenings we read aloud from a chanting book in the main meditation hall for a few minutes, along with an audio recording. The chanting book had a series of fairly standard Buddhist Pali chants, transcribed into the Thai script, and while I wasn't familiar with all the chants, I recognized mindfulness in a few. One spelled out a blessing with a Thai title followed by the rhythmical tone of Pali:

> *Phaun chattumanakkha nieoranghchithjai chit-anu sati sankha-anu sati chi-rachanusati arahaltan anu sati bapphachanusanusatikhantiyanu sati chattu-makhala satto bukkatachatima nokanchakatasukkho tilopoti.*[12]

I recognized some Pali-Thai words I knew, like *chitjai*, heart-mind, and *sankhāra*, sensations or phenomenal qualities favored by Goenka, and others that pointed to the chant as a reference to the list of *anus-sati*—as the *Navakovada* put it, moods to recall, or things to be mindful of. But I didn't spend too long trying to figure it all out. I figured I would ask one of the monastics after I was done with the retreat to explain what it meant. Instead, I focused on the meditation. As with the other retreats, I didn't write things down or read, though I could have; it just didn't seem very important. I could read some of the chants, and could read a few other things around the monastery, like the ingredients on the packaged foods, or the signs commenting on the dhamma nailed by past recluses at the monastery onto the trees in the woods: "*Kot matawa suk leti: Kha khwamkrot dai yu pen suk*" one said by my *kuti*, in a mix of first Pali and then Thai: *Kill anger and you will be with happiness*. But I didn't crave these signs as much as I had before. I could see that at some point writing and reading wouldn't be as much of a distraction after all. I was slowly becoming more comfortable with the practice—not necessarily to integrate it into the life I already led but to alter that life a little bit in a different and more mindful direction.

Only once did I hear the three monastics break the general silence. While we were eating our meal one day I heard one say to another something almost in a whisper, and they chuckled. I thought I caught a few words about politics, that something had happened again with the government, but I figured I had misheard them because of the casualness of the speech. Rather than anxiety or worry, they talked about what those government people are up to now almost humorously, and I didn't think anything of it. Only after I left a few days later and was trying to cross the border into Burma did I find what they had been talking about: there had been a coup d'état, and the country was now ruled by a military junta.

At the time when I heard them comment on it in passing it didn't seem worth paying attention to. Instead I focused on the breath, on walking slowly, on working on not trying to rush the time. I continued to work on training my body and mind to be in the space they were in, and if my mind wandered away I "recalled" it back from wherever it had gone, gently, and continued on. I thought of the air just a few inches from my skin, the way my breath or the slow movements I made as I walked seemed to ruffle the space. I felt a sense of calmness at Wat Mae Long, and not just calmness but also a kind of power and capability. I had started to feel this at Wat Tham Thong, but it had even there seemed at odds with the fact that it came from basically sitting around all day, seemingly doing not much at all.

After the seven-day period that I had set aside to meditate was over, I went to speak to the two female monastics, to formally thank them for permitting me to stay. We talked quietly for a few minutes about the monastery and their lives there. They showed me pictures of their latest trip as *thudong* wandering forest monastics, clad in their dark red robes surrounded by the jungle and mountains.

"Don't you worry that people will think it's odd that you're wearing the dark robes?" I asked; usually only the male monks as *bhikkhu* are permitted to wear such robes.

"Oh, when we go into town we'll wear white," the younger female monastic said cheerily. "That's what people expect. But here in the monastery or when we're traveling out in nature we wear the dark robes, because otherwise the white ones will get dirty!" I laughed—I had spent the week imagining the radical symbolism of the women's outfits, as a kind of subversive activist move against the patriarchal system of the Thai sangha, but they put it all in much more practical terms. I had come across other women who had similarly stated that they didn't much care that they couldn't ordain as equals to men, and had even read about it in an article by two (male) Buddhist studies scholars who recounted the same narrative. One of the central Buddhist virtues is considered to be nonattachment and an understanding of non-self; fighting for personal status went against this. But unlike those who left the matter at that as a kind of acceptance, or on the other hand acted against the system and demanded that women think differently, these women were creating change within the system around them without overtly fighting against it. It was "just" because of the dirt of the jungle, they said, that they wore the darker robes; but I could see that they were also (and possibly only coincidentally) treated with more respect from male monastics and visiting laypeople than I was used to seeing at other monasteries with white-robed *mae chi*. I realized that compliance with and acceptance of a subordinated position isn't the same as agreement with it, and these women were acting this out on their own terms.

Rather than talk about the politics of the robes, the two women asked me about my own story, my reason for coming to the monastery.

"Aren't you bored yet, Julia?" the older of the two monastics asked.

"Bored?" I replied, not sure what she meant.

"Bored with the world," she clarified—*buea lok*. "I used to be a desk attendant at a fancy Bangkok hotel," she explained, "for years. I spent my whole life there, saw my kids grow up, and now my grandchildren. I still see them, but I like the monastery." Like Phra Thēp and Phra Mon, in talking about the reasons for her lifestyle she was thinking of her own experiences as much as recalling the Buddha's emphasis on retreating from the world as a response to the inevitabilities of sickness, old age, and death.

"Not yet!" I replied, laughing. "There's still a lot to do and see out there." I was a little uncertain, though, already starting to think about what it would be like getting back on my motorbike and finding my way to who-knew-what at the Burmese border.

"Give her time, she's still young!" the younger one admonished the older one, smiling. The younger one, though, looked even younger than I was.

After speaking for a few minutes more I thanked them again for allowing me to come to their monastery and for taking the time away from their meditation to speak to me. They said I could come back again, and if I wanted to I could ordain and shave my head as they had. As I said goodbye I could see them turn back to the papayas they were peeling for the morning meal. Near my motorbike at the entrance to the monastery I stopped by to thank the head monk, Luang Po Odom. He was sitting on the porch at the front of his *kuti*, where he seemed to spend most of his time. After thanking him for the stay I wasn't sure what else to say, but wasn't quite ready to leave. I asked him about sati.

"Yes, sati is very important," he said, nodding to show that this was an appropriate topic to talk about. He told me in similar words the things I had heard from so many other monks, in definition and illustrations: "Sati is to pick something up," he said, using the Thai phrase *yom rap*. "If you lose your sati, then you don't know anything about what's going on. It's to recall your body and mind, *raluk tua*."

I figured that Luang Po Odom had spent a long time in the monastery, or at least had grown up in the area, but in our conversation I was reminded again how nonprovincial most places actually are. Luang Po Odom used to be a driver like Phra Thēp, and not only in so faraway a place as Bangkok but in Lebanon. He had driven construction trucks until about ten years ago. "If someone is driving," he said, "like when I was in

Lebanon driving my truck around the construction site, if I lost my sati, that was bad." He explained more: "Really, if one has no sati it means one is crazy. With sati you remember where you are. Like, you're a particular way, you can remember what your name is, that you're Julia, that you're a woman, that you come from America." He linked the idea of mindfulness to memory and also to morality: "Sati is to know and remember," he said. "Is some particular thing good? Like, should I drink alcohol? With sati you can remember to do what's good, not what's not good. To remember: good or not good."

After he finished talking I was about to get up and leave but remembered one last question.

"In the mornings," I asked him, "I remember chanting this one chant that mentioned mindfulness. What did it mean?" I showed him the picture of the chant I had taken that morning after packing up my things: "*Paw raw jattumanakcha . . . jit-anu sati, sanka-anu sati.*"

"Well, they're about mindfulness," he began, pausing and then continuing: "I know a lot of the meanings of the chants, but I don't know the exact meanings of those ones. I benefit from the chants, but I don't have a lot of training in the Pali language."

"Oh, it's OK!" I rushed to reassure him. I was worried he might feel embarrased at his level of language ability. "I have a professor friend in Chiang Mai who can help me translate the chant," I told him. "He knows Pali well."

Luang Po Odom nodded, but then corrected my impression of his response: "That's good that he can do that," he said. "But really Pali as it was spoken at the time of the Buddha and Pali as it is represented here in the chants is not the same if you translate it into meanings in the modern language." He thought for a minute of a way to illustrate his point. "Maybe it's like your Old English and New English. The representation of it today only gets a small bit of the real qualities of it across. The sounds, the intonations, the teachings had a different rhythm to them than just a word-to-word translation would allow. Sit in meditation, chant, and you can translate. You can translate from your mind."

I thanked the monk again and got up to leave. I was happy to be reminded that the paths followed in mindfulness practice are multiple wherever one went. It reminded me too that different styles of mindfulness practice have different consequences for the learner. The unfolding of mindfulness, it showed, isn't contingent necessarily on any one particular skill, even Pali training. I left the monastery, refreshed from the experience of meditation.

The five meditation retreats I participated in taught me collectively how mindfulness can be practiced and improved on, from the difficulty of first sittings to the relative ease and peace of later ones. They all were free (taking donations at the end), they were all a little bit different, and they all helped cumulatively to find what mindfulness looks like in practice.

I had done each of these meditation retreats before meeting Kay at the restaurant that evening in Chiang Mai and hearing about his experience at Wat Rampoeng. From talking with Kay and other ordained and lay meditators in Thailand like him, I realized that if I hadn't done any of these retreats, and had thought about the teachings only in the abstract in texts or through others, I wouldn't have as much of a visceral appreciation of what people actually went through. I wouldn't understand the difficulty, nor the benefit, as much.

A few days after I met Kay I went to talk to Phra Suphan, the head monk of Wat Rampoeng. I had done a short three-day meditation session there a few years earlier but couldn't remember much from it. Returning brought back vague and amorphous memories. I remembered lodging in the new dormitory-style building with the Thai meditators, instead of the purposefully rustic cabins the international meditators usually stayed in, and hearing the middle-aged women whispering together at night. I remembered sitting and walking in meditation along the centuries-old bricks of the grounds for hours, as the meditators sitting and slowly walking around were doing now.

Even with the workings of the monastery to run, Phra Suphan took some time from his responsibilities to talk with me about mindfulness at the monastery. During our conversation I felt appreciation for the work of meditation even more: the relatively small amount of meditation I had done helped me to get a sense of the different world that he lived in.

While we were talking I could tell that Phra Suphan was actively speaking to me in terms he felt I could understand, not in some kind of a-cultural abstract sense about the "truth." He spoke about sati similarly to the ways Phra Thēp and Phra Mon had, with his own interests and emphases. As I sat there scribbling notes, he spoke comfortably and straightforwardly of mindfulness's connections with morality, recollection, and well-being.

"I remember learning about mindfulness in books and in meditaiton," Phra Suphan said. When I asked when he had first become interested in it, he told me: "Just growing up. As I was learning how to practice it I saw the benefit of it, how it supports a good life, to improve one's life, to have *phalang*, energy. Right mindfulness [*sammā sati*] helps us to do good. It supports life to be good. *Raluk*, recollection, this is to do good. It helps us to be cleaner inside, free from desire and craving, and improve mentally. It helps us to have a wholesome, positive mind, one that allows us to do good and not bad. It changes a bad mind to a good mind, and a good mind to be even better. . . . When we recall the mind with sati," he said, "we can change from an unwholesome mind, can change our wrong desire."

"How does one do this?" I asked him.

"Well," he said, using a metaphor I hadn't heard before, "it's a lot of factors. It's like the mind is a battery, a motor. Everything has to work together. When a mood comes up, we use sati to change it. We have to train in sati meticulously, through learning by doing, not just listening or reading. We do it through the Four Foundations of Mindfulness."

I told him a bit of what I knew of the Four Foundations of Mindfulness, and said that I had heard different variations of them, and different kinds of meditation. "Should everyone learn from these the same way?" I asked.

"No," he replied. "Every person is different. It depends on one's life experiences. What is good for each person isn't the same. It's very close to the same, but it's not the same. So when I meet with each meditator [during a few minutes in the afternoon or evening] I suggest different courses of action. The effect of each technique [of sitting, walking, or meditating on different foundations of mindfulness] will have different results, different effects for each person. I watch the cause and effect for these techniques. For example, for countryside people, sati might develop through attention to memory, or wisdom [*paññā*], but for others [presumably monks and other meditative renunciates] it's the ultimate truth [of the teaching, to lead to nirvana]. . . . International meditators, they usually come in for existential reasons, a sense of looking for something in their life. Thai meditators are usually more concrete, they're dealing with some particular problem. So, it's different."

Every few mintues as we were talking someone would come into the room and hand Phra Suphan a piece of paper to sign, or offer him a glass of water. But even with these distractions Suphan seemed very at peace and at ease. I had a very comfortable, even happy feeling as I sat there talking with him. It's hard to explain why—his responses to my questions weren't particularly new or different from those of other people I had spoken with, and he didn't seem to be adhering to some kind of extreme monastic ideal of distancing from society. He seemed quietly comfortable, even casual, in talking about these issues.

Before leaving I asked Phra Suphan one last question: "Why do you think so many people like this monastery?" I had heard of Wat Rampoeng often, in Chiang Mai and in books at home, and wanted to hear why it was so popular from the mouth of the head of it. I thought I would hear about an approach that was taken that was especially good, or even the best or the most correct one, but Phra Suphan didn't say that. By this point I shouldn't have been surprised at a show of humility, but his answer was like that of so many others: "Well, the monastery here isn't too far away from the city," he said, "and it's not too close to downtown, so it's not too crowded. It's easy to come and go. And it's comfortable. . . . And about 80 percent of the meditators here are women," he added, citing a slightly higher number than the usual even gender split, and I remembered hearing how he supported *mae chi* taking positions of power in the running of the monastery, "and being a safe place is a factor, too. People can meditate on their own but still check in with me as their teacher, so that's a draw too."

Instead of saying that he had a particular perspective that was especially sought after, or that an especially good technique was taught there, Phra Suphan was essentially saying that the location, comfort, and practicality of the place were the reasons for its popularity. It was a nod to the "grocery store" theory I had heard about as a reason for practicing at one place or another, though there were also additional significant issues of reputation and technique. After a while I thanked him for his time and left the monastery, passing meditators in their white outfits slowly walking or sitting around the monastery grounds.

Meditative TAPES

From learning about mindfulness of sensations in Goenka's retreat, and the breath in Buddhadasa's, from learning about walking at Wat Tham Thong, and putting it all together at Wat Mae Long, I developed an appreciation for the larger task as well as some of the varieties of meditative practice. I found a few new, straightforward lessons about mindfulness from these Thai retreats. I found that meditation, and mindfulness with it, are difficult but get easier through multiple iterations—a lesson easier to agree with in principle than learn in practice. I found that there are different styles and interpretations of generally followed ideas about mindfulness, and that people follow particular styles and incorporate them as they choose. I learned that different styles pay attention to different aspects of embodied experience, and that these different techniques add up to what can be different kinds of subjective engagements with the world, but also that in general they are similarly pointing to a shared sense of experience. This sense of experience can be useful for everyday purposes, but it can also be very intense and extreme, of a kind I only glimpsed from the amount of meditation I engaged in.

Monks don't usually describe their personal felt encounters with meditation, but even they struggle in the beginning before gaining skills that make the practice easier. One monk who was more candid than others in describing his experiences explained the process as one similar to what I had gone through over a period of years. The monk was the head monk of a monastery in Lamphun near Chiang Mai, and he related how during his studies at Mahachulalongkorn monastic university in Bangkok he had to spend a minimum of ten days doing meditation retreats once a year for each of the four years he was enrolled there: "It was very difficult at first," he said, "because I wasn't familiar with this before I ordained as a monk. My body hurt so bad and I felt heat on my skin and my mind couldn't stay still and I was sometimes sleepy, like you're probably familiar with. I spent half the day in sitting meditation and half the day in walking meditation, and would meet with the dhamma teacher for a few minutes in the evening, and he would teach me how to deal with my feelings. It's called *sup arom*, like a 'mood examination,' to see what I gained and didn't gain each day." After a time dealing with these difficulties he had gotten used to it. "To get better I would ignore the discomfort and concentrate my mind to gain sati and *samādhi* and be patient, and then I would feel calmer and more relaxed, and overcome the pain. Now when I meditate I feel free, cool, light, almost floating. If I talk about the feeling of meditation, well, before it was very difficult, but now my emotion is still; I stay still, and my mind is free from attachment. It's called *chit praphatson*, like *piti*, a quiet kind of joy." These kinds of phenomenological descriptions of meditation as embodied through training are similar to the experiences that I too had glimpsed in practice. They help to show the connections between mindfulness and meditative training, and in understanding why so many monks in Thailand reported in their interviews that in order to understand mindfulness, "it would be good to meditate."

Through my meditation practice and from hearing about that of others, I picked up some more clues about human experience in sati and well-being in a cultural context, rather than an a-cultural context, especially in terms of what I have called the TAPES of mindfulness. I came to understand more about the TAPES of Temporality, Affect, and Ethics. And while Power wasn't yet an explicit part of training, I also gained a stronger sense of the ways that Selfhood becomes implicated in practice.

T—Temporality

As monks like Phra Thēp, Phra Mon, and almost all the others I talked with in Thailand had pointed out, mindfulness is about the subjective relationship to time. It is both about the past in the sense of remembering, and about the present in the sense of using this memory to be aware of what is happening now. As my friend Gaew said when I asked her why she was about to go to a ten-day meditation retreat at a monastery near Mae Jaeng, "Well, I'm doing the retreat because I'm so forgetful! It will help me remember better."

Understanding mindfulness as recollecting the mind to the present helps to reconcile the term's attention to the past and to the present, because it could be said that through recollection one "remembers" what one is doing now. Yet the meditation retreats also taught me that there is more to it than just the attention to the moment of the past or the present. They taught me that the way mindfulness relates to time may not be especially about either the past or the present, but rather about the way one experiences time in general. This ties in to the TAPES of Affect too: the reason why mindfulness helps to construct emotionality in a particular way is that it helps one to pay attention to the constant changes that are happening to the body and mind, and through that attention realize that attaching to some feeling about a sensation is futile. This was what Goenka was teaching us when he repeated "*anicca, anicca*"—changing, changing—at the end of each hour of meditation, using the Pali term to refer to one of the central "characteristics" of existence in Buddhist thought. Mindfulness trains one to "be" in the present, but more than that it seems to train one to recognize the past in the present, and anticipate the future from the present—to recognize in a sense the continuity of time in any one moment. The breathing meditation at Buddhadasa's retreat and the walking meditation at Wat Tham Thong both trained in this too, through noticing the constant movement of the breath or the body, and slowing things down. It was somehow only once I got better at how I related to the passing of an hour, not as "being" in the hour but in seeing the time move, that I altered the experience of meditation. Especially right after each meditation session I was acutely aware of this movement and myself as part of it.

A—Affect

Phra Thēp and Phra Mon had talked about mindfulness as helping them to construct affective dispositions that were calmer and better-controlled than they might be otherwise. In the meditation retreats I learned a little bit more about what this looks like in practice. I had wondered if the result of mindfulness was happiness, on the one hand, or a kind of emotionless state on the other, but I found that neither was the case. The meditation courses helped me to understand how the process of constructing emotion itself is differently understood through meditative training. Rather than one experiencing "an emotion" and then regulating it or managing it, as I usually thought of affective processing (but had come to realize wasn't the case in Thailand), the story of affect in mindfulness seemed to be one of altering the sense of attachment and craving that one typically feels about a sensation, and thereby avoiding the negative clinging effects of emotional states. The monk at Buddhadasa's meditation retreat had said that when a bee stings, the feeling is unpleasant, and by recognizing that the feeling will go away, the negative feeling doesn't become an attachment. The same would be said about positive feelings too: one decreases emotional engagements through a recognition of impermanence.

In discussing the relationship between experience and emotion, the monk was offering an illustration of an idea that is also offered in many textual accounts of the teachings, such as one that says clearly, "When an instructed noble comes into contact with a painful feeling he does not feel the secondary mental feeling" (sutta 6, Vedanā Saṃyutta)—that is, emotion. Mindfulness is understood to help in this. According to Tse-fu Kuan, in a lengthy analysis of sati in the early Buddhist canon, "The Satipaṭṭhānas [or Foundations of Mindfulness] enable one to surmount emotional agitation and achieve equanimity (*upekkhā*) through transforming *saññā*" (2008, 33, citing the Saḷāyatanavibhaṅga Sutta and the first sutta of the *Anuruddha Saṃyutta*). Through awareness of impermanence and changing one's attachment to the sensation, Kuan tells us, perception (*saññā* in Pali terms) helps in achieving feelings of calmness, or "equanimity," of being neither overly happy or overly sad but rather calm and unagitated. Nonattachment is key: as a popular dhamma book I found at a library in Chiang Mai put it, "If we don't have sati we'll *sep dtit*, get attached, think a lot; sati allows us to know our feelings, to know what to say, to not get attached" (Prawet wai 1984, 3).

It is this complex process of affective development through mindfulness as a tool for nonattachment that Phra Mon had been speaking of when he said that practicing mindfulness helped him emotionally to become less angry and more calm. It is also what Goenka and his lineage teaching was pointing to with his "mentalist" interpretation of *vedanā* as the feeling of sensation. As many Buddhist teachers point out, Goenka had described how even pleasant experiences when clung to turn negative, and he also pointed to it when he instructed the meditator to use the technique of *vipassanā* to disintegrate feelings of emotion and recognize them as wavelets. At the Goenka retreats, I had first noticed that fixating on a thought or on my discomfort in sitting didn't help the time pass, and that actually it made the time go even slower and the agitation more acute. At Buddhadasa's retreat I learned a similar lesson, where the dhamma talks in the evening were about the wheel of dependent origination, and the way that clinging to feelings attached to sensations can be destructive. "Once you're aware of what happened, catch the breathing again," he had said, "gently bringing it back to the breathing." In my experience there I put this into practice by starting to not crave the time to pass or be angry for following a thought to pass the time. In the retreats at Wat Tham Thong and Wat Mae Long I continued to put these instructions into practice, working to separate a feeling as sensation from a feeling as emotion. Happiness wasn't the result, or the goal, but neither

was a sense of emotionlessness, at least not in a cold, affectless interpretation of that term. Instead I felt a sense of calmness, and peacefulness, that
came from practice.

E—Ethics

Attention to change and the mindfulness that develops from it were said in
the meditation retreats to be good things. This goodness was not just spoken of; it was also implied bodily through the ascetic rigor of training. By
disciplining the body, practicing mindfulness is felt to be not just an intellectual exercise but also a physical one. And this physical act is considered to be about doing what is good and moral. Phra Thēp had said that
moral behavior along with wisdom is the foundation that mindfulness
grows from, working together "like a chain of friends." Phra Mon had
said that mindfulness helped him to be not just calmer but also more kind
and "good." In the meditation retreats there were lessons on both of these
connections with morality in mindfulness, though as with the monks'
reports, most of the ethical component was implicit. The strict following
of behavioral guidelines at the meditation retreats was required because, it
was said, it would allow the practitioner to benefit the most from the practice, though it took time to realize why. I had thought of the not-speaking
in the retreats as having the purpose of not being distracted, and this was
part of it, but I also heard from people that not speaking means that one
is less likely to say something untruthful or bad. I did find that following
the requirements helped, especially in the silence, and the not eating after
noon (which provided alertness rather than sluggishness from large meals,
and also prevented the hunger common to more ascetic practices), and the
keeping a simple lifestyle. They helped not just because they facilitated the
development of mindfulness, but also because they helped me feel good in
the practice. And, as I was learning, feeling good enables one to do good
more easily. In each of the retreats it was taught that clinging to a thought
or perception wasn't good to do, and, in the sense that judging an experience can mean clinging to it and fixating on it, then the training did
involve a sense of non-judgment; but mostly mindfulness was connected
to these kinds of direct approaches to moral goodness.

At the end of each hour and at the end of the retreat the meditators
were also taught to meditate on loving kindness to others, to "share the

benefit of the practice," a Theravāda version of the Mahayana emphasis on compassion. This was explicit in the Goenka and Buddhadasa retreats, and was understood to be part of the practice at the retreats I did at Wat Tham Thong and Wat Mae Long. At the end of the chants in the mornings and evenings at each monastery, a moment of this kind of meditation was brought in, adding a more social awareness to the ethical practice.

S—Selfhood

In addition to these TAPES of Time, Affect, and Ethics, the experience at the meditation retreats taught me especially about the role of the self in mindfulness. The monks I spoke with had pointed to a theory about the self through their discussions of nonattachment to static time and affective training toward calm emotionality. There is a social need to talk about the self in everyday life, even in the relatively sequestered life of a monastic setting, but underneath the colloquial uses of self was a radical view of the person, one in which there is no self at all. Meditation in these settings takes place within complex social contexts; but the relative separation of individual experience from other interpersonal engagements allows this view of the person, or rather the non-person, to become more explicit.

I had gone into the first meditation retreat years before partly because the world had seemed so chaotic to me, and I wanted to focus on finding out who I was in it. Meditation, after all, I had heard, gets rid of layers of baggage and shows you who you are: "Wherever you go, there you are," as the famous book on mindfulness by Jon Kabat-Zinn suggests (1994). But I didn't really learn about this in the meditation retreats at all. The focus on letting go of feelings about sensations didn't seem to leave much room for self-reflection. The emphasis in each of the retreats on noticing time and the changing of time suggested not just that my thoughts and feelings weren't really "mine," but that there wasn't really a "me" there at all. This, of course, is the teaching of *anattā*, or non-self, one of the other main characteristics of phenomenal experience in Buddhist thought. I don't remember hearing a lot of talk about this teaching explicitly at any of the retreats I went on, and in the interviews and conversations I was conducting on mindfulness people told me it is an especially difficult topic to really understand; yet it seemed to underpin a lot of what I was learning and experiencing in meditation. There was something about it especially that I felt the night at Buddhadasa's retreat when I realized how different it would be to really see the teaching through. And Mae Lah had pointed to something that to me felt unusual about a theory of personhood when she said that the opening-of-the-karma ceremony at Wat Tham Thong was for seeing one's past lives—but only if one's "spirits" were strong through the power of mindfulness. The construction of selfhood in meditation wasn't perfectly clear to me, but it was definitely different from what I had been taught previously to think of.

A year after the meditation at Wat Mae Long, in June of 2015, I visited the monastery again on the way to Mae Jaeng, to say hello and make a donation. Luang Po Odom was receiving offerings from some laypeople, and the female monastics were busy in the back of the monastery grounds when I arrived. I made my offering, bowing, and could tell that Luang Po Odom didn't recognize me at all. "I was here a year ago," I said, "and just wanted to say hello and thank you." He recognized me then, and said laughing, a little abashed, "Oh yes!" It was charming to me that I was so unmemorable to him, and it felt good to think of how little of an impact I had made at the monastery, and how unimportant I was in the everyday scheme of it. One of the female monastics I had met, the older one, had since left the monastery to go live with her grandchildren, and the elderly one that had been in the hospital was back in her *kuti*. I thanked Luang Po Odom again, and left.

From the experience of these meditation retreats, and from other experiences of meditation I've had and heard about over the years, it has become clear that continuing to meditate would mean developing mindfulness more and more. The path is alluring because of the practical clarity that the training provides, and I wanted to keep the role of meditation present in how mindfulness can be understood. But I also realized that the path suggested by meditation isn't something that most people can or want to follow fully. Most people take mindfulness in pieces, in popular culture or meditative moments, and apply it to much more secular pursuits than those of the formal setting of the monastery. To find out how mindfulness works not just in the form of meditation itself but for people outside of the monastery, and learn what these understandings might say about practices and processes of well-being,

I would have to move outward again into the wider world of social life in Thailand. I would have to insert the element of power into the middle of the TAPES, and examine how mindfulness works more explicitly as a tool for mastery over the self and others in different aspects of social life. I turn to this now, in "Power and the Ghosts of Insanity in Lay Thai Life."

3

Power and the Ghosts of Insanity in Lay Thai Life

One late afternoon during the rainy season Santi, Justin, and I were sitting at a coffee shop in Chiang Mai going over the day's mindfulness interviews. As we watched the rain fall outside we listened to the audiotapes and recorded the words of the monks and laypeople, and after a few hours the battery on Santi's laptop died, and he realized that he would have to drive over to a friend's house to borrow a battery cord. He was nervous about driving in the rain, though, and said so.

"I just learned to drive," he told us, "and with the roads wet out, well, I'm afraid I don't have much mindfulness."

He headed out into the rain anyway, and when he still hadn't returned in an hour Justin and I started to get worried. After another hour had passed he finally walked back into the shop, wet from the rain, and announced excitedly, "The guy was totally OK, but I just ran into a pedestrian with my car!" The man Santi had bumped into was a foreigner, a tourist walking across the street near the city's main gate. Though the man was unharmed from the light bump, he had been upset, and I could tell that Santi was shaken up too.

"I told you!" he said triumphantly, smiling. "I told you I didn't have mindfulness!"

We laughed at the unfortunate serendipity of the moment and got back to work. Santi's experience was mostly forgotten for the rest of the evening, but it stayed in my mind afterward. I kept coming back to it while thinking about mindfulness in the lives of people outside the monastery. I kept thinking about it partly because someone could have gotten hurt, and also because in the interviews and questionnaires that were coming in from the Thai students, villagers, and hospital staff we heard stories again and again about mindfulness in relation to driving. We were asking people to tell us about times they did and times they didn't have a lot of mindfulness, and the most popular response by far was to illustrate both with examples from when they were operating a motor vehicle. "Yeah, there was one time I was driving a car and I turned right and my car hit another car," said one student, "and this was a time when I didn't have sati." "Lets say I've been drinking and I drive my motorbike," said another. "If I kept driving there would be an accident. But if I had sati, I would never drive a motorbike while drunk." Even monks (who don't drive vehicles) mentioned driving as examples of times when they did have a lot of mindfulness and stayed safe, or alternatively when they had gotten into an accident on account of not having much mindfulness at all. Phra Thēp in Mae Jaeng and Luang Po Odom from Wat Mae Long both had been drivers professionally before they ordained, and like others, both had talked about mindfulness as part of those experiences.

Santi's comment was memorable, because he had announced that he was lacking in mindfulness right before he went out and got into an accident; it was a prescriptive *in situ* moment rather than a retroactive one reflectively recalled. Santi was thinking of mindfulness because he was working on it with the project, and had made his comment almost comically on account of it, but he was not someone who struck me as invoking Buddhist ideas like mindfulness in casual conversation; it was even one of the first times he had mentioned his own state of mind to me. Santi is unlike Phra Thēp or Phra Mon, or even unlike Kay or my host mother Mae Daeng, all of whom spend time at the monastery regularly. Santi was very open about not being interested much at all in Buddhism, though as a Buddhist Northern Thai person he follows it as the religion of his parents. His graduate school project at Chiang Mai University was about Gayatri Spivak's perspectives on the subaltern (Leksakun 2014), and he visited

Europe whenever he could, having spent time there as a teenager. Even in Chiang Mai, Santi preferred the social scene of the city to its monasteries and meditation retreats.

Why would mindfulness be associated so much with something so ostensibly typical, and unreligious, as driving, even in Santi's mind? And why would anyone bring up mindfulness at such a nonreligious moment? Kay had talked about the power of mindfulness, but what does this power look like in practical, everyday terms? In some ways a connection seemed intuitively obvious: one should be "mindful" when driving because it can be dangerous, in the same way that signs saying to "mind the gap" or "mind your head" suggest a general call to pay attention. Driving takes focus and concentration, and so it makes sense that being a good driver means to be a mindful one. With the precariousness of motorcycles, the often chaotic traffic patterns, and the new incentives from the government for first-time drivers to buy cars, there are good reasons to be mindful while driving in Thailand.

Given what I knew about mindfulness from monks, from the feeling of competency developed through meditation, and the chaotic streets of Chiang Mai, the link between mindfulness and driving didn't at first seem to be much of a puzzle. Yet the efficacy of mindfulness in Thailand is about more than just about watching out and being careful and aware. The nurse Ta at the psychiatric hospital had said that mindfulness can help people be mentally healthy, and my friend Sen had said too that the

Figure 7. "Have good sati. Drive well," reads a street sign on a road by the Mae Ping River in Chiang Mai. A small boy and his mother pass by in a makeshift extended motorbike as a new car drives down the winding street in the other direction. Photo by J. L. Cassaniti.

main reason people were at that same psychiatric hospital was that they didn't have sati. Even the military leader of the country, General Prayut, who had assumed power after the coup I first heard about at Wat Mae Long in 2014, said that what he was doing in taking over the country was to give mindfulness to the people. He was using the concept of mindfulness to refer to a kind of psychological strength for the Thai people, and was wielding his own strength in doing so. As one of the psychiatrists at the hospital put it baldly, "If we have more sati, we will have more power." Inserting Power into the TAPES of Temporality, Affect, Ethics, and Selfhood allows for an understanding of the development and efficacy of mindfulness that is much more than a simple "getting by" for the purposes of self help. The mindfulness that is considered so necessary to drive well is the same mindfulness that is seen as a key practice for enlightenment. It is also a way to stay sane, to keep away spirits, sell products, maintain the social fabric of community life, and even attain supernatural powers. All these connotations are implied, to different degrees, in the relatively casual, colloquial ways that sati is brought up in everyday Thai life.

The power associated with mindfulness is created and disseminated in multiple forms. Mindfulness is taught by parents and teachers to children most often in a general sense of being careful and gaining self-control, a kind of low-level power of survival; ideas about mindfulness are traded with friends and circulated in popular culture as reminders in everything from getting A's in school to staying calm and not getting into fights. In a political sense mindfulness is disseminated by the media and the government to sell products, control populations, and exert and promote particular kinds of citizenship from its people. In a "supernatural" sense it is used for its potency to keep one's spirits gathered together and keep away the negative, "crazy-making" energy of ghosts. And in a scientific sense it is used in increasingly global discourses by mental health professionals to promote particular ideals of psychological well-being. Understanding how power is wielded through mindfulness in each of these perspectives helps to make sense of why someone like Santi would see a lack of mindfulness to be tied to a car accident, and why mental health in Thailand is so closely tied to local and global ideas about a mindful person.

Practical Powers: Getting A's and Avoiding Accidents

Unlike the slow and steady looking inward of monks and meditation, the typical "householder" (a Buddhist term used to refer to laypeople) engages in life goals that compete with aspirations of enlightenment. People don't always want to develop nonattachment to the point of full disinterest in social life. Influences and interests are more jumbled together, with distractions that can feel as chaotic as the vehicles on the streets. Yet even within this context it is felt that people need to watch where they're going at all times, as Santi should have been doing when the foreigner he hit with his car moved across his path in the rain. Within the cacophony of distractions that make up the lay life, Buddhists in Thailand think about mindfulness as being both obviously natural, akin almost to "instinct" of the kind that every (sane) person has (as Noi had told me on the motorcycle on the way up to see Phra Thēp), and at the same time so complicated and profound that it requires years of religious scholarship and meditative practice to attain. Buddhadasa Bhikkhu made famous a particular way of thinking about this distinction in what he referred to as the language of conventional truth and ultimate truth. In Buddhadasa's telling, mindfulness and many other concepts like it can take on either quality, depending on how they are used. Mindfulness can mean both obvious instinct and deep knowledge. A dhamma book I came across in Chiang Mai pointed this out explicitly. "Sati has two types, qualities," it said: "(1) *sati lok*, the sati of the world (for everyone everywhere has sati. This is the everyday sati, and you can have more or less of it, depending on your karma from the past. If you have a little sati you'll benefit a little, if you have a lot of sati you'll benefit a lot) . . . and (2) *sati tham*, the dhamma sati" (Thammaraksa 1987 [2530], 42–43). In interviews some people referenced this kind of thinking, too, as when a monk said, describing what his parents taught him about mindfulness: "They taught me the basic things. Like when I did something wrong, they would tell me 'use your sati,' but they didn't teach me directly, because sati is a dhammic word. Ordinary people may not know what it is, or may not think about it, but my parents taught me to think before doing anything." This reflects a fairly common distinction made between everyday versus religious kinds of teachings. But while a dichotomy of conventional and ultimate ideas for mindfulness can be useful in understanding how mindfulness is used in formal religious contexts as opposed to the more informal lessons of life, usually people are thinking of some blend of both when they bring mindfulness to mind.

People are often thinking about mindfulness in both senses when they raise the term colloquially, as Kay did after he got out of his meditation retreat, and as Santi did after he ran into the man with his car. Because I was listening for it, I overheard talk of mindfulness more often than if I wasn't doing research on it, but even without my seeking it out, it was clear that people use the concept often. When someone isn't paying attention to something, she might say by way of explanation, "Oops, *sati taek*—I lost my sati for a second there!" If someone hears some unexpected news and finds he can't concentrate, he has "*khat sati*" (to cut one's sati), or "*sia sati*" (to lose one's sati). *Tang sati* is to "compose" one's sati, much as one would compose oneself after getting rattled at something. Tripping while walking might elicit a comment about one's sati, and if someone got drunk or just acted crazy the verdict might be "*rai sati*"[1] (to be mad or crazy).

Growing Up with the Power of Mindfulness

The power of control and mastery of the mind through mindfulness is taught to children in Thailand at a young age. Most of the people I spoke with about their early exposure to mindfulness said that they learned about it most formally at the monastery, but they also said that they just grew up learning about it from parents:

> When my parents would say, "Be careful," well that's how they taught me about sati. For example, when I had to carry heavy things like a bowl to wash and my parents would say "Be careful, or you'll break it." Or when I would have to walk somewhere, they would say, "Be careful, or you'll fall down."

> When I did housework, I was taught to do it very carefully. When I would do the dishes, my parents would tell me not to break anything because I might cut my hand.

> I used to be a very hot-tempered person, and my dad said that I should cool down. By acting hot-tempered I made mistakes.

My parents taught the basics, of walking and eating with mindfulness, like that. Like, that if I ate fish without sati the bone would stick in my throat. Or when I was walking, to watch out for nails, and be careful not to step on a nail. That is the teaching about sati.[2]

Secular schoolbooks for children in Thailand are also full of talk about mindfulness. I was surprised by this at first, because when I asked Santi what he learned about mindfulness in school growing up, he said, "Nothing—we don't learn about it there, we learn it from our parents, or from monks." I asked my Chiang Mai housemate Thong the same question one evening, after a day of interviewing, thinking that Santi perhaps wasn't a good representative of the majority of Thai people. But Thong gave the same answer. He didn't remember learning about sati in school. Maybe mindfulness is either too obvious or too complicated to be taught to children at school, he told me. But a few days later when Thong and I went to the DK bookstore in Chiang Mai, which distributes the city's public schoolbooks, we found, surprisingly, talk of mindfulness throughout many of them, in textbooks for courses on either "Buddhism" or "Religion and Society." The two of us brought back to our house all of the books for each school year from one of the most popular publishing lines, regulated by Thailand's Ministry of Education, and found mindfulness in multiple places in each, and for each year of school, from elementary school to advanced grade levels. The more advanced levels discuss mindfulness in more technical terms, describing the teachings of the Satipaṭṭhāna Sutta and different angles on Buddhist thought of the kinds discussed in the *Navakovada*; but even the very beginning levels for children only five years old in first grade (called *bor* 1) include lessons on mindfulness. Mindfulness is brought up not just once but in multiple places, on multiple pages.[3] And as with lessons learned from parents, mindfulness is taught from *bor* 1 to *mor* 6 (the last year of high school) as a way to be careful, especially to develop a sense of mastery and mental power and control, and to succeed in school and in the world. There are discussions involving temporality:

Sati means to recollect, or knowing all the time what one is doing. (*bor* 1, p. 43)

Sati is recollection, noting, and not being blurry, to be able to control the mind with things you're concerned with. (*bor* 3, 26)

And affect:

To practice sleeping in the way of having sati is to practice the mind being calm. While you are sleeping you won't have nightmares, and you'll feel refreshed when you wake up. (*bor* 4)

In developing *vipassanā*, practitioners must practice to use sati in controlling feelings. (*mor* 5, 142)

Through mindfulness one becomes a person who is easily happy, and has moods that are stable and controlled. (*mor* 5, 142–49)

Ethics:

The Buddha taught people to uphold not doing bad deeds but good ones instead, and to make the mind clearer and pure through sati. (*bor* 1, 13)

Practice doing good deeds until the root of goodness has grown in one's mind in three aspects: no greed, no anger, and no delusion. Exercising the development of wisdom in this way will make the mind have mindfulness, concentration, and wisdom, and you'll know what to do whenever you encounter a problem. (*bor* 5)

Selfhood:

We should try to decrease our attachment to ourselves; having sati we'll remember the real Dhamma, that everything changes all the time, that everything that arises will change. (*mor* 3, 74)

Throughout all the lessons too there was an emphasis especially on Power, with teachings about developing mindfulness as a way not to be careless, to develop mental control, and to be successful:

Having sati will make the heart and mind be controlled, to not be excited or frightened . . . to have a good memory, and be able to control oneself to not do bad deeds, with the result that one will find success in everything, such as work, and study and more. . . . Playing while having sati makes us have fun, and if we play without sati, it may cause an accident and be dangerous. (*bor* 1, 44–46)

To clear our mind is to practice sati to control the mind to concentrate on things we do, by realizing what we are doing and how to do it. (*bor* 4)

When you consume [alcohol and other disordering substances] things can happen that are dangerous for your body, and you aren't able to control sati. (*bor* 5)

To practice sati is to practice in gaining sati to prevent failure. (*bor* 5, 35)

When we lose something, at work, or are being manipulated, or suffering, be sure to not lose sati; persist in your mind and attempt to solve all the problems you encounter with full capacity. (*mor* 5, 57)

Sati is the awakening tool of the world. (*mor* 6, 96)

From the time of childhood most people in Thailand are surrounded by these messages of mindfulness. This is true in a general sense of everyday lessons like being careful, and in a religious sense of going on long meditative retreats, and often too in messages that integrate the two. When Santi said he was worried about driving in the rain because he didn't have mindfulness, he was internalizing these messages.

Popular Powers

As people in Thailand grow older they will come across mindfulness in messages not just from family, school, and the monastery but also as powerful incentives for thought and action in popular media. When I asked friends in Chiang Mai to help me gather some of these popular references to mindfulness they quickly told me about dozens of them circulating socially. In one typically melodramatic Bangkok soap opera being broadcast across the country at the time, a man fighting with his brother and mother pulls a gun on them, and his brother promptly exhorts him in reaction, "Mi sati na"—"Have sati, man!" In this short expression the man meant a lot of things: for his brother to put down the gun, to remember where he was and whom he was with, and to calm down.

In a public service TV advertisement sponsored by Lion laundry detergent, mindfulness takes an even more central stage: A young Thai man is angry after someone cuts him off in his car on a busy urban road. After jumping out of his car and imploring the hapless other driver to get out and fight, the man suddenly pauses and remembers his mindfulness, and desists. "The second you lose sati—" the narrator intones over the stopped action, as the man freezes mid-punch and a pause-button signal beeps on the screen, "just stop. And think. What will be the result of this moment? What will be gained? What will be lost?" The sound of a meditation bell goes off in the background, almost as the sound of a light coming on in the man's head, and he relaxes, smiles, and *wais* respectfully to the driver: "I'm so sorry, my elder brother," he tells him. "I'm sorry too," the driver says in reply. As the young man gets back in his car, now with a smile on his face, the narrator tells us: "Use sati to walk along the path of life."[4]

The incident in the public service advertisement is a modern moment, one that is as much about the global use of discourses of mindfulness as it is indirectly indexing their Buddhist roots. It is significant, however, that the man is young: his prominently displayed dental braces signal his relative immaturity in not already employing mindfulness, as much as they show his wealth in affording the expensive cosmetic health aid. And even with the obvious marketing purpose of the advertisement, remembering one's mindfulness is seen as a powerful, socially good thing to do.

Memory is part of these kinds of popular accounts. In a film called *Sati taek sut khua lok* (Lost mindfulness at the edge of the world), a group of teenagers have a series of adventures by re-experiencing their past lives. The title refers to people whose souls don't have places to go, and therefore they wander without a calm and peaceful mind. In a TV advertisement for a popular band's concert the announcer says, "*Tang sati* [compose your mindfulness] before you scream, *tang sati* before you laugh!" Mindfulness comes up in pop love songs, such as one I heard one afternoon on the radio: the singer Phongphat intones in the song "FanFuan" (Frantic), "Suddenly you left me. . . . The hurt is too much to handle. . . . If I can prepare, and accept being frantic and have my mindfulness disordered, well maybe then I'll forget you." In introducing Phongphat's song, the radio announcer prefaced it with a comment on mindfulness: "Dear audience, don't forget, when you decide something in life, anything, you should have mindfulness before you decide it." And in an older but still very popular song called "Live and Learn," Kamala Sukosol tells the listener (author's translation), "One day our life comes to the point of change, so soon that our hearts aren't ready for it. / Joys and pains, no one knows when they'll come, and how much truth we will be able to face. / Because that is just life, things come and go. / There's success, there's failure, laughter and fears, they happen every day. / With learning and acceptance, follow the way of thinking with mindfulness, / live with what you have, not with your dreams, and live with it to the best of your ability."

There are many more of these kinds of examples. Collectively they point to a shared sense of mastery of the mind (and one's life) through sati, and a sense of losing that mastery when mindfulness goes away. They provide a sense of what it looks like to be psychologically well. One Thai friend, who perhaps not uncoincidentally had just been turned down for entrance into the grad school he had his heart set on, offered a pertinent example of the kind of message about mindfulness typically offered in the media: "The media will say things like, if you don't get into the school you want, don't give up, recollect yourself! They'll say you've got your future still, your life will be like this. It's to gain your self-confidence back." Mindfulness is used as a positive tool for dealing with these difficulties, and for creating future change.

While circulating socially, these practices are often cultivated in relative privacy. When people spoke about moments when they feel especially mindful, the most common response was, not surprisingly, in meditation:

I had a lot of mindfulness when I went to the *vipassanā* course, because I had a chance to observe my mind, to observe my thoughts, to concentrate, and practice.

When I'm doing meditation is when I have more sati. Because we have to focus on our breath. When I forget what I'm doing I'm lost.

But people also talked about having mindfulness at times when they were engaged in more everyday activities: reading, or in class or studying or taking an exam, or while spending time alone, walking slowly, and even, for a few people, when online:

Since I practice the dhamma it makes me feel like I can control my body, and have sati all the time. To not be angry or distracted. Like, when I walk, I know I'm walking.

When I went to sit for the exam, and when I studied my textbook, I tried to have sati. I try not to think about other things, and focus on the textbook for the exam, to get an A.

When I'm reading, reading makes me calm. I like to read novels or meditation books, things like that.

When I wake up in the morning I have a lot of sati . . . and when I'm avoiding doing bad things, and when I think of my parents. And when I think about the Buddha, the dhamma, and the sangha, that's when I have sati.

I have sati when I'm online, playing video games.

Conversely, the times people said that they had especially low levels of mindfulness were when they were upset, or angry or confused:

A few years ago I got really angry at a friend who borrowed my motorbike at school without asking me. . . . When I found out about it I was angry and I hit him, and my friend lost two of his teeth. I didn't have sati then. But then I got over it. . . . We've become friends now again, like we used to be.

When I am mad, really angry, and confused, I might sometimes do something harmful like using bad words to other people. Especially when I'm angry I might take something from another person without thinking carefully. We express our anger through our body or our words. That's why we need sati: to control ourself.

The feelings of unmindfulness were expressed most often not as a kind of rage, but rather as a sense of being disordered and unclear, almost like a mental blurriness. Many of these moments of lacking sati had a similar quality of being without a sense of power or self-control, such as when one was feeling tired, scared, distracted, drunk, or sick:

My grandfather died, and I couldn't control myself. Everything felt like it was crashing down. That was a time I didn't have sati. I couldn't control myself, and I didn't want to listen to anybody. . . . Or when I went out to have drinks with my friends, this was a time also that I couldn't control myself.

When I am frightened. For example, once when I was walking in the forest and a tree fell down in front of me.

Three kinds of times: when I have greed, when I'm angry, and when I'm lost. Especially when I'm angry. Like when I'm in class teaching and some students aren't listening to what I'm saying, that's when I've lost my sati.

I can forget sati at any time. Losing sati does not only happen in a critical situation, but it can happen anytime. For example, we are talking
right now, and my mind, and my mind could wander to something else.
I may be speaking to you now, but I may be thinking of my temple or
my work.

The training that one engages in while practicing mindfulness is cumula-
tive over time, whether in informal or formal contexts. People try to have
mindfulness as much as possible, but monks especially noted that it's not
expected that one can have mindfulness all the time:

Once when I was in a hurry for class, at that time I thought about getting
to class on time and forgot what I had to do to prepare for that day. If I had
had sati with me . . . but of course we can't have sati all the time because we
are not enlightened yet.

Sometimes when I'm walking and suddenly I just forget why I am walking. Or I go to get a pen and then forget where I am going. Or I want
to get the phone and while I am walking I forget why I am walking. It's
not that everybody has sati all the time. Except for an *arahat* [an enlightened being]!

I used to have that feeling of not having mindfulness often before I went to
the monastery. It's like when things aren't like what I expect of them. It's like
I have desire, and desire is anger—that makes one feel angry and neglected.
Now I understand more. Desire brings suffering. And I learn from suffering.
Dukkha [nonsatisfactoriness] is suffering.

Mindfulness may be cultivated in private, but it is used especially in
social situations. In Thailand, where general etiquette, politeness, and
deference to one's social superiors and others are especially shared
values in one's community, being mindful is about more than just self-
cultivation. It is about helping the group as a whole. This social quality of mindfulness, while seen as good and beneficial in general, can
also be used to keep people from speaking up about their own personal interests—at least not until they had thought carefully about
what the implications might be.

Figure 8. "Playing on social media = practicing sati." This public service message, sponsored by the Thai Ministry of Public Health, promotes the practice and benefits of mindfulness for a contemporary setting. *Top left bubble:* "Don't rush to like/share: when you receive a good message or picture or video clip, take some time to read it, and think about the people who sent it to you, and make yourself aware [*ru suk tua*] of the intention of the people who sent it." *Top right:* "Don't rush to respond. When you receive a message or video that you don't like, take time to realize your anger, your dissatisfaction, and then stay still with your breath for a moment; take it easy, relax, little by little, and from there you can decide what you want to do next." The bottom text offers "four advantages of practicing sati from playing on social media": you know ahead of time your heart and mind; prevent your mind from thinking of something and take measure of your mind to allow yourself to do something appropriate; prevent having anger; be able to solve any problem more easily." The bottom left corner offers a toll-free number for those who would like to consult the Thai Ministry of Public Health's Department of Mental Health about sati.

Governmental Powers

As mindfulness at a personal level is thought to help govern the individual, mindfulness at the political level helps to govern the people. Some of these broader, power-laden instances are for specific public services, as in the commercial about the young man and road rage in the crowded city streets, or during a flood in Bangkok, in a commercial I saw during the same rainy season when Santi got into his minor car accident. The public service announcement from the Ministry of Public Health at that time aired on television a message to help combat the rising waters that had started to infiltrate even rich Bangkok homes. "Don't know what to do when your house floods?" the announcer spoke with a deep, Bangkok accent. The camera panned over the inside of a living room with a foot of water in it, bags of rice stacked at the door in a futile attempt to stop the flooding. The answer was superimposed over the screen: *Mi Sati*, it said—"Have mindfulness." How would *that* help? I thought, laughing dismissively at the message. But I realized that in an important way it *would* help: it would help people gain equanimity in what was a stressful situation so they would be able to think clearly, and, perhaps just as important, it would help the government not become inundated with irate demands that something be done about the rising waters. I imagined a similar kind of message being broadcast to people after Hurricane Katrina in New Orleans, telling them to be "mindful," but imagined it probably wouldn't help at all, because people in an American context might take it as emotionally dismissive or insensitive, whereas in Thailand, where being "mindful" is more religiously and culturally resonant with personal beliefs, such a message might be found to be more emotionally helpful.

The political use of mindfulness as a tool for governance goes beyond the kinds of public service messages that suggest using sati in times of personal or social difficulty. There is a long, popular, mythologized history of Buddhism's ties to royalty and governance, starting with the first retelling of the Buddha's life story as a former prince and continuing through the ancient era of King Asoka and into the present day. Rulers in today's Buddhist-majority nation-states promote the memory of these associations and make use of them in their own circumstances, often claiming moral legitimacy of their rule through powers associated with Buddhist practice (Tambiah 1976;

Jackson 1989; Jory 2002, 2016). Even in the very short summary of the whole of the Buddha's teaching compiled in the *Navakovada* I found an entry that claims an explicit link between mindfulness and the continued success of the country. The entry was written by King Vajiravudh (Rama VI) at the turn of the twentieth century, when Thailand was still known as Siam. It is called "Siam-anu-sati"—the Mindfulness of Siam:

> If Siam is to continue for sure
> The people will also continue to live
> If Siam is destroyed the people cannot live
> We'll have lost our Thai family and nation.
> With the mindfulness of Siam
> Thai people will fight to the death
> Lose our blood, be sacrificed, lose our lives
> But nevertheless our names
> Will be honored and remembered.

It is only with the "mindfulness of Siam," the statement proclaims, that the Thai nation will not be lost. And the connection of mindfulness that links Buddhism with the power of the government continues today. In the years after the coup in 2006 there was a series of political protests in the country, from a takeover of the Bangkok airport to an occupation of a main commercial area of the city. The political problems at that time were complicated, but they can be (oversimply) understood as a struggle between the "yellow shirts" (stereotyped as elite urban pro-royalists) and the "red shirts" (stereotyped as poor rural democrats who supported the ex–prime minister Thaksin Shinawatra).[5] When I was in the country during each of these periods of civic unrest I would inevitably hear at least one Thai friend or informant say that the protesters weren't being very "Thai," or weren't being very "Buddhist." What this meant wasn't drawn out specifically, but there was a sense that it somehow wasn't "Buddhist" to make waves and demands on the government, or very "Thai" to do so either, whatever that meant. Thai Buddhists, the implication was, do not usually behave this way. Rather than the active quality that Buddhist ideology took on in local communities, popular governmental contexts seemed to suggest it as promoting a kind of political passivity in the citizenry.

Even more explicitly than in the passing social commentary of the post-2006 coup protests, mindfulness has become part of the rhetoric of the country's present military government, which took power after the coup in 2014. The use of mindfulness by the current regime suggests even more of a connection between mindfulness and power, extending past the person to society at large. Months before the coup, I had seen friends in Mae Jaeng grow more politically vocal; this wasn't particular strange, as the political situation was getting increasingly tense overall, but it did feel unusual that even friends' older relatives, who were usually silent or dismissive about politics in Bangkok, were watching the growing, loud rallies on TV with enthusiasm, often nodding and proclaiming loudly their agreement with red-shirt activists who demanded equal representation. Around this time General Prayut Chan-o-cha, who would become the military junta's leader but at the time was the commander in chief of the royal Thai army, began promoting what he called "mindfulness for the people." In a speech titled "Yak hai khon Thai thuk khon mi sati" (I want to give every Thai person mindfulness)[6] he declared that he wanted people to receive the "good decisions" that were being made for them. Days after the 2014 coup, I turned on the television at a guesthouse by the closed Burmese border only to find that all the stations showed the same blue static screen, with a slogan across it that read: "Khana Raksa Khwam Sangop Haeng Chat"—National Council for Peace and Security. The screen in essence announced the coup and told everyone to be calm, using for "peace" the term *sangop*, with its affective connotations of quietness and mindfulness, rather than the more typical Thai word for peace, *santiphap*. It seemed to be at least indirectly using Buddhism, in its reference to calmness, to create the rhetoric that a good citizen was a silent, peaceful one. A few days later I was back in Chiang Mai, playing badminton with my neighbor Lek, and I asked what she thought of the situation. "Oh, they're giving the people mindfulness," Lek said. "They're doing what needs to be done, so people can have *samādhi* and think clearly." *I bet you heard that on the radio*, I thought to myself, but I didn't say anything to her, scared as I was about the new injunction against criticizing the government. And soon after that I did hear almost verbatim the message she had echoed: that the military was taking over the government because the situation in Thailand with all the protests was causing people to get riled up, and that what the authorities were doing was giving people mindfulness so they can feel peaceful and think clearly. Lek had been repeating the message to me—and to herself.

This powerful rhetoric continues. On July 24, 2015, a full year after the 2014 coup, the prime minister Prayut Chan-o-cha gave a long speech on "returning happiness to the people," in which he discussed the political situation in the country, how the government was dealing with foreign news journalists and foreign affairs, how farmers were suffering from drought due to water shortages, and how to be happy and get along in the country.

As part of the talk he said,

> To solve any problem, it will be impossible if we don't have love and unity, or do not listen to each other. If we have misunderstanding we will return to the circling around of the conflict [that brought about the coup] and get stuck in our own trap. The citizens must know and be aware and listen together. Therefore continue to think with sati, on your own. Do not let anybody lead or misguide you; you must listen from both sides. I ask you to cooperate and listen some and find the way out. [I] do not want to use my power or law to make us reach the point of confrontation in every issue, or the country will abruptly stop again.

The mindfulness raised by Prayut Chan-o-cha here and elsewhere could arguably be seen as a tool of political persuasion. On the other hand, it might be that he is simply invoking a power seen to be connected with mindfulness that is in agreement with how many people in Thailand think about living well. Yet through innocence or cunning, by aligning himself with mindfulness and saying that people should listen to him and not be swayed by other people's opinions, he is in effect manipulating the symbolic social value placed on mindfulness for his own political ends. Mindfulness is clearly connected to power, as a way of thinking that is seen as powerful and good. This takes on the form of being "good" Thai citizens: such citizens are supposed to have mindfulness in the things they say and do, and what they should say and do is, not uncoincidentally, what the government wants them to say and do. It is a different kind of "power" from that developed through meditation in the monastery, or cultivated in school and everyday social life, but it is nonetheless power that is associated with mindfulness, and a potent kind at that. Invoking mindfulness in politics is a way of giving power to the people and articulating ideas that are locally meaningful to them, but it is also a way of legitimizing one's own relative position of authority.

Mindfulness clearly isn't just a formal religious term to be read about in Pali texts or practiced only in the cloistered halls of meditation monasteries or by being a monk. Mindfulness is also something that people in Thailand make use of to create particular ends, and political power clearly is one of these ends. The corralling of Buddhist ideologies for ends that are not equal for everyone is a classic move in Thai politics. The *Setthakit phophiang* (sufficiency economy) program is a good example of this: in a widely popularized campaign from 2007, people were told that they should want only as much as they need. Bowls with "just enough" rice were shown on billboards as preferable to bowls overflowing with rice. The intention was to curtail extravagance, but to many it could also be interpreted as suggesting that rich people "need" more and that poor people should just be happy with the little they have. Debates about whether the sufficiency economy program is good or not still continue in Thailand, but it is in ways like this that Buddhist messages of living well, including those of mindfulness, get manipulated, their signifiers redistributed for economic and political aims.

Ghostly Powers of Sanity

Mindfulness is considered as necessary for everything from getting by to staying sane to influencing others, but why? Why is it thought that mindfulness will help one deal with floods, or with exams, or with virtually everything else? Where does this power of mindfulness come from? The practice of mindfulness is thought to provide powerful protection, not just in avoiding accidents, getting A's on tests, or even in political maneuvering. It is also about staying sane, and keeping away the crazy-making influences of ghostly encounters. In one sense the efficacy of mindfulness is derived from its being a socially valued practice; because it's a shared value, people are rewarded for having it. But there is more to it than that: people will talk of a kind of clarity and ability in mindfulness to "see things as they really are," helping them to move past mental barriers and biases, especially affective ones, that can distort experience and lead to danger. When people say that the mind is "recalled," I found that they couch their understanding of what this looks like within a range of other ideas about how power works.

This is especially so in relation to the "spirits of the person" that keep one healthy and well. The Buddhist teaching of *anattā* (non-self) is relevant here. *Anattā* suggests that the feeling of stability of the person is an illusion, and that the mind is part of this always transient, insubstantial illusion of the self. It is a teaching that is often considered to be too abstract for a person to fully engage with, and this is as true in Thailand as it is elsewhere. If recognizing that our feeling of having a self is an illusion was easy, I was told, the Buddha wouldn't have had to teach about it.[7] Yet for many the teaching is important to attend to, and mindfulness is considered helpful in recognizing the truth of it. For many, having mindfulness helps one to understand this Buddhist teaching of non-self. This was the case across the board in interviews when I asked explicitly about non-self and its connection to mindfulness, and it was also the case in the questionnaire data. In response to my direct queries "Do you think sati is connected to ideas about non-self [*anattā*]? How?" 131 (75 percent) of the 175 responses answered in the positive. Their responses included "Yes, sati is a practice that helps you understand *anattā*" (the most common response); "Sati is related to the three characteristics of *dukkha*, *anattā*, and *anicca*"; or "Sati helps at the point of death when you realize you become nothing." Only 59 (or 34 percent) of the responses checked the other options of "They're related but I'm not sure how or how to explain," "I don't know what *anattā* is," or "No, sati is not related to *anattā*." When I asked them more specifically to explain how mindfulness connects with non-self, most people, from monks to students to villagers to psychiatric hospital workers, explained that practicing mindfulness helps them understand non-self especially by helping them pay attention to change:

> Sati is to determine knowledge because we will know what is true and not true and then we will learn that life is not certain. People will die and get hurt, and we all know that life is going to be like this. I mean, our life is impermanent, but if we have sati, we will know everything. Sati is to determine our perception, that we are without a self. Now we are young, and we have our sati to determine that later we will die. We also know that in the past we were without self. . . . We are here because we were just born

from something, and sati is in our self like a fire. It is up to us to determine whether the fire exists or does not exist. (a monk at Chiang Mai's Wat Suan Dok)

If we use sati to consider things, we'll learn that things are non-self. To practice mindfulness is to know how to control the breath. When we breathe in and breathe out, if we have mindfulness we'll learn that these breaths in and out are impermanent because the breath goes away. To relate mindfulness to non-self, I think mindfulness helps us to learn that everything is impermanent, and if we understand these concepts we'll understand *anattā*. (a student at Chiang Mai University)

Practicing mindfulness, for these people, is about a particular kind of knowledge that comes from attunement; by attending to the fact of impermanence, they said, one is able to clearly understand the insubstantiality of the person. The understanding of how this works, though, varies from person to person. One of the psychiatrists I spoke with at the psychiatric hospital in Chiang Mai put it this way:

Without sati it is difficult to see *anattā*. That is, to understand the non-self. Like, I am talking to Julia. But it's not—it doesn't exist. We think that we're in this room right now, but we're not. Because if we distinguish reality we will see that there are just things gathered together here. If we cannot think of *this*, if we can't think of *anattā* we will fear loss.

He pinched his arm, gesturing to his corporeal body, when he said "this." The psychiatrist spoke of "just things gathered together here." But what are these things that are gathered? One reading is that what is said to be "gathered together" to make up the illusion of the self are the *khandha*, the five aggregates that are thought to contribute in their own partial, insubstantial way to the illusion of the person. They are form (*rūpa*, also often translated as "body"), sensations/feelings (*vedanā*), perception (*saññā*), mental formations (*saṅkhāra*), and consciousness (*viññāṇa*). These aggregates loosely follow the foundations of mindfulness in the Satipaṭṭhāna Sutta. Yet, importantly, the work of mindfulness is not thought to be about gathering these aggregates together to form some complete or full person. Rather, it is in recognizing the transience and instability of each aggregate.

While some people think about the aggregates that make up the feeling of a self, few people articulate the self as such. It is not assumed that one needs each of them to feel mindful, or that the aggregates go away and need to come back. When one woman told me in Mae Jaeng what had at this point become the familiar refrain, "Sati is about the feeling that controls our body and brain. . . . With sati everything is gathered," I interrupted her to ask, "But *what* is gathered?" I expected her to answer with "*jit,*" the Thai word for mind (from the Pali *citta*), or to talk about these aggregates. Instead she said, "*Khwan.*"

Khwan is a concept followed by Tai people in mainland Theravāda Asia (not just Thai but "Tai," referring to a wide ethnic group in Thailand, Laos, northern Burma, southern China, and northeast India [Formoso 1998; Eberhardt 2006; Terwiel 1978]). The concept of *khwan* theorizes the self or mind as made up of multiple "spirits," which are usually encased in the body but can also at times wander away and get lost, and which need to be called back to keep the person healthy and well. *Khwan* is seen as part of Buddhism in that it is incorporated into Buddhist practice, but it is sometimes considered a "pre-Buddhist" idea about the spirits of beings. *Khwan* is difficult to conceptualize; they are single and multiple, personified but not given names. They are us, in a sense, but they can wander and get lost. I often think of *khwan* as a kind of personified "wits," similar to when English speakers say "to keep your wits about you" to refer to having a kind of mental fortitude, or "you've lost your wits" to refer to a kind of scattered mental state. In Thailand it is thought that when one's *khwan* are gone, having dispersed by becoming surprised or fixated or somehow unfocused, one is more susceptible to illness, both mental and physical. Ceremonies called *hong khwan* or *riak khwan* ("calling back the *khwan*") are performed to help one regain one's *khwan*.

There is a good deal of variation in how people understand *khwan* in northern Thailand. Some people emphasize an intentional and animated (even "animistic") interpretation of *khwan*, as beings, while others "psychologize" them. One informant psychologized *khwan* as "mental support, and confidence. These are 'spirits' of the person that can wander, get lost, and find their way back. When one's 'spirits' are scattered or weak, a person is more susceptible to being ill and vulnerable to the influences of other forces. It is when these spirits are totally gone that one has no

mindfulness at all, and when one is thought to have lost one's sanity altogether. . . . The ceremony to call back the *khwan* is really a ceremony to
help us feel better."

While separate in some senses, *khwan* are also about the spirits of
the mind, and mindfulness is part of this. Understanding the *khwan*
helps to make sense of what so many people were saying about mindfulness as "recalling" the mind, recollecting it and bringing it back. It's not
just "you" that wanders, it is suggested, but the many parts of you that
make up the feeling of being a person, and bringing the mind back is less
about gathering a stable "you" and more about, almost paradoxically,
a recognition of there not being a "you" at all. I again asked the woman
in Mae Jaeng who had said that everything is gathered with *khwan*
to tell me more about it, and she replied with an example. "Let's say
some fireworks unexpectedly go off in front of us," she said. "When the
loud noise and lights erupt, people who don't have sati will be startled
and run at first [maybe thinking it's purposeful violence of some kind],
but people who have sati will look and consider what the situation is
and will know how to escape if it's something dangerous, or if it's just
fireworks will know to stay. When someone is weak [without a lot of
khwan], the monk puts the *sai sin* [a white string bracelet] around the
wrist, it's like good medicine, and they come back to normal." I noticed
this kind of startle reflex one day while I was sitting at lunch in Mae
Jaeng, in an outdoor eating area crowded with people. At another table
nearby sat a monk. At some point someone dropped a glass, which
made a loud crashing noise as it shattered on the pavement. We all
started at the noise, but I happened to be looking at the monk when it
happened and noticed that he—presumably immersed in mindfulness
practice—didn't start at all. It is this susceptibility to being shocked or
not being shocked that for many people is connected to what mindfulness looks like.

White string bracelets are tied around wrists by monks and revered
elders to help keep in one's *khwan*, especially when one isn't feeling
well, or is about to go on a trip, or is prone to be in a situation that
does not invite a lot of mindfulness. Each time I was about to leave my
field site of Mae Jaeng to return to America, my host mother's mother
would quietly chant as she tied a white string around my wrist to wish
me well and remind me to have mindfulness. The same thing happened

Figure 9. A group of monks gather throughout the night at a monastery in the town of Mae Jaeng to perform a ceremony to "open the eyes of the Buddha [statue]." The white strings hanging above the monks' heads and wrapped around the monastery symbolize the power and strength of mindfulness as connected to *khwan*, serving to keep the energy of the space together. These strings are considered practically efficacious in addition to their symbolic power. Photo by J. L. Cassaniti.

when Sen's brother Noi left for Australia, and again when he returned to visit. For similar purposes white strings are put around other things too, including new motorcycles, cars, houses, and even monastery buildings, to help keep the mental spirits of them and their users gathered together.

Once, while Sen was staying in Mae Jaeng's local hospital after returning from a series of hospitals in Chiang Mai, a *mo phi* (spirit doctor) named Nan Jan came in from his office at the back of the Mae Jaeng hospital grounds to perform the ritual. With chants circling Sen's body he sent away the "ghosts" of alcohol that had been attached to Sen, to restore his mindfulness by returning his *khwan*. I talked to Nan Jan after the ceremony and asked him to tell me more about *khwan*:

"Sati is related to the spirits that wander around," he told me. People perceive different kinds of connections between *khwan* and mindfulness, from their being not related at all to being the same thing. For the doctor they are intimately intertwined. "When our *khwan*—and *khwan* is the same meaning as sati—are weak, the spirits will come to you. If your *khwan* is strong, your mind is strong. *Khwan* is our mind. If our mind is strong, nothing will come to us. If our *khwan* is weak, we're always sick or ill."

Others also saw a connection between the two, and linked them to the body and experience in different ways:

> Well, from my understanding, sometimes when I'm frightened I say, "Come back *khwan*, come back *khwan*!" And, really, this means, "Come back sati, come back sati!"

> It is about mind. We have this ceremony to call *khwan* back to our body. That is to call sati and to clear the mind. *Khwan* and sati may be the same thing, and it affects all minds. When something bad happens, or when there is something wrong and we've lost our *khwan*, that means we've lost our sati.

> *Khwan*, from my understanding, is like sati. There are *khwan* in every part of our body—our ear, our nose, our tongue, trunk, heart. . . . Losing *khwan* is like losing our ability to perceive, and that makes our body weak and get sick. Our heart may beat fast. This is a body without sati.

> I think when we lose our *khwan*, it means we have lost our sati. It's like when we are frightened and we may do something strange. *Khwan* is like sati. When we lose one, we lose them both.

Khwan are important for thinking about what it means to stay sane and powerful in Thailand because of the ways they invoke local models of the mind. Many think that when *khwan* are weak and scattered (and mindfulness is gone with them), one is more likely to be affected by negative forces or events, and that it is this disordered state that causes suffering. Some people see the dispersal of *khwan* as the negative natural consequences of mindlessness, such as an accident that occurs when your mind is "somewhere else," as Santi's was during his drive in the rain. Others connect mindfulness to more supernatural consequences, in the energies of what are thought of as "ghosts."

Figure 10. Piyawit Moonkham, a graduate student at Washington State University, speaks with a man in Mae Jaeng about his experiences with mindfulness. In the interview the man relates how he once almost drowned in the river near his house, but with the power of mindfulness was able to escape the situation. He described the incident as a moment when he really learned about what mindfulness was, and how there was an uncanny, almost supernatural feeling that went with it. The white strings on Piyawit's wrist and strung across the space are thought to help keep one's "spirits" of self from scattering and losing mindfulness. Photo by J. L. Cassaniti.

Ghosts (*phi*) in Thailand look very different from how they are conceived in the United States. The energy of ghosts is also tied to mindfulness, with the centering of *khwan* and mindfulness together helping to keep away the scattered, disorienting influences of others' attachments, most commonly known as ghosts. Ghosts are thought by many to be everywhere in Thailand. "[Ghostly energy] is just in the air around me," one friend put it—"I can feel it on my skin."

Understanding ghosts is important for understanding a wide range of issues in contemporary Southeast Asia, from politics and social inequality (Johnson 2014; Fuhrmann 2016, 2009; McDaniel 2011; Morris 2000) to explanations for sickness and death (Aulino 2014; Stonington,

Figure 11. The author listens to a man discussing his encounter with the ghostly energy of his brother-in-law, who had recently passed away; in his telling the man recounts how he heard a bird fly through a window into his house, and how he felt powerfully that it represented the energy of the spirit of the deceased man. He recounted speaking to the spirits and sending them away, and about the importance of being mindful in these instances of potential vulnerability. Photo by Piyawit Moonkham.

forthcoming). There are thought to be many kinds of ghosts in Thailand, among them tree spirits and guardian spirits and hungry spirits. But in all their iterations they are thought to be in large part constituted by the feelings, whether living or dead, that escape the body and mind and travel in interpersonal space. Thai movies are full of ghosts, often as part of larger Buddhist stories. One common image is for monks in forests to be brought in to exorcise a malicious spirit that is "haunting" a person or a community. Ghosts speak to the intense interpersonality of Thai society, where people are very aware of others' intentions, and of the influences these intentions might have on them.

One story, *Nang Nak*, tells about a woman killed in childbirth, and the psychological ties her husband has to her that bring back her spirit to haunt him.

Figure 12. The Thai romance and horror movie *Nang Nak* relates what is likely the most famous ghost story in the country. Here a screen shot from the film shows some forest monks helping to exorcise the spirit of Nak, a woman who has remained attached to her husband (or, her husband who has mentally remained attached to her) after her untimely death.

At the end of the story, as is common in these kinds of tales, the mindful chanting of a forest monk puts these haunting influences to rest.[8] Descriptions of magic and the supernatural in Thailand are sometimes pitted against more "rationalist" modern readings of Buddhist thought, but connecting them to the powers that come from mindfulness in meditation helps to show how for most people in Thailand there isn't a problematic divide between one reading or the other of religious experience.

The ghostly connections of mindfulness, however, was a difficult topic for me to broach, especially to monks, in large part because of a general monastic Buddhist tradition of avoiding it. One monk, whom my research assistant Piyawit and I were interviewing at a remote hilltop monastery in Mae Jaeng, told us at length about his feeling of levitating after meditation, and of the ghosts that he, like Phra Thēp, hears in the woods sometimes at night. But almost in the same breath he said to Piyawit, "Don't you know you shouldn't be asking these kinds of questions?" The American foreigner, it was clear, was too much of a lost cause to be taught, but Piyawit, he went on, should know better. Didn't Piyawit have a master's degree? Didn't he know his Pali teachings? Abashed, we withdrew from the interview, but the comments the monk made lingered. The *vinaya* injunction against talking about supernatural abilities was cited for the most part by monks who didn't feel inclined to speak on the subject. This was usually couched as simply a rule to follow, but some said also that attending to "these kinds of questions" is a distraction from the work of walking the Buddhist path. This is important, because attending to ghosts is in large part understood to mean that you have allowed yourself to be affected by the feelings and intentions of others, both living and dead. It means you don't have mindfulness. As one older man in Mae Jaeng told me, "It's about practice, to gain power, like the monks who go to the forest to meditate and collect the inner power. It requires practice, meditation [*phawana*]; that is *parithat* [theory], practice, and concentration meditation; and walking meditation. But the monks can't talk about this, because it's against the rules of monks. It's against the monks' precepts [*phit sin*]." The entire monastic enterprise is about becoming more and more proficient at nonattachment and the letting go of these affective influences.

It is this "supernatural" kind of power that partly explains the ghostly politics of sanity in lay Thai life. Most people have encountered the manifestation of ghostly energy personally, or know someone who has, as affective pushes and pulls on one's body and mind. Even in a classroom I visited one afternoon to talk with students at Chiang Mai University, where the British teacher told me he had just taught the students that ghosts don't exist, and that I wouldn't hear any "ghost stories" from them, I found that almost everyone had one to share. One student spoke of encountering a Khmer (Cambodian) couple in a rice field, who had passed away in that spot, and who had caused her to start speaking a language she didn't know; another related hearing scary sounds at an abandoned house by the beach while on vacation in Phuket after the 2004 Indian Ocean tsunami. Yet another student said that right after her grandmother had died, and she was thinking about her, a ghostly vision appeared: "It was my grandmother," the student said. "My mind was all over the place at that time. . . . She told me to have mindfulness."[9] In each of these stories, individuals are understood to be vulnerable to ghostly influences precisely when their mindfulness has left.

The ghostly energy that is kept away through the presence of mindfulness (and *khwan*) is the same ghostly energy that can cause someone to trip up, get into an accident, or become mentally unstable, even "insane."

When people meet a ghost, or when they meet very bad things, the sati in them goes away! And this means the *khwan* disappears too. *Khwan* is like *kamlang jai*, the motivating or supportive energy in us. (a psychiatrist in Chiang Mai)

Khwan is sati, it's the same thing—it's like someone with weak sati has weak *khwan*, and strong *khwan* is having very strong sati. And people with strong *khwan*, nothing can harm them. Ghosts can't do anything to them. Can't make you feel anxious. Truly, I think they are the same thing. The old people talk about weak *khwan* and strong *khwan*. It's like when we do meditation, and if we're calm nothing will scare us. We'll have no fear if we have sati. If we have sati it will make our mind strong. (a layperson in Chiang Mai)

Whether momentarily through fright or distraction, or built up over time, the ghostly energy that is kept at bay can come and affect people when their *khwan* is scattered and their mindfulness with it is weak. In *Tort, Custom, and Karma* (2010), David Engel and Jaruwan Engel write about a man who had passed by a car accident on his way to work at a factory in Bangkok and, distracted thinking about the man who had died in the accident, cut his arm on the factory machine. He understood this to have happened precisely because his mind was distracted and the energy of the man in the accident had come to do him harm. Even my Christian Thai friend Poi, whom I wrote about in *Our Most Troubling Madness: Case Studies in Schizophrenia across Cultures* (Cassaniti 2016), told me about the spirits she felt she would literally see come out of the spirit houses that are in front of virtually every home in Thailand, causing her mind to become sick.

Not everyone I spoke with in Thailand follows or believes in *khwan*—some associate it with a kind of "old fashioned" traditional thinking, one that is usually seamlessly integrated into everyday Buddhist thought but that in some modernist readings is incongruent with the formal teachings of Theravāda Buddhism. Others do believe in *khwan* but don't see it as connected with mindfulness. But most people (especially those born in Northern Thailand) whom I asked whether and how *khwan* and mindfulness are related said they are related, and most of those said that when a person has a lot of mindfulness, his or her *khwan* are also strong. A few people also talked about *khwan* in relationship to Buddhist ideas about the spirit of *winyan*, sometimes considered to be the "soul" that transmigrates over lives.

Not everyone integrated all these different perspectives on ghosts, *khwan*, sati, and the many related cultural constructions of the person in the same way, and not everyone believes in ghosts (*phi*), though most do.

A monk in Chiang Mai connected ghosts to a person's spirit, while also reiterating that *khwan* (and sati) are about strength of mind:

> Phi is, from my understanding, the *winyan*, but there are layers of *winyan* in Buddhism. The *winyan* that has a lot of merit is able to transform or display itself for people to see, but sometimes they can just be the wind. So if you ask "Are ghosts real?" well, I have never seen one. I went to do meditation in a cemetery, but I never saw one. So, I think the idea of *phi* is our illusion. For example, if one is afraid of the dark and if one were told in the dark there is *phi*, that person would be terrified. *Khwan* may be related to sati. *Khwan* is something that is hard to explain. When something bad happens or there is something wrong and we have lost our *khwan*, that means we have lost our sati. "Come back *khwan*, come back *khwan*" is to call sati back. . . . But for those who have lost their *khwan*, we call them "*khwan*-less."

In contrast to the mental instability that is understood to come with scattered *khwan*, mental health and even mental power are thought to attend strong *khwan*, and strong mindfulness. Those who have strong sati, and the *khwan* are gathered together, are thought to have the power to control their own mind, and even have the power to influence others, even ghosts, and even their feelings at the moment of death. A monk at Chiang Mai's Wat Chedi Luang linked ghosts, *khwan*, and mindfulness like this:

> When people talk about *phi* they are talking about fear. But those who have very good mindfulness will never fear *phi*. About *khwan*, I'm not sure. . . . But *khwan* may be something that can cheer people up. People who don't have sati are the people who are lost. If people have sati, they will understand what the truth is so they can solve the problem. Like, if we are going to die and we have sati at that time, then we will be able to accept it. But for some, who may need support, they may have a ceremony to call *khwan* to make them feel better.

Many of those I spoke with iterated the point that having mindfulness at the moment of death is extremely important, and that training in mindfulness throughout one's life may have its largest purpose as preparation for that time. On one hand the idea of being able to accept one's death by practicing mindfulness seems clearly practical rather than supernaturally significant; but the implications of the ways that people understand it are that it is not just for this life that acceptance is beneficial. It is thought that if one has sati at the time of death, then the outcome of what happens after death is more likely to be good. One woman offered the following typical perspective: "If I don't practice sati, then when I die I'll be scared—I mean, everyone is scared of dying. . . . If I don't have sati when I die I'll feel stressed, I'll create *jit* [mind] that will leave my body and go and be a hungry ghost. But if I'm a person who practices sati, if I practice the dhamma, my mind will go out and find a peaceful place." And the way that mindfulness ties in not just to life but also to afterlife, and even previous lives, is also important. I came across this perspective in a local dhamma pamphlet, of the kind that Phra Mon had said are so commonly handed out for free at monasteries: "Practicing mindfulness," it said in a northern-inflected Thai, "will help us be able to recall our past life; we'll be able to see it." Mindfulness is a power that moves through intersubjective space, and even extends past life.

Scientific Powers: The Power of Mindfulness in the Psychiatric Hospital

It is in this power that mindfulness really finds its place in local theories about well-being in Thailand. It is what Phra Thēp was referring to when he said, "The precepts are like discipline. They're the method for making people be mentally healthy, and not crazy. People without sati are crazy people." These powers of mindfulness help to connect mental health to the multiple, potentially wandering "spirits of the self," and this in part helps explain why my friend Sen said that he was in the psychiatric hospital in Chiang Mai because of a lack of sati.

For a variety of reasons Sen's *khwan* had left, and with them his sati too, leaving him mentally weak and vulnerable to illness. For their part, the forty doctors and other hospital workers I gathered data from reported feeling a connection between mindfulness and a sense of power and mental mastery, especially in relation to their work:

> When I'm in the lab, I use sati when I'm recording things, so I don't make mistakes.

> When a patient accuses me of something, I have to remember to have sati, to not get mad.

Figure 13. The entrance to the Suan Prung Psychiatric Hospital in Chiang Mai, Thailand, with a Buddha statue just inside the front gate. The Buddha statue was installed in 2013 with a large ceremony and parade. I took its installation as a clear sign of the hospital administration increasingly connecting its approach to Buddhist thought, but when I asked a nurse at the hospital about it, I was told, "It's more that someone on the board wanted to make merit for himself." That this "making merit" reason was not seen as a marker of Buddhist values permeating the hospital points to one of the challenges in incorporating mindfulness practices into contemporary Thai health-care settings. Photo by J. L. Cassaniti.

One described a moment when he said that it would have been especially easy to lose sati, but he didn't:

> I remember one time a client came into my office for a session, and as we were talking suddenly she took off her shirt! She was very seductive. I was distracted, I can tell you! But I thought about sati, to use sati, to be calm, and I just sat there calmly and continued talking with her. When I remember to have sati I feel better, like I have competency, to be careful.

For many of these doctors and hospital staff, mindfulness is couched in scientific terms. As one said, "When I come in to work here, it's like going into the lab of mindfulness." Many of them incorporate mindfulness into their therapeutic practices, in their own ways.

> The Buddha teaches not to attach to God, but to sati. . . . In medicine often we doctors think that the problem the patient has with the body is caused by illness. But the mind is hard to explain. According to current data on suicide rates, people are killing themselves more now than before. What we're doing here at Suan Prung is to try to decrease that number. We do this mostly with pills, because that's the best way to help people. But this is because people fear their pasts—they fear those situations in the past and are scared the situations will come back again, and it's this that makes people want to kill themselves. But sati is in nature. The Buddha discovered it, he didn't invent it . . . and we can use it. Actually, sati is the foundation, the groundwork, of all health care.

Mindfulness, clearly, is considered relevant and important for mental health. In a cultural landscape rich with connections between mindfulness and mental health, and in a hospital where the doctor and staff were virtually all Buddhist, and comfortably stated their admiration for mindfulness, it seems self-evident that therapeutic techniques that incorporate mindfulness would be part of recovery practices. But for the most part, they weren't. Sen told me that the doctors didn't teach him about mindfulness, and I didn't hear about explicit programs about it being used for patients either.

In a very straightforward and practical way, it's possible that the relative absence of mindfulness's messages in the psychiatric hospital is because mindfulness may not help mental health patients as much as it is sometimes claimed to do, at least not as many patients or to such an extent. Scott Stonington, an MD and PhD at the University of Michigan who conducted fieldwork in hospitals in Chiang Mai, has found that Buddhist practice (including that of mindfulness) is actually considered unhelpful by some people with chronic pain (Stonington 2016). This type of finding suggests that mindfulness, and Buddhism more generally, may not be as practically useful for the average Thai person as the official and authoritative Buddhist sangha or the Western scientific community might think. There is some merit to this reading. Some staff at Suan Prung did feel that mindfulness's potential was limited. One staffer, a policy and planning officer at the hospital, told me that "it depends on the patient, if they can learn [and benefit from mindfulness]. It depends on their personality, and their problem. Some can get benefit from it—like, for example, people who are suffering from stress [*khwam khriat*] or are anxious [*kangwon*]. . . . But [for others] I'm not sure. For alcoholics I think it could help too. . . . For these people I think the doctors could teach it."

"It's good for anxiety," Pumin, a neurologist, said, "and for depression. But not for psychotic patients. For them it can't help." There is a body of emerging scientific evidence pointing to some of these findings. For the doctors, an awareness of mindfulness's strengths and weaknesses shows a level of nuanced reflection that I didn't at first understand when I encountered Ta and her mindfulness program at the hospital. In this sense of recognizing mindfulness's limits as well as its strengths as a therapeutic aid, and perhaps based on a long familiarity with the concept, the staff at Suan Prung are thoughtfully hesitant to apply mindfulness-based trainings with their patients on a large scale. Yet even as the limitations of mindfulness's potential may be one reason for its relevant absence, for most of the staff, even when applying it thoughtfully rather than as a blanket cure, mindfulness is seen as a helpful, even crucial idea. After all, as one of the doctors said, mindfulness is considered "the groundwork, the foundation of all health care."

Instead of not finding mindfulness to be useful, I think the reason that Sen and others like him were not benefiting from therapies that involve mindfulness may have more to do with what is seen as acceptable in the scientific context of the hospital. The supernatural, spiritual powers of mindfulness not only help to explain why Sen was in the psychiatric hospital; they also, as part of a larger power-laden discourse of mindfulness, help to explain why he wasn't aided more from mindfulness-based techniques while there. A scientific alignment with mindfulness may exclude the very connections between mental health, spirits, and local concepts of the person that would be especially useful to the overwhelmingly rural and relatively mid- to lower-class patients who find themselves at Suan Prung. Connections that are meaningful to patients between mental health, spirits, and concepts of the person may not be seen as acceptable in the scientific context of the hospital.

This deference to the scientific technologies of global therapies is an explanation that, as with media and supernatural influences, has to do also with issues of power, though of a different and more socio-structural kind. All of the staff I spoke with at the hospital know about mindfulness and think it is good to have, but they did not always prioritize incorporating it into their practices in ways that would especially resonate with their patients' understandings of it. Most of the professional staff are from Bangkok, or went to school there, and align with a Bangkok-focused, global elite of scientists and modern thinkers. It may be for this reason, and because of the globally hegemonic discourses about medical science they learned there, that they do not teach mindfulness to their patients; or when they do, they do not teach it in ways that align meaningfully with the people they are helping, as part of the vulnerability of *khwan*, the ghosts of insanity, or the many other colloquial uses that mindfulness takes on in Thai social life. Instead, they make use of it in terms of its more doctrinally philosophic renderings, or its demonstrably scientific meanings. "I teach sati to the patients," said one doctor, "but simply. I teach them how to have sati, slowly, to pay attention to their breath, to do that often and continuously, and that then they'll get better and understand more. I teach them to apply it, and to have awareness. I don't expect the patients to get to a high level with it, but to just understand the concept."

To this doctor, patients required simple lessons, which were seen as relating to meditative practices of the breath. Another told us how he brought in monks to teach about mindfulness, but that they were thinking of discontinuing the program because the monks' discourse was "over the heads" of the patients. I wondered what kind of discourses the monks were using. They were not, I was sure, talking about mindfulness as connected to the *khwan* that must be called back in times of vulnerability and weakness, which were ways of talking I heard more in colloquial, lay accounts of the concept. In this sense the doctors preside with a kind of cultural capital (Bourdieu 1986, 1984; Chung 2015) that carries the weight of prestige but that also serves as a disadvantage, in the sense of their position of power obfuscating their ability to connect with their patients in more empathically meaningful terms. These positioned discourses are connected to a global and globalizing conversation about mindfulness that carries a kind of power of its own, a power that is as much if not more powerful than the parallel powers of politics, charisma, and the supernatural attainments of meditation. As authoritative arbiters of what mindfulness is and how it can be gained, the hospital staff, in their

ideological orientations to science and its Western associations, influenced
the practices employed in the hospital.

TAPES in the Social Power of Mindfulness

P—Power

What I found outside of the monastery is something felt only tangentially
in it: that mindfulness is directly connected to power. Power, of course,
takes on different forms in different contexts. The power of mindfulness
is a power of mastery over the self in ways as small as avoiding tripping or
getting into accidents, and as large as staying sane, and it is also a power
of mastery over others through the deployment of political or therapeutic tactics of influence. It is a power over the natural and even supernatural world, allowing for an ability to keep away the "ghosts of insanity"
and even, perhaps, attain nirvana. And in Thailand, as elsewhere, power
is especially social. Taken together, the power and potency of mindfulness
speak directly to theories of mind that relate to local ideas about mindfulness and what it means to be a sane, safe, and healthy person in society.

I have argued in this chapter for the importance of inserting the concept of power into the practices and purposes of mindfulness, not just in
mindfulness's potential for self-empowerment but also for a wide range
of additional areas. The TAPES of mindfulness suggested by monks and
meditation are reinforced in lay Thai life through the manipulation of
their symbolic meanings for psychological, educational, political, commercial, and even supernatural powers. The way that temporality is
understood to work, and the leveraging of these understandings, are part
of mindfulness's power: being aware of the present means remembering
what happened in the past, and what the consequences of that past are
for the present and future. Affect is constructed in part through this temporal awareness. Ethics is not enacted the same way everywhere, but the
assumption in making public claims about mindfulness is that mindfulness is good, and that gaining mindfulness will create good results, not
just in the sense of ethical goodness but also in efficacious goodness, of
being a powerful tool to get things done. Selfhood in lay life is very much
about a Buddhist attention to non-self, but it is also more plural than

a focus only on non-self, with mental health tied to the keeping together of these potentially scatter-able and dangerous spirit "selves." Inserting Power into the middle of each of these TAPES of mindfulness reveals how each of them works in practical, non-monastic (and even in monastic) terms, as people use the potency of mindfulness for their own social and personal ends. The potency attributed to the development of mindfulness helps to explain why and how it is practiced, and what its benefits can be.

Although I had not noticed it explicitly in the meditation retreats or in conversations with monks, the TAPES of power also came up within the monastery as well as outside it. Power was part of monks' depiction of their own experiences, and part of the meditation retreats, even if it was not often explicitly acknowledged. There is a real social power at play in the inequalities between teacher and student, as when a young novice monk voiced his preference for the same style of meditation that the head monk of his monastery had no doubt instructed him to do, and this is gained not only from typical social hierarchies like age but also from a reputation of being strong in mindfulness. Power differences were even more explicit when a powerful monk expressed a desire (and sometimes an action!) of hitting a disobedient novice on the head. The relations of student to teacher are always power relations, and this is as true even in the "solitary" act of meditation as it is elsewhere.

Social power is only part of the potency of mindfulness: there is also a sense of power over the self and others that comes about through meditative training, even as part of that power is in a recognition that the "self" that one gains a sense of mastery over is an illusion. In moments when I was feeling especially successful in my meditation, I could feel an almost uncanny sense of power, as if the awareness I gained in mindfulness had real effects in my ability to interact in the world beyond my own body and mind.

The social and meditative powers associated with the formal religious sphere are also part of lay life. Religious and lay spheres in Thailand are porous and overlap; people who ordain as monks for a while often do so to garner some of that (moral, spiritual) power to then use later in social life, and people go to the monastery to make merit to get a small dose of it for luck and good fortune, along with positive karma.

These powers associated with mindfulness help to explain not just how and why people understand how to rule their minds. They also help to explain how people rule each other, in part through the social value placed on this type of mental cultivation. As we were playing badminton a week after my meditation retreat at Wat Mae Long, my neighbor was so confident that the post-coup government was doing good for the people, harnessing mindfulness as a political tool and powerfully distributing an image of a socially, mentally solid populace, that I don't think in my much less socially powerful way I could have persuaded her to question her views. Monks are the idealized representatives of the Buddha's teaching, but Buddhism and governance have been intertwined for a long time (Ünaldi 2016), and the powers that come from these associations extend to the way that leaders justify their own authority.

People gain mindfulness in order to access power, I found, as protection for themselves and as a way to control their environment and their minds. In some scholarly and religious circles mindfulness is thought to help one see the world "as it really is," apart from mental biases or distortions. It may partly be that, but I found that it is also about exerting influence and creating change through the psychological and social manipulation of the mind. I found that mindfulness is about affecting the world as much as seeing what the world looks like. And the ways that mindfulness is inscribed within that world of influence are multiple. They are changing over time, with different versions always at play.

During a long interview, the head of the psychiatric hospital in Chiang Mai discussed his views on Thai Buddhist belief, framing large historical movements and their representations in his own personal way. Dr. Pari talked about mindfulness and *vipassanā* training, the Thai sangha, and the influences of India, Burma, and Sri Lanka over time, as well as global and globalizing views on Buddhist practice. His conversation was open and honest, full of thoughts about the ways that he sees people in Thailand making sense of the many cultural and religious influences over time. His was the only one of the fifty formal interviews conducted in Thailand that was spoken for the most part in English, a choice he made that itself alludes to a kind of deference to global (English-privileging) powers. He offered thoughts that privilege what he sees as local Thai understandings of Buddhism but that at the same time privilege other influences, particularly Burmese ones, alongside and even over them. His conversation, though long and wandering, points to the complex mix of overlapping global and regional influences on past and present forms of Buddhism in Thailand. The doctor said, in part:

Buddhism in Thailand in my opinion is very unique. It has special develop-
ments, just like in other places in the world where people believe in supernatural powers. It involves the power of ghosts [*phi*] and demons [*phi sat*],
the power of the trees and earth. And we took Indian culture in the form of
Brahmanism and Hinduism to mix in, and it mixed in our way. We brought
the power of nature into the idea of deity and the Indian gods, and then
Buddhism came. . . . And so Buddhism in Thailand therefore doesn't emphasize the real Buddhism. And in what the Buddha said about sati. Or
about liberation or being independent or the absolute truth. So it became
local Buddhism, that the local people got from the influence from Hinduism. And [like in] Hinduism, they think that the Buddha, like an avatar,
is another form of their God. So they think that Buddhism is one of their
gods. . . . Buddhism was lost for a while. It was brought back by the Lankan
monks. But not really the real Buddhism, either. But people adjusted. But
actually there is one good thing about that, because it helped Buddhism
survive. . . . Later, during the reign of King Rama V, which is when Thailand was encountering globalization from the West, the king tried to cen-
tralize the power [to combat colonization], and it affected the religion too.
So they divided the Buddhist governance—the king governed the people,
which is against the power of the West. But there were also disadvantages
to the modernizing reforms . . . especially in the exams of the monks, for
which monks had to do intensive intellectual and meditative work. They
said that *vipassanā* was very difficult, so they left it. And learned about theory, *pariyat*, or from the Tipiṭaka. That's why the monks from the Northeast didn't have the same education as the monks in Bangkok. They didn't
have to learn the exams, so they became forest monks. . . . Which is different from the monks from Burma. They still all practice *vipassanā*. So they
have stronger practice. Later on in the period of King Rama V they brought
the Burmese monks in to teach, and there were many outstanding, good
masters that learned from Burma. Like Ajarn Tong [of Wat Rampoeng and
Wat Chom Thong fame], and Goenka, and Ajarn Cha [a famous Northeast monk] and others. So [that is how] meditation was lost from Thai Buddhism for a while.[10]

Many of the doctor's points were about laying an intellectual foundation to incorporate secularized mindfulness practices into therapeutic
programs in the hospital. His views reveal a power of perspective that
needs to be connected to complex regional and global communities to be
understood. They point to a more globalized stance on what Buddhism

is (referring to some practices as being more or less "real") than I heard from others, but in many ways they reflected a shared sense of multiplicity and enmeshed history of Buddhism in the region.

Narratives about the influences of Buddhism from Sri Lanka and Burma (and elsewhere, including Cambodia, Laos, China, Japan, Tibet, and India) are common in Thailand. They point to a shared history of monks and laypeople who over history and still today move around and across the national borders of Asia for the purposes of religious training. At present, mindfulness practices are often articulated within the terms and languages of contemporary, bounded nation-states, but they point to more than just national boundaries of experience. International networks and movements of ideas travel not just from the "West" to the "East," or the "developed" to the "developing" world; they also circulate across regional space. The practice of sharing ideas through regionally international monastic exchange programs is as popular now as it was in the past (Borchert 2017); today a special category of visas are available to those who wish to spend time in monastic settings.

I met a monk who was doing just that at a small monastery near my house in Chiang Mai right around the time the Thai part of the mindfulness project was wrapping up, and I was beginning to look past the borders of the country. The psychiatric hospital had started the trip into mindfulness in Thailand, and through Phra Thēp in Mae Jaeng, to meditation and the city of Chiang Mai, it had returned me there. I was ready to broaden the lens. Phra Ñeyya, or rather Sayadaw Ñeyya, to use the conventional honorific title appropriate for a Burmese monk, had been living in Thailand for the past five years, and before that had spent a few years in Bengal. I met him one morning while out making merit with my neighbors, and asked him how he liked living in Thailand. He said he liked it, but he also told me that most people in Thailand can't understand what sati really means. "Because sati is in the *Abhidhamma*," he said by way of explanation, "and that's not popular here." I replied that I didn't necessarily feel that a lack of emphasis on the *Abhidhamma*, the third "basket" of the Buddhist teachings, would mean that one doesn't know as much about mindfulness, but I added that I did notice that the *Abhidhamma* was not raised all that much by people in Thailand. He nodded. Some monks and laypeople in Thailand had mentioned the *Abhidhamma* explicitly, but not nearly as much as I would find in Burma, or as much as Sayadaw Ñeyya was used to. Whether the *Abhidhamma* holds more secrets about sati or not, the monk's comment, and other comments he made about memory, awareness, and ethics during the course of our conversation, did point to the ways that different texts and teachings gain traction in different settings over time.

To understand mindfulness as practiced "on the ground," I didn't want to just take what I was learning about how mindfulness works in Thailand as representative of all Theravāda culture. I wanted to know too how mindfulness is experienced in other areas where it is also considered to be a dominant part of the contemporary social and religious world. I wanted to see how and why (and whether) mindfulness is understood to be powerful and efficacious in other nearby countries, and as the Buddhist monk Sayadaw Ñeyya had indicated, what kind of variations might exist.

Part II

Myanmar (Burma) and Sri Lanka

4

BURMA: A FINE MIST,
OR A CAVE IN THE WOODS

"But the Burmese are scary," my Thai friend Jieb said when I told her I was going to Burma to learn about mindfulness. The two of us were sitting at the back of her porch in Mae Sot, a border town to Myanmar (formerly Burma), a few months after my meeting with Sayadaw Ñeyya in Chiang Mai. I had met Jieb in Mae Jaeng years earlier, and we had stayed in touch after she moved to the border. She now worked for an international NGO helping Burmese refugees settle in Thailand. "They won't be friendly, I bet." In all her time at the border town she had never been across into Burma. Like a lot of people I knew in Thailand, Jieb had an image of the Burmese that reflected a long history of neighborly animosity. Cartoons in Thailand often pictured Burmese people, with dark skin and red eyes, sitting on the backs of the most ferocious-looking elephants, as if the two nations were still in the throes of historical wars. "But I'll go with you," Jieb continued. "I'm curious what it's like, and even without knowing Burmese or English, I can help you out as you start the research there. We can find a place to stay, and meet people, so you don't have to go alone."

I agreed to the plan, and the next morning the two of us walked across the border into Burma and rented the border guard's motorbike on the other side. We made it only ten kilometers, though, before a police checkpoint turned us back. Since that visit the restrictions on entering further into the country via land routes have eased, and I have heard that buses take people all the way from Mae Sot to Yangon a few hundred kilometers away; but at the time we wouldn't be able to get in overland, the man at the checkpoint informed us. So we headed back to Mae Sot and took a bus the few hours south to Bangkok, then flew in to Mandalay the next morning.

As the plane descended we saw the landscape turn a dusty green, stretching out in all directions, with a river to one side of the city and the streets carved into a long series of tan grids. The two of us checked in to a ramshackle guesthouse in the old part of the city, and after renting a dubiously legal motorcycle from a family that lived around the corner we set out to explore the town. The streets were more crowded than the previous time I had visited, fifteen years earlier, but compared with the packed roads of Chiang Mai they were relatively peaceful, and felt full of adventure. A few cars, motorcycles, rickshaws, bicycles, and ox-drawn carts rambled by. Kids played *chinlon*, a Southeast Asian form of hacky sack, on the street corners, spread out between mobile food stands selling all kinds of fresh, diverse, delicious foods that would put LA's food-truck reputation to shame. From the minute we landed, people were welcoming and kind. "Everyone's so nice here!" Jieb pronounced conclusively by our first afternoon.

We contacted a woman named Tiri after we had settled in; a friend in Thailand had put me in touch with her. The friend had worked as an English teacher in Mandalay for a few years and had taught her at his school; she might be able to help me carry out the interviews, he had said. Because of colonial histories, English is spoken more in Burma (and Sri Lanka) than in Thailand, though it is still relatively uncommon. Tiri agreed to meet with me when I called, and after we talked for a while at a café near our guesthouse, she agreed to help over the course of the next month with the data collection.

"Sati is so important," Tiri told Jieb and me as the three of us sat down at a street vendor's shop the next evening. She spelled out sati the common Burmese way, *thati*. "It's a regular word here," she explained. "Like, people will say '*thati tha*'—to notice; '*thati hlut*'—to forget; '*thati ya*'—to remind; and there's '*thati may*'—to forget to do something or say something while doing something else; '*thati ne thaw*'—to remind some-one to go with mindfulness; and '*thati ne pyaw*'—to remind someone to speak with mindfulness. There's even a famous Burmese saying about it," Tiri concluded: "Thati ma mu, gu ma myin. Thati mu gah, myu go myin— 'If you don't have sati, you can't even see a cave in the woods. If you have sati, you can see even a vapor particle of a fine mist.'"

I knew it was just an idiom, but I couldn't help wondering: How would having mindfulness allow one to see a particle of fine mist, or not having it prevent you from seeing something as big as a cave? How would people consider the relationship between the type of memory invoked through sati's historical meaning and the ideas about attending to the present moment? How would the ideal psychological states thought to be developed by mindfulness be described, especially as they related to affective practices? And how would power, ethics, and the concept of the self come into the equation, of self-mastery, of ghosts, of society, and of mental health? I had come to Burma to learn about what mind-fulness looked like there; this was the Buddhist country, after all, that spawned much of the world's modern *vipassanā* movements, including and especially those that emphasized mindfulness. I would use the same interviews and questionnaires I had used in Thailand (translated into Burmese) and would keep a few central questions of the TAPES in mind as the research unfolded.

I wanted to know if people in Burma would suggest practices that were similar to those elsewhere—and not in the elite, internationally oriented centers of monastic and scholarly learning only, but as incorporated into everyday contemporary Burmese life. I wouldn't be able to learn as much in Burma as in Thailand without spending years in the country learning more about the language and culture; but with many of the same Pali terms used, and the help of a Burmese-English-speaking assistant, I would be able to pick up on some of these similarities and also some of the slight differences of mindfulness in the country.

Tiri was twenty-three years old, a student at Mandalay University working toward her master's degree in business administration. On the side, in the afternoons, she also volunteered teaching English to schoolchil-dren in her neighborhood, and also somehow managed to help her friends at school with their homework, on top of helping me. Unlike my Thai research assistant Santi, who was (or professed to be) initially uninterested in the formal practices and philosophy of Buddhism, Tiri loved to go to the monastery for meditation retreats. She told me how she visited the monasteries around town whenever she could. During her vacations from school she would go on retreats there, especially during the water festival (in April), the lighting festival (in October), and the long December holidays. "A lot of young people do this," she said, then laughed and added, "I can avoid all the parties that way!"

I had read about famous meditation traditions in Burma (Braun 2013; Jordt 2007), both in the metropolis of Yangon (Rangoon) and in Mandalay and elsewhere, and was curious which of them, if any, were connected to ones Tiri followed. The well-traveled Burmese monk Sayadaw Ñeyya whom I had met in Chiang Mai had told me about two main famous meditation traditions in the country, as he spoke with a mix of Thai, Burmese, English, and Pali phrases: "There's the Mahasatipaṭṭhāna style of Mahāsī Sayādaw," he had said for the first one, "which focuses on strong breath, learning to breathe in and breathe out; and Mogoke *vipassanā*, the other, which uses a secular diagram to map out ignorance [*avijja*] and craving [*taṇhā*]. Goenka is the leader of that one; it says that whatever you do you must have mindfulness." For "mindfulness" Sayadaw Ñeyya had used the Pali-influenced Burmese verb term *sati-hta*, which indicates mindfulness as action, "to act mindfully," or "notice." He said that a lot of people went to monasteries that followed these two traditions, and that there were centers, which weren't monasteries, for meditation specifically for laypeople, "and to learn about the *Abhidhamma*. Mostly they're in Yangon . . . but they're working on it in Mandalay."

Yangon is the center for these more internationally famous traditions, for sure, but Tiri told me, "Most people go to the monastery regularly here in Mandalay—to offer donations, celebrate birthdays, meditate, learn the Buddha's teaching from monks, volunteer to clean the monastery or wash the monk's robes. The relationship between the monks and the public is so good they even call Mandalay the 'monk city'!"[1] She went on: "If you want to learn the Buddha's teachings well, as U Janakābhivaṁsa, the former head of the Maha Gandayon Monastery has said, Upper Myanmar— and especially Mandalay—is the right place to go."

Tiri listed some of the famous monasteries in Mandalay and in the areas bordering it: the Old Masoeyein Monastery, the New Masoeyein Monastery, Mya Taung Monastery, Maha Gandayon Monastery, Dhammasara

Monastery. I asked which she felt most connected to, and while she told me these ones are the most well known, she herself didn't prefer any of them: "I like to go to a little monastery outside of town, not a famous one. I knew someone who went there and recommended it to me." Some of the monasteries that people listed as being influential to them had strict academic environments and particular monastic-lay relationships (Dicks 2015); for others, monastery affiliations are more practical. Choosing a monastery based on personal connections, convenience, and even aesthetics is as common in Burma as in Thailand.

Figure 14. A young family visits the Mahamuni Pagoda, one of the many Buddhist monasteries around Mandalay city. Photo by J. L. Cassaniti.

It wasn't that Tiri was ignorant of the major and famous traditions; she knew the different traditions in the country, but didn't really see a big difference between them.

"Mogoke and Mahasi are really famous, and Ledi Sayadaw is famous too," she told me, pretty much echoing what Sayadaw Ñeyya had said but emphasizing the similarities rather than the differences between them:

> Mogoke has us focus on the "breathing in and breathing out" to get concentration; Mahasi has us focus on the abdomen, how the abdomen gets bigger when we breathe in and how it gets thinner when we breathe out; Ledi has us concentrate on the tip of the head, which means to put all our mind on the top of the head in order to get concentration. Mogoke, Mahasi, Ledi's teachings are said to be different because those are the practices mainly used by the respective monks, which then came to be known as that tradition. But those names aren't included in the Buddha's teachings. Even though the approaches are different, the way of going about them is the same; all aim to get to only one target, nirvana.

As *vipassanā* mindfulness meditation has gained global popularity, scholars are increasingly writing about these Burmese monks, who have been influential not just in Burma but in the development of contemporary and popular forms of meditation throughout Theravāda Asia and around the world.[2] Like many people today in Burma, rather than following one tradition in particular, Tiri combined different teachings from the main traditions around her, integrating teachings like impermanence of the body, and using the idea of the movement of the breath to allude to the movement of everything. She went to her favorite monastery for a few days or a few weeks when she could, and visited other ones too, based on relations with the monks and nuns that she established at those monasteries. Later, when we were in the throes of data collection, she talked a little bit about her own practice, and her perspective on Buddhist meditation:

> It's about concentration. After gaining concentration we can see things truly, as our body shows us. Like, things [cells] appearing and dying out and inside our bodies. We'll see impermanence through seeing our bodies, and even thoughts. If we're getting to advanced stages of meditation, we'll even know how our own thoughts come in and go out in detail. We'll get to know that nothing in this world is permanent, either living or nonliving things. We'll get to understand that everything is changing, nothing is staying constant

forever. Based on that we'll know in depth about the *anicca, dukkha,* and *anattā* of everything we see or feel. Then we'll understand that nothing is essential and nothing is permanent. If our thoughts are filled with the impermanence, the path to nirvana is close. And if we reach the nirvana stage, we'll be in the Arya [*arahat,* an enlightened one] group.

I could tell Tiri enjoyed meditating; her face seemed to glow enthusiastically when she talked about it. "I'm probably a bit more into it than others," she admitted, laughing almost sheepishly when I asked if this impression was true, "but a lot of people here go to the monastery. It's really normal!" And it wasn't just during meditation that she felt the benefits of the practice—as many others would, she connected the everyday use of mindfulness of not making mistakes to social activism and to nirvana as the ultimate purpose of the religion. "For social movements," she said,

> if we could live life according to what the Buddha taught we'll be able to notice—*sati-hta*—to do things with mindfulness in whatever we do, so we'll make less mistakes. We can even reach nirvana while carrying out our daily routine if we can control our mind and live life with sati. Reaching nirvana isn't just concerned with sitting in a meditation center and meditating for long hours. We can reach nirvana only if we have sati and keep practicing *vipassanā*; and *vipassanā* means to me not just sitting but knowing things as they are happening. To be acting, to be knowing impermanence.

In the course of telling me about her own perspectives and practices in regard to mindfulness, Tiri brought up a lot of the ways that others in and out of the monastery would talk about the idea. The Pali-inspired Burmese term *thati* (sati) is known by virtually everyone in Burma. As with other colloquial Burmese words rooted in Pali, like *douqkha* (*dukkha*) for suffering, where people will pronounce "Douqkha beh!" (Just *dukkha*!) as a common expression after some daily inconvenience, *sati* has an even more localized ring to it than I observed in Thailand, possibly pointing to a more Buddhist-integrated social culture.

Tiri and I were ready to start the interviews, but before beginning, Jieb and I took a trip to Bagan, the ancient capital in the middle of the country. We wanted to see the sights, as this was Jieb's first trip to the country, and get a sense of the historical, cultural context that mindfulness is part of in Burma. As we arrived, the valley's thousands of stupas took on a hauntingly beautiful glow in the sunset.

Figure 15. A girl plays on top of a pagoda's tower, on one of the thousands of stupas spread across the central Burmese valley of Bagan. King Anawrahta established Theravāda Buddhism in Bagan as the state religion in the eleventh century, though Buddhism in its different forms had made its way to the region through traveling monastics much earlier. It was around this time that Anawrahta and others engaged in a massive project of constructing the thousands of temples scattered across the vast plains; today the most spectacular of them host tourists that gather every sunrise, cameras ready. Photo by J. L. Cassaniti.

The plains were dusty and dry. The stupas made the scene look ethereal at any time of day, but especially at sunrise and sunset, as the Irrawaddy River flowed placidly and timelessly alongside. Bagan hadn't changed much at all since the first time I had visited, fifteen years earlier. But there were more people now, especially tourists, and it was clear that changes were under way. The country was just opening up to an international community that had long shunned its military government; and Bagan, like the rest of the country, was trying to figure out how to manage it all. Even with the fifteen years' difference, though, I tracked down the family I had befriended on my first, pre-Facebook, pre-internet visit, just through an old picture I had brought with me and word of mouth with people in the area. The family was still working as painters at the same temple and still living in the same house in a village to the north of town, and while their young son was now older and married, they continued to live as they had before. On a day trip, we talked about the region and the changes in our lives, as a boat brought us to Buddhist sites hidden in caves along the

Irrawaddy. My friends told Jieb and me how the government was involved in new temple construction projects and was even building a giant hotel nearby. They had different perspectives on whether that was a good thing or not: as in the ancient past, Buddhism continued to be very much tied to economics and the state.

It was so beautiful and peaceful in Bagan that we didn't want to leave. But I had to start the mindfulness interviews, and Jieb had to get back to her work at the Thai-Burma border, so after a few days of exploring the fields on our bikes and eating meals with our friends we got into another bus and returned to Mandalay. After a few more days Jieb flew back home, but not before making plans to meet up with her new friend Tiri in Bangkok a few months later, when Tiri would take her first trip out of her country. They continue to meet up regularly.

After a week more of translating and transcribing the research protocol, and making hundreds of copies at one of the very busy copy centers in the city, Tiri and I set about figuring out just whom to talk to. As I had done in Thailand, we intended to find forty monks at one monastery, forty at another, forty university students (at Mandalay University), forty lay people, and forty people working at the psychiatric hospital, conducting in-depth interviews with ten in each instance and gathering questionnaires for thirty more. We enlisted the help of Nyein, a local man who had once been a Fulbright fellow in Seattle and later a political prisoner, along with his friend Moh, who taught at a monastery near the old town. Over the next month, Nyein, Moh, Tiri, and I carried out the data collection at Moh's monastery, translating and transcribing the interviews in the evenings; and Tiri and I and her cousin Ken carried out a second set at a nearby institute called the Intensity Center that brought monks together from other area temples. The monks at the institute were there to study for the Dhammasariya exam, the stepping-stone exam for Burmese monks who want to pursue advanced education. As in Thailand, the state-sponsored monastic education system is complex, but I was told that in general monks must pass three basic levels (called Pathama Nge, Pathama Lat, and Pathama Gyi) before they are allowed to sit for the Dhammasariya exam. On passing this exam there are two higher degrees, the Tipiṭakadhara and Tipiṭakakovida. Only a handful of famous monks, people said, have passed either or both of these. From my subjective impression, more monks were actively pursuing these degrees than

I felt were doing so in Thailand, though that may just be that there was more discussion in the public sphere (including in conversations with me) of them in Burma, including billboards along the streets announcing the monks' accomplishments.

After each day of interviews, Tiri and I sat down together to listen to audio recordings and transcribe and translate and talk about what they had said.

Monks Remembering to Do Good

The first monk we interviewed was Sayadaw U Thilasara Bhiwuntha (Pali: Silacara Bhivamsa), a straightforward, factual teacher at the Aungchanga Monastery near the city's old walled center. When we arrived at Aungchanga for our first interview, the courtyard was crowded with the young monastics making their way into their morning class. Sayadaw U Thilasara Bhiwuntha motioned for Moh, Nyein, Tiri, and me to sit on the floor in one of the large rooms of the monastery, and he too sat cross-legged on the floor in his dark orange robes in front of us. After we had explained a bit about the project, and received his permission to conduct the research there, he told us about mindfulness. Mindfulness means to "remember good deeds," he said, and explained that it is especially practiced through Satipaṭṭhāna meditation.

"There are four foundations of mindfulness," he told us, and listed each of them, for the most part as the same straightforward list I had heard in Thailand, but with the term *vipassanā* instead of *paṭṭhāna* added to each: *kayā-vipassanā* (insight into the body), *citta-vipassanā* (mind), *vedanā-vipassanā* (feelings), and *dhamma-vipassanā* (dharma concepts). When we asked him to tell us more about these four foundations, he explained them in detail, using his own interpretation and meanings. He emphasized especially a relationship between the mind and feelings as understood through the changes of the body. *Kayānupassanā*, he told us,

> means looking at the body with your mind. For example, thinking about your hair. *Cāgānussati* is watching the mind, and what's going on in our mind. When there's no sati, we don't know. When there is sati, we'll

know how we are feeling, if there is good *citta*, or bad *citta*, fast or
slow, and we pay attention to our mind in this way. After practicing this,
sati grows stronger. *Dhammā-vipassanā*, apart from *citta* and *vedanā*,
there are a lot of *sankhāra-s* [sensations]. Belief, *saññā* [perception], and
vedanā. According to the *Abhidhamma* we can pay attention to the *nama*
[name] of things—there are a lot of *nama* [named] concepts. Lastly, the
most vivid one is *vedanā*. In understanding *vedanā*, one will practice
meditation. It comes out. So, it comes very vividly, like a backache,
things like that. This is *dukkhavedanā* [nonsatisfactoriness of feelings].
The thing that becomes distinct is being watched by the means of sati.
Then the *vedanā* is gone, and after contemplating on that *vedanā* many
times, sati becomes stronger. These are the four ways the Buddha told us
to develop sati. If we are contemplating like this, the passions—*kilesa*—
will be destroyed. The things that will trouble people will be destroyed.
Then greed and hatred—*loba* and *dosa*—which are ruinous, that can affect our mind, will not come. Then we'll have peace in our mind. We
won't happen to do things that are *a-kusala*, unwholesome. Our mind
will be clear, and then we'll do only good things. And when our sati is
stronger we change our attention to *anicca, dukkha, anattā*. . . . Then
you can experience *nibbāna*, which is free from *dukkha*. And then there
is no *rupa* or *nama*, no name and form.

I recognized in Sayadaw U Thilasara Bhiwuntha's attention to notation
the *vipassanā* technique taught at Wat Rampoeng, based on the Burmese
monk Mahāsī Sayādaw's lineage. I recognized Goenka's teaching in his
description, too, emphasizing as it did the idea of thinking of *vedanā* as
sankhāra-s, as tiny fleeting sensations on the skin. The Satipaṭṭhāna, Sayadaw U Thilasara Bhiwuntha was saying, can be especially followed by
understanding how sensations are tied to feelings, and how being non-
attached to these sensations and recognizing their impermanence keeps
one away from suffering. And like Phra Thēp and Phra Mon, Sayadaw
U Thilasara Bhiwuntha had also tied mindfulness in with moral goodness. By destroying "the things that will trouble people," that "affect our
mind," he was saying, unwholesomeness is avoided, and peace is formed.
Put another way, by destroying attachments, and thus feeling emotionally
peaceful, one would be less likely to do bad things.

"Do you feel like you have mindfulness a lot?" I asked. I was curious if this
practice is something he saw as happening only during meditation, or all the

time. He answered as if mindfulness was a kind of current that one can enter into, a state that one can be in or, without the right effort, can easily be out of.

"Only when I'm meditating do I have sati," he told us. He explained: "According to the *Abhidhamma*, we are not practicing mindfulness when we're not practicing meditation. Things we're usually doing, they go on by themselves, and there is no sati. Other than those moments we're engaging in meditation [and he used the term *bhāvanā* to refer to it],[3] other than those moments when we're looking at our minds, the rest of the time is without mindfulness. When I'm meditating I have mindfulness. It's like the mind is washed, it's being washed with sati."

Feeling washed by meditation was an evocative metaphor; I often felt after sitting for a period of meditation that I was cleaner, that it was like a bath for my mind. It was this feeling that kept me wanting to go back to meditation, and improve in it. After telling us that it is only in meditation that one can experience sati, though, Sayadaw U Thilasara Bhiwuntha clarified, adding that it wasn't just by sitting in silence that he felt one could be in this meditative space: "Sati is really just being watchful, and meditation isn't limited to sitting. You can go about working on things, and as long as you have attention to your mind this is meditation [here using the term *kammathana*]. When you walk, and even when you speak, you watch your mind, and you try to know your mind. That's where there's sati. The moment you're rid of that attention, then there's no sati. While walking, teaching, and every moment I pay attention, until the moment I get into bed, if I'm watchful, there is sati."

This constant being in, and only sometimes falling away from, mindfulness felt like a state to keep as long as one can, something to develop maintaining for longer and longer periods, and was susceptible to slipping away. It was as if the development of maintaining this quality of mind for longer and longer periods was one of the goals of practice.

Sayadaw U Thilasara Bhiwuntha did not elaborate on what he did precisely to cultivate this practice of mindfulness, but other monks whom Tiri and I and the others spoke with did. Like their counterparts in Thailand, monks in Burma comfortably talked about their own and others' preferred practices:

> I try to meditate with *ānāpānasati*, to get a peaceful mind. By breathing in and breathing out I have the mind in body. . . . If you want to have the

stable mind, we can practice the *ānāpānasati*. From doing *ānāpānasati* we
will have that peacefulness.

When I'm walking I try to remember the goodness of the Three Jewels—the
Buddha, the dhamma, and the sangha. At that time I have sati. By thinking
about those three jewels I'm safe.

Reading and reciting the *Patthana* [the last book of the *Abhidhamma*]—
there are forty kinds of *kammathana* there. And by keeping Buddha in
mind, and saying beads [a kind of meditative counting].

In order to have sati we must have concentration [*samadhi*]. In order to
have *samadhi* we have to count the beads. And practice our mind to be
calm. That's why our Buddha went to the forest and tried to have lots
of sati.

In order to understand sati we must keep our mind calm. For example,
whenever we meet a crisis or a problem we have to think "how can we solve
this problem—which is the right and which is the wrong?" Whenever we
feel afraid we have to keep our mind calm and try to get out all the fear, and
figure out how you're feeling actually. If you keep doing this continuously,
you'll get mindfulness. . . . It's not so difficult for Buddhists to cultivate sati,
because we're already familiar with it.

The most popular kinds of practice raised by monks were the techniques of mindfulness of the breath in particular (and the noting of sensations of the breath more specifically), and the general doing of things
calmly and carefully—especially things that are "good" to do. Thinking of
the Buddha, reciting chants, and counting beads were also popular ways
to train in mindfulness. The *Abhidhamma* and its many commentaries
were mentioned especially often, usually generally rather than in specific
references. Some monks said they read versions of the *Abhidhamma* that
are written in Pali using the Burmese script, and many monks (and laypeople too) pointed to summaries they have read in Burmese. These relatively
popular, contemporary works address some of the controversies about
what mindfulness means in practice.

As in Thailand, the way monks talked about the cultivation and purposes of mindfulness combined an almost rudimentary, everyday carefulness or consciousness with a feeling that mindfulness is an especially

difficult and most profound teaching of the Buddha. It was tied to memory in the sense of not forgetting what one is doing or what is going on in the proximate environment, and to goodness in terms of good actions allowing its development. And in a mutually reinforcing sense, they also spoke of mindfulness as resulting almost automatically in doing good actions.

In a sense, sati was thought of as developing a kind of basic life-instinct for remembering and getting by successfully:

> When my parents told me "Don't let it fall," "Don't leave it behind"—that was the time I learned about sati.

> My parents told me not to forget to do my school lessons, to not forget to do good things. Or to not forget the things I meet with everyday. To not forget what one is doing. Like, "That dog is going to bite you—take care of yourself!"

> I once ate some food that I knew I'm allergic to, and I went to the hospital for a week. The reason I had to go to the hospital is that I put the priority to my appetite. If we have too much priority to our mind we will be *sati-hlut*—being in the stage without sati.

> If we don't have sati we will face forgetfulness. For me, I usually forget things. In order not to forget to answer for this interview, I try to focus on sati, on not forgetting. Like, to come to this interview!

> When I'm in a rush I tend to make mistakes. Because I miss my sati. I lose hold of it.

While very pedestrian ways of talking about mindfulness were common, often monks also talked about mindfulness in a related sense as very profound, even as everything the Buddha taught and leading to nirvana, the ultimate Buddhist goal of enlightenment:

> I know more about sati as I am going to sit for the exam, on the twenty-eighth of March I'll have to answer questions about it in the exam, and also I'll have the mind, the sati to study for the lessons. My opinion here is that all things have their own endings. Our *samsara* [the Buddhist idea of the cycle of ongoing suffering of existence through birth and death] has an end. In order to reach the end we must have sati.

> Mindfulness is like salt—everyone needs salt to eat. The same as that, sati is the one that everyone needs. If people don't have sati, they can make some mistakes. Sati is also like the footprint of the elephant. In the footprint of the elephant every kind of animal's footprint can enter into it. If we are going to summarize what the Buddha said, we only have the word "sati." There is nothing we could compare with sati.

The examples of mindfulness as being like salt, and like the footprint of an elephant that encompasses all the "footprints" of the Buddha's other teachings, speak of mindfulness as both as common as everyday experience and as important as the most profound teaching of the Buddha. A twenty-three-year-old monk named Dhammapiya, who had been ordained for the previous ten years, made the point that sati is not comparable to anything else. Like the others at the Intensity Center and at the Aungchanga Monastery, he was studying for the national Burmese monastic Dhammasariya exam. He had learned about mindfulness when he was young, from his parents, he told us, and had studied it formally at the monastery. But he really started to understand it, he said, by experiencing it in his regular life.

He described one instance that helped him to appreciate what mindfulness is, and understand how to use it to keep his mind calm. A few years earlier he had been present at an incident that involved the government, though he didn't relate the specifics of what it was. He didn't know if the place he was staying would be bombed or shot at, and as a monk he had recited a *metta sutta* on loving kindness to the people who were scared and crying. It was then, he said, that he recognized that he was also scared. "And as soon as I knew that I was scared, I was no longer scared. I wasn't any longer scared to die. So that's how I started to know about mindfulness: mindfulness told me I was scared." The military government of Burma has carried out a long series of crackdowns on lay and monastic protests; the monk at the Intensity Center was unclear about whether he was speaking of one of them, but it was likely that he was.[4] Most monks didn't have such extreme examples of when they felt and learned about mindfulness, but they were living in a social space in which the teachings of the religion were, similarly, part of their larger personal and cultural environment.

Lay Life, from Seeing a Can of Coke to Not Forgetting to Water the Fields

Laypeople in Mandalay incorporate mindfulness into their everyday experience, too. For the most part they have less formal training in mindfulness than the monks, but more practical everyday experience. As in Thailand, many laypeople in Burma have spent time as monks or as other kinds of renunciates, though sometimes only for a few days. As in Thailand, most men in the country spend time ranging from a few days to many years as temporarily ordained monks. Women are also ordained as renunciates of a similar, though lower-privileged, position.[5] After the monks' interviews, Tiri and I started seeking out the non-ordained too, to find out how often and in what ways they used mindfulness in practice. On the old motorbike that Jieb and I had rented in town we drove about an hour outside Mandalay to a village called Yekyi in Patheingyi township, and wandered around the tea shops and back roads finding people to talk with about mindfulness. We also went to Mandalay University, where with the help of a professor of history we approached students studying for their exams at a sprawling outdoor café on campus. From old women in flowered sarong and *thanahka* tree bark face powder to two teenage girls at the university sporting bright blue nail polish and bright spiky punk hairstyles, they told us about their thoughts and impressions on sati. Perhaps not surprisingly in a country in which Buddhism is so dominant and so few other perspectives on the world are available (though this, of course, is changing quickly), we found that laypeople were for the most part very aware of mindfulness and thoughtful about how they developed it in their lives. A few of the people we spoke to in the village said they weren't very familiar with the idea of mindfulness (even though they had thoughts to share about it), and a few others had many elaborate ideas, but overall mindfulness is considered a fairly regular part of life.

In our last interview with a monk, the head of a rural monastery outside Mandalay told Tiri and me that regular laypeople wouldn't know much about mindfulness, and that if we wanted to know the best information about it we would want to talk with monks, especially learned and senior famous monks. I had heard this kind of affirmation of authoritative sources in Thailand too. The monk was suggesting that some people would know more about the topic, that I might do best to, say, go to

Yangon, where the most famous international centers are, or find the most learned reclusive monk; and while this in some ways would be true, I also wanted to know what other people who weren't part of this social structure of official knowledge might think about mindfulness. A bit hesitant and skeptical of our own plan, Tiri and I had approached a man having tea at a dusty pavilion at the edge of the village. Children were running around, the television was on in the corner, and an old woman was taking a nap in a hammock. Instead of the casual references to mindfulness I had been led to expect from laypeople after the relatively technical summaries from monks, the man surprised us by talking extensively and passionately for the next four hours. His interview, though longer than the others, shows the idiosyncratic, textually influenced but personally interpreted meanings of mindfulness in Burma.

U San La was forty-nine years old, and after being a monk for many years he was now a semiretired doctor of traditional medicine. He drew up an elaborate system of perception involving mindfulness, combining dozens of technical Pali terms with very practical illustrations drawing on the tea shop around us. He started off summarizing the well-known list of the five aggregates, called *upadana-khandhas*, that are thought in Buddhist philosophy to constitute the illusion of a self.[6] He went on to discuss the connection between an object and the sensory experience of it:

> Sati starts from *thi wein nyin. Thi* is from knowing, *wein nyin* is mind consciousness. Sati is knowing your mind. For example, look at this Coca-Cola can sitting here in front of us. Only if we combine the mind [*citta*] and the object [he used the term *citta-tikha*, referring to the objects that the six sense doors of sight, sound, taste, smell, touch, and thought can perceive] will we really see the can. Or, I have an ear, and your voice comes into my ear, and it's called hearing. So to see or hear needs two things: *citta* and *citta-tikha*. If we don't have sati at a point of time, then we won't know there are voices out there. For example, from the TV over there.

He pointed to the television in the corner.

"Do you hear those sounds?" he asked us.

"Yes," Tiri replied.

"Do you know what they're saying?"

"No," she replied, indicating that she was focusing on him instead.

"People are talking all around you. But you don't hear them because it depends on what you accept. There are a lot of things around us—the chairs, the trees, that grandmother lying in the hammock in the corner. But you don't see her. That's because the eye from you and the things from the outside that come to you, if they meet together then something like hearing or seeing or feeling occur. Because of *citta* and *citta-tikha*. To say it briefly, you can only sense things if the two meet together."

"How does sati come in, then?" I asked. "Is it only about things you want to see or hear or feel?"

"Sati is something that's there to mend, to heal," he told us. "For example, let's say you're feeling unwell. If you're unwell you have to drink water. How do you know you have to drink if you're feeling unwell? It's because of sati. The sati reminds us of the *citta-tikha*, if you're feeling unwell. It's like reminding."

U San La talked for a long time, much longer than the monks we spoke with, and covered a wide range of issues, from the fire of ignorance (which he talked about using the Pali term *moha*) to wisdom (*pañña*), and how to attain the four stages of sainthood (*ariya*) through extinguishing the flame of ignorance, and how to understand impermanence (which he illustrated by comparing the life of a person to the leaf of a tree that gets old and falls down), and three different kinds of nirvana. He talked about *sīla* and the Eightfold Path, the four brahma *viharas*. At the end of the interview we got up to leave, and he asked us one last question.

"Did you come here with sati?"

"Yes!" Tiri replied confidently.

"I see your motorbike parked over there," he said, gesturing to the shady spot near the pavilion. "How many steps did you take when you walked over to sit down with me?"

"I don't know," she said.

"Then you didn't have sati. Let me ask it a different way. When you got off your motorbike, did you step off with your right foot or your left?"

"I don't know!" she said again, laughing and nodding.

"Then you didn't have sati! Let me ask it again. When you got up right now, which leg did you start with?"

"I don't know—maybe the right one. Maybe the left one, I don't know. OK, let's say the left."

"OK," he replied, "now mark it. Every time you get up, start with the left side, the left foot will start walking. That's what we said in the military: 'Left, right, left . . .' It's to train on mindfulness."

Tiri and I thanked U San La and headed out into the hot sun. Tiri was glowing from the conversation, inspired by the man's way of connecting abstract, even esoteric, ideas to very practical everyday concepts. We drove on our motorbike for a while down a dusty, shady road, pausing to give some coins to a group of people raising money for a village festival, and stopped at the side of a road to get a cold soda and relax after the long interview. While we were there chatting with the older couple that ran the stand, we asked if we could interview them too about mindfulness. Unlike the more formal interviews we had done with monks at the monasteries, we wanted to see what regular, random people in the countryside thought about sati, and here were two of them sitting in the shade with us. The two responded to our questions with good humor, although they weren't anywhere near as elaborate as U San La had been. They scrunched up their foreheads a bit when we asked what sati was, and said "To be careful?" in reply. But even they and others we talked to related ways that they made use of mindfulness, and gave examples of when they especially did and didn't have any. As was the case in Thailand, many of these examples were about driving—that in driving one usually has a lot of mindfulness, and when the mindfulness is gone one can get into an accident. It is not just inattention that is seen to cause these accidents, but also fear and the idea of a mind that can wander away. When we asked people to tell us about times when they learned about mindfulness or had a lot or a little of it, many referred to these kinds of moments at the wheel.[7]

> When I was learning to ride a motorbike I was eager to know how to drive, so I didn't put lots of sati into driving the bike, that's why I ran into a lot of things. And starting from that time I knew about sati.
>
> Last month I had an accident with a car, because of not having sati—*sati-hlut*. I saw the car was coming toward me, but I thought I could pass the car without having an accident. My mind was going to another place, and I couldn't concentrate. So, I had an accident with the car. That is because of *sati-hlut*. That is something that our mind reached to other areas that we are not doing right now.
>
> When I'm driving the motorbike I have to look forward and take care of myself not to encounter accidents. I drive with sati.

Laypeople also talked about times when they had a lot or a little bit of mindfulness in comparison to other times, such as when they got angry or distracted or drunk or in other ways "lost it." Driving was an example that had not come up in the preliminary research when I was putting together the questionnaire a year earlier, so it wasn't listed as one of the options that people could pick from, but it was the most common example in the interviews, and a frequent write-in in the questionnaires.[8]

These moments of losing sati were similar to other instances of having a distracted, unsettled mind. One older man told us how he had once been in a program to become a general in the military, but that he got into a problem with one of the senior staff members and had hit his superior.

"I couldn't control my anger," he told us, as I tried not to look surprised, "and after I hit him I was supposed to sit for the exam, but another senior officer said to me, 'Do you really want to bother sitting for the exam? You've made such a big mistake hitting that guy, who's senior to you,' so I told him I'd just go home, and I took my bags and went back home and quit. I was so wrong, I shouldn't have done that. I did it just because of the anger." The man didn't say if it was the hitting or the quitting that was especially wrong, but he marked it all as having been because of a lack of mindfulness.

The man selling soda from a cart on the side of the road also told us about the practical repercussions of losing his sati. In addition to selling soda, he was a farmer, and each year he usually put some pesticides on his crops after a big rainstorm, but last year he forgot. "We were having a big festival at that time," he said, "and I was drunk and didn't notice that I hadn't put on the pesticides. That was because I didn't have sati."

These instances of losing sati or feeling that it was weak were tied to instances in which, going by U San La's framework, one's attention or awareness did not accurately perceive the correct object of focus in a way that would allow proper remembering to occur. This was true for all kinds of objects, inside the mind as well as out. The "object" of the senses in these cases was as material as the dog that one man said he almost hit while driving, and as immaterial as the social reality of the senior government officer or the potential well-being of a field of crops.

In Burma anger is thought of as a "hot" kind of feeling. In a way similar to the aspirations of affective nonattachment in Thailand, the "heat" of affective experiences may be a more relevant and meaningful category for emotionality than the state names of one emotion or another. All "hot" feelings are seen as negative, and according to one informant, all result from a lack of sati. A common compliment in Burmese is to say someone is "*aye*," or cool and peaceful, suggesting that that person does not lack sati in responding to stimuli. Some feelings are themselves divided into hot and cool types; love was offered as an example. This was explained as hot love being driven by lust and possession and cool love being driven by *metta*, a kind of loving-kindness or compassion.

In contrast to these "hot" moments of losing mindfulness, the times that people said they were especially mindful were when they experienced the coolness of *aye* feelings. Not surprisingly, the most common times people reported feeling mindful was during meditation. Other times when people reported feeling especially mindful were when chanting, driving, studying, reading, and doing things slowly and alone. People often combined the practice of meditation with stresses and everyday experiences:

> Especially when I'm doing *vipassanā* I have more sati than usual. My [university and monastic] teachers also remind me to go with sati, eat with sati, arrive with sati. As I have a little bit of pressure from my teachers, I usually have sati while I'm in the meditation center.

> I have more sati when I sit for the exam. If I just wrote down all the things that I think then I will get low marks. I also have more sati when I meditate. Because when I'm meditating I can concentrate more.

> I have more sati when I have to go to some dangerous or adventurous area, some area that's strange to me. Because I don't want to face any accidents.

People talked about meditation in Burma using a lot of the same phrases as in Thailand, but there were slightly more references to *bhāvanā* and *vipassanā*, along with *samatha*; and *ānāpānasati* meditation, as in Thailand, was the most popular form of meditation among both ordained and laypeople. A method called *pom peng* was also cited, which was described as a focus on the breathing of the stomach, "like when we blow some air and it'll be big like a balloon and we let it out."

In some ways the examples that people offered of the meanings and purposes of mindfulness felt obvious: being careful, concentrating, and attending to one's environment. But they also point to mental power and ability, over forces both natural and supernatural.

Figure 16. Two women on the outskirts of Mandalay discuss their experiences with mindfulness while they rest from the midday sun. They relate how mindfulness helps them generally to remember to do things, and to do them well, from selling soda on the side of the road to biking into town and working in the fields. Photo by J. L. Cassaniti.

This power of mindfulness is in some sense about everyday successes; but it was also more than that. A monk noted that mindfulness is one of the *bala*, or "powers of the mind," listed in the *Abhidhamma*.[9] Tiri told me how she sometimes could see ghosts while meditating at her monastery during retreats, and how it felt powerful. She didn't interact with these spirits, she told me, but she told me how strange it was, and viscerally real to her. Being mindful not only helps to keep away unwanted influences, it seemed; it also allows for a control and even mastery over them, as it permits the ability to see and engage with them. As in Thailand, others also talked about how mindfulness allows one to have control over ghosts (and other unhealthy forces), whether through the choice of being able to see them or the ability to keep them at bay. Although there was a lot of variation in how people connected mindfulness to supernatural forces, the majority of people felt that a mind that is weak, sick, or overly attached will be more likely to be affected by these preternatural powers.

There is a significant degree of variation in connections between mindfulness and spiritual powers. Some people told us that they did not believe in ghosts. Some told us that they did but that mindfulness had nothing to do with them. Others talked about whether they thought ghosts could have their own sati. This last issue of ghostly sati did not come up at all in Thailand, where ghosts may be considered more amorphously consisting of diffuse energy rather than as autonomous beings. Burmese *nats*, whose statues often depict them as having distinct histories and personalities, take on these more autonomous qualities. For example, when we asked about whether there is a relationship between mindfulness and ghosts, the monk Dhammapiya, who had talked about fear during the government incident, said, "I have never seen a ghost, but most Burmese will say that they have seen them. Some people think that the appearance of the ghost is fearful. But I don't know. . . . As the ghosts have their own life, they may somehow have their own mindfulness. The mindfulness that the ghosts are having and the mindfulness we are having may not be related to each other." The other general connection between mindfulness and the supernatural had to do with, as in Thailand, what is thought to happen after death. It is thought that when one has a lot of mindfulness in life (and especially at the moment of death), one will be reborn in a good place. Morality was also invoked: as one monk put it, "Sati and ghosts are related to each other, because if we do good things, then after we die we'll reach the good place, and if we do bad things we'll reach the bad place, like hungry ghosts, like that." Laypeople also talked about meditation and the positive powers of mindfulness in not just this life but the next.

Mindfulness for laypeople in Mandalay isn't as tied to a concept of *khwan* as in Northern Thailand, but it is similarly connected to keeping away the spirits that can cause distraction and even illness. There are many ways to talk about these spirits, or forces that fall under the umbrella category of the supernatural referred to in the Pali Burmese term *para-loka*. The *para-loka*, or "other world," encompasses a wide range of spiritual forms, from *thewada* (angels/deities) to the traditional Burmese spirits called *nats*, to *byahma* (described by Tiri as spirits "higher than *nats*") to *seta-hse* ("spooks"), and *peta* (hungry ghosts; *pret* in Pali) that wander around because of excessive attachments left over from life. These "ghosts" are part of everyday life for people in Burma, in invisible and even sometimes visible ways.

"If you have sati," the monk Sayadaw U Thilasara Bhiwuntha had told us, explaining the connection between the energies of others and one's mindfulness, "well, because you're relying on your mind with sati, ghosts can't approach you. Because you're paying attention to your mind. That notion is very evident, and so the ghost can't appear in your mind. They can't scare you, they can't haunt you. Only when you're free of sati, independent from sati, when you're feeling small, feeling sad, they can come and haunt you, because you don't have sati." Conversely, having a lot of mindfulness can not only keep ghosts at bay but also suggests a power or ability over them. Most people we talked to followed this same pattern that was described by Sayadaw U Thilasara Bhiwuntha:

> When you engage in meditation, you have to have sati. When there is no sati, there are ghosts around you. If there is sati, those ghosts disappear.

> People without sati can be possessed by ghosts, but if you have strong sati, they can not possess you.

> I don't believe too much in ghosts, but maybe there are. Somehow sati and supernatural things are connected. If we are overconfident, we may lack sati. At that time we can reach to some extreme point, and we may face troubles.

> I think sati and ghosts are related. If those who practice *ānāpānasati*, those who practice sati, they have very high mind power, then they can see the ghosts.

One afternoon Nyein's friend Moh brought me out to a small countryside community to watch a *naga*-possession festival at a local monastery. He was fascinated by the event and was sure I would be too, with my interest in mindfulness, spirits, and Buddhism. When we arrived we found dozens of middle-aged women swaying to music in the central monastic pavilion surrounded by statues and paintings of the mythical *naga* serpent. The entire monastery was dedicated to the creature. The women danced until they fell over and began rolling on the floor, possessed by the serpent spirit that was said to reside on the monastery grounds. We spent the afternoon listening and watching, and talking with people. There was no talk of mindfulness explicitly that afternoon, but it was clear that the women were understood to be influenced by external forces, and that their mindfulness was far away, taken over by the spirits.

In a sense the energy of "ghosts" or spirits like these is the energy of distraction, of feeling influenced by others' intentions. It is a way of thinking based in large part on ideas about the dangers of attachments, over which the power of mindfulness helps. These attachments have ramifications not only for life but also for death, and for what happens after death: a woman told me about a monk at a meditation center who taught her that the ability to maintain sati at the moment of death is part of what determines what one will become in the next life, alongside one's karmic stock. More than at any other moment, the ability to let go of attachments is part of what enables someone to achieve this mental state at such a tricky time.

> Two or three months after my grandfather passed away we took a ride on the bull cart with my grandmother. We had just passed the cemetery, and I thought I saw a spook [*seta-hse*]. . . . Maybe I had some strong attachment [*asweya-*], that I was too attached.

> If someone is in his last moment of life, if he doesn't *sati-hta*, he can be attached to something, and after that can become a *peta* [hungry ghost].

These difficulties and successes in the attachments of mindfulness are directly tied to mental health, not only in future lives but in this one. In Burma, as in Thailand, mental problems are seen to be in large part due to having a lack of mindfulness. The connection is circularly reinforcing: mental disorder breeds a lack of mindfulness, I was told, which in turn breeds mental disorder. It was a connection implied rather than stated by most of the people Tiri and I talked with, but one monk said explicitly: "A lot of people are faced with mental disorders, because of not having sati. And so doctors have to train their patients intensely to have sati." Another spoke similarly, though less directly: "In order to teach those who are abnormal, we have to train them to have mindfulness and concentration. We have to train them to do things regularly." He offered his ideas on how one might do this: "For example, you have to train a person to come and hold something, a particular thing, every day at, say, eight o'clock. If psychologists want to train someone who is a little disordered, they can train them by having them focus on touching one thing every time at the same time in the morning. It has to be the duty of the patient. And after that he will remember what to do, what is his duty. So it's like giving sati to him." It reminded me of studies that show how people in nursing homes tend to do better when they have a plant to water or a pet to feed (Rodin and Langer 1977, 1976): it's the responsibility for a living thing that is helpful. It seemed this monk was saying that it was also helpful because of the focus, or mindfulness, that came with it.[10]

Psychiatric Implications

To find out how mindfulness might be tied more formally to mental health, and especially to mental health care, Tiri and I went to the Mandalay psychiatric hospital outside of town. Of all the places in Theravāda Asia I went to learn about mindfulness, this was the one I was most hesitant about. Psychiatric hospitals can be tense places to spend time in, because of the states of mind of many of the patients and because of the institutional red tape that surrounds them. Beyond that, the Burmese government wasn't known as being very keen to allow foreigners access to much at all. I was told it would be almost impossible to get the staff there to talk to us. After driving up to the front gate on our first trip there, failing to find the mental fortitude to enter, and returning to Mandalay, Tiri and I made the hourlong trip on our motorbike a second time the following day, and this time went in cheerily, keeping elaborate, casual smiles on our faces. Tiri was inspiring to me in this. At just twenty-three years old, she was very sweet and quiet, so quiet that she felt too shy to sit down at the tea shops lining the streets in Mandalay ("because there are so many boys there!" she said, even when I teased her about doing her part in dismantling the institutional sexism around us). But when it came to carrying out the interviews, she boldly walked in and inquired directly if she could ask the staff some questions.

The staff members at the Government Psychiatric Hospital who met us at the entrance at first said they would have to talk with their boss and that we should come back another day. When we appeared again the next morning, they led us to a back room, where this boss welcomed us and asked what he could do for us. The first half hour in the hospital was the most difficult. As the staff were figuring out what approach to take with the strangely impetuous foreign and local researchers, the alarm went off and bars came down from the ceiling to block many of the entryways around us. The boss laughed when he saw the alarm on my face and said that it was just an incident with the inpatients, and that it would all go back to normal in a few minutes. I looked over at the inpatient ward around the corner: people were hanging their arms out of the bars, and I could hear yelling and howling in the back. At the front halls of the hospital, quiet-looking parents and sickly looking teenagers were sitting on the benches, waiting to be seen. Mostly, the head of the hospital told us, the people being treated were there for drug addiction, their concerned parents bringing them in. I thought again of my friend Sen, and how, to someone visiting who hadn't already known him for years, he would appear to be just another sick inpatient in need of help in an overburdened mental health system.

The members of the staff at the Government Psychiatric Hospital answered our questions about mindfulness in ways that were very similar to how monks and laypeople had responded. Like the majority of monks and other laypeople, they said that sati is to remember and act carefully. Almost everyone in Burma discussed mindfulness as memory, carefulness, or both, but one person at the hospital discussed mindfulness explicitly as related to the future. "For example," a young senior psychiatric nurse said, "if I'm about to make an injection to a patient, at that time the patient can also harm me. So if I'm going to inject such patients, I need to have sati. Even while I'm injecting him he could kick me with his other leg. These are the kinds of things I can predict, that we should be expected to see. I prevent myself from danger by having sati." People at the hospital said they have a lot of sati especially when they are at the monastery, and that they have especially low levels of sati when they are angry. They said that sati is related to the supernatural but that they weren't sure exactly how, or how to explain it. They also said that mindfulness is connected to impermanence, and that doctors should use mindfulness in their work and teach it to their patients.

All the psychiatrists and psychiatric staff members Tiri and I spoke with said that mindfulness was a good thing to have and was good to incorporate into therapeutic practice. This was similar to how psychiatrists talked about mindfulness at the Suan Prung Hospital in Thailand, but there was less of a sense that it was a new or especially "scientific" technology. This seemed to me to be a good thing, but it also meant that they didn't necessarily see mindfulness as something for doctors to have to teach. For the most part they seemed delighted that a foreign researcher would take an interest in such a local concept—though perhaps my interest in it was particularly welcome because, through my foreign, professor status, it somehow made more legitimate or potentially acceptable the idea of incorporating it formally into practice. Most people said that as they and most of the patients were Buddhist, there was no need to teach mindfulness formally to them, since the patients already knew about it and could learn more from monks and others outside the hospital.

Dr. Soe, the senior mental health specialist at the hospital, was especially interested and straightforward in his discussion. We sat in his air-conditioned office with its new copy of the internationally famous *Diagnostic and Statistical Manual of Mental Disorders* (DSM-5) on the desk (considered the global standard guide for diagnosing mental distress), the patients and their families on the benches outside, as he talked about his struggles with and thoughts about mindfulness. He told us how he used to lose mindfulness a lot when he would go out and drink with friends. He brought up one time in particular in 2007 when he had drunk too much during the annual spring water festival and started a fight: "I'm so lucky I didn't die!" he told us.

"Whenever we're out of sati, problems come to us," he said. It was similar to the way others talked about ghosts. He didn't specify the problems that he said can come to one who is out of sati, but he said that his brother once saw a ghost, and he connected mental health to the powers of mindfulness explicitly. "If we have sati, bad things won't happen to us, because we won't feel afraid of problems. When we meet with the things that arise in the world [using the Pali term *loka dhamma*],[11] if we have sati we won't feel afraid. Even if the house is on fire we'll know that it's impermanent, and we won't feel attached to that." He told us that sati is the thing that controls us—a kind of self-control. "Especially I need to have sati when I have to talk with government people," he said.

"How do you get this sati at those times?" I asked.

"I have sati by practicing *vipassanā*," he replied. "And more than that. By trying to have sati in whatever we do, later we can reach nirvana. Like, when we're walking we have to look carefully at how we walk. It's like

Figure 17. A desk at the Government Psychiatric Hospital is cluttered with papers, signature stamps, and assorted medicines. Even in this relatively remote area of Burma the DSM (the standard *Diagnostic and Statistical Manual of Mental Disorders* used in the United States) has made its way to the medical professional offices of psychiatric centers. Photo by J. L. Cassaniti.

a habit." He went on, referring again to a kind of power that sati brings: "Whenever something good or bad happens to me, I usually say '*bud-dhang, saranang, gachami,*'" referring to the classic chant that marks a Buddhist follower by announcing the taking of "refuge" in the "Three Jewels"—the Buddha, the dhamma, and the sangha. "I feel like if I'm say-ing that, like if I whisper that, I feel like I'll reach a good outcome, a good place, even if I die."

Even with this clear connection between mindfulness and the ability to keep away negative experience and gain the powers of clarity and calmness, Dr. Soe did not think that doctors at his hospital should nec-essarily teach mindfulness as part of their treatments. But that wasn't because it was too "local" to be part of international scientific tech-niques unless it was "stripped of cultural baggage," as the nurse at the psychiatric hospital in Chiang Mai and so many others have suggested. Instead he said that it just wasn't necessary, because "as this is a Bud-dhist country, most people know about sati already." He added, though, that "to not have problems, the doctors should teach by giving exam-ples. Like, doctors can share their problems, and if we know how to solve problems in particular situations, we'll have sati." His discussion of his problems with drinking and the need to have sati, especially when he talked with government people, was in this way put into the context of his own pedagogical practice of teaching his patients, his staff, and even the foreign researcher and her bold research assistant. Before we left, we asked if there were any questions he had about the research we were undertaking, and even though he had said that mindfulness wasn't something he imagined would be useful for doctors to teach explicitly in their practices, he told us he was excited that I was doing the research, and that he had heard of this idea of bringing mindfulness into the hos-pital in more formal ways than the "everyone knows about it" approach he was advocating. "I have a friend in Yangon," he told us as we were packing up to go, "a colleague, who's doing something like a mindful-ness-for-mental-health program, to learn how to use it in the hospital. It sounds interesting. I hope I hear more about it!"

Like Dr. Soe, other members of the psychiatric hospital staff expressed interest in mindfulness, said it was important, but didn't talk about teach-ing mindfulness explicitly as a remedy for their patients' problems. They did, however, follow his tendency to bring up situations in their own life to illustrate what they saw as a link between the two. Especially in the area of emotion and affective problems, they discussed how mindfulness helps one to be mentally well. The senior nurse in charge of all the other nurses at the hospital told us,

> I have a lot of responsibilities, a lot of people who depend on me, and not just at work but at home too. Sometimes having too much on my shoulders causes me to get too worried and depressed. Due to this I stayed in bed recently for three days in a row with a lack of sati. *Sati-hlut*—I had lost my sati.

In these illustrative, almost taken-for-granted ways that mindfulness was connected to mental health, the staff at the government hospital saw the Buddhist concept as relevant in their own lives and work.

The TAPES of Mindfulness in Burma

T—Temporality

Most of the perspectives on mindfulness that I learned about in Burma were shared by the majority of the people, and agreed on as central qualities of the practice. But one area of mindfulness's implications did reveal an apparent discrepancy: the issue of temporality as part memory and part present-moment awareness was not expressed in the same ways by everyone. In America, there seems to be a very present-centered focus to the practice, whereas in Thailand there was more a sense of recollection, or memory. Since American concepts of mindfulness have been heavily influenced by recent Burmese meditative traditions (Braun 2008, 2009; Cook 2010), I had been curious if there would be more attention paid to the present moment in Burma, as compared to the relatively unproblematic "recollection" of mindfulness in Thailand. I was surprised to find that mindfulness understood as "memory" (*asomaya*, or *sati ya*—to remind) was even more prominent in Burma than in Thailand, but "attending to" or "noting" (*sati-hta*) and its present focus was also very prominent. While most people incorporated the two together, there were some people who talked about one perspective as being better than the other.

In Ashin Janakābhivaṁsa's book *Abhidhamma in Daily Life*, the text most often brought up in the Burmese interviews and questionnaires as being influential in teaching about mindfulness, the place of morality and the controversial role of memory in mindfulness practices are at the fore. I was told that this book is well read by both monks and laypeople, and this seemed to be the case: at the nationally famous Maha Gandayon Monastery in Mandalay, where over three thousand monks reside at one time, there was a little book stand where a monk was selling copies of it, along with all the other books that the author had written as the founding monk of the monastery and the writer of dozens of commentaries on the *Abhidhamma*. When Tiri and I went into a crowded bookstore in Mandalay, we saw the same book prominently displayed, standing out amid the many other books packed on the shelves, a clear best-seller. In the English translation of the *Abidhamma in Daily Life*, Ashin Janakābhivaṁsa writes, among other things,

> Recollection, remembering or heedfulness, are definitive terms for mindfulness which is known as sati in Pali. There are various forms of sati. For example, one recalls the meritorious deeds performed in the past; one listens attentively so that one can remember the Dhamma discourses. While meditating, one concentrates deeply not to lose the object of meditation. Such is the nature of sati. Sometimes you look forward to meritorious deeds to be done tomorrow or in the future. You take care to observe morality (sīla) and do not breach any precepts. You are mindful to restrain the arising or greed, pride and ignorance. You recall the counsels of your teachers. Only such forms of mindfulness concerning wholesome matters are collectively called sati (mindfulness). . . . Mere Remembrance is Not Sati! When a person remembers his relatives, when lovers yearn for one another, when friends remember to keep appointments, when one recalls some precious moments, etc. all such remembrances have the nature of attachment. . . . When one remembers to take revenge for injuries done to one, when one keeps in mind atrocious plans; when one pays heed to possible dangers that may befall en route to a destination; such cases reveal hatred (dosa) as the base. Any form of the aforesaid mental factors being accompanied by attachment or hatred, cannot be classified as true mindfulness (sati). (Janakābhivaṁsa 2009)

"Mere Remembrance is Not Sati!" the text stated in bold letters, and explained how remembering is just part of mindfulness. This may be a reflection of the concept's changing meaning in the contemporary meditative scene in Burma. In bringing up morality and especially the contentious question of the role of memory in sati, Ashin Janakābhivaṁsa recognizes that many people have and do think of mindfulness as meaning memory, but he also says that it is not "mere memory." People I spoke with reiterated this point, with some saying that they used to think of sati when they were young as "remembering" (such as "I *sati ya* my parents when I'm away"), but now they think of it more as "noting" or "attending" (such as "I *sati-hta* to do well on the exam"). "When I was young I would write letters to my friends saying 'I miss you,' 'I'm thinking a great deal about you,'" Sayadaw U Thilasara Bhiwuntha told us, "and that is *sañña* [perception], not sati, even though I would use the word *sati*. So when I was learning the *Abhidhamma* seriously for the first time, I had trouble distinguishing *sati*, *sañña*, and *citta* [mind]. Sati really means not just longing for something but being aware of things."

Although a half dozen people distinguished the two aspects of sati as memory and present-notation, most saw them together, as when they said "I *sati-hta* to remember the facts—like what time I have to go to a meeting." Memory isn't usually brought to mind when an English-speaking person in America thinks of mindfulness, but they were central to a lot of the ways that people talked about the concept in Burma. This was surprising to me, especially given that the ideas that influenced American (and global) forms of mindfulness practices in large part come from Burma. Part of the connections to memory, though, were ideas about the present and the way in which one can train to "note" the things around them, and gain mindfulness through doing so.

A—Affect

Talk of specific emotional states (especially anger and using the power of mindfulness to decrease it) was slightly more common than the more amorphous affective feelings described in Thailand, but there was a similar theory about how affect works and how mindfulness can positively improve it—not as "happiness," but as part of ideal states of calmness. Even good feelings like "happiness" (and other general states of excitation) are seen as part of the kinds of emotional feelings that lead to mindlessness:

> If we have sati we will be more calm, peaceful, successful, and more stable.

> Whenever our mind is meeting with defilements, we seem to lose sati, because our mind is happier in defilement. At that time we have to train ourself to be more stable and comfortable.

> The time when one is feeling excited, they'll also lose sati. They'll have more sati when they're calm.

The reasons that calmness is constructed through and representative of the presence of mindfulness are many. The connections in some ways felt self-evident, given my own cultural sensibilities of how being calm and "collected" allows one to be more careful and "mindful," but they also tie in to larger cultural issues about time, ethics, power, and selfhood. They have in large part to do with a kind of power or ability to see things clearly, but are also based on shared ideas about the importance of not attaching to things that change. Strongly formed feelings—whether happy, sad, or angry—were all seen in some ways to reflect a lack of mindfulness; conversely, mindfulness was seen to help develop the kind of calmness that allowed for its power to be expressed. For example, the nurse who described having sati as resulting in calmness explained her reason in the following way:

> It's because things are changeable, so situations can change. If someone is too busy they can forget to do things, and when someone is feeling excited they'll also lose sati. They'll have more sati when they're staying calm.

Others also explained calmness as tied to sati through an awareness of change:

> My mind is also changeable. My mind is tough to control while I'm feeling sad or happy. If we could *sati-hta* in times of feeling sad, we'll not feel sad anymore.

Of course, people told me over and over again that within this larger truth about change and the worthwhileness of not craving things, it is good to keep sati with one, to not lose it, to not let it get lost. It was perhaps the one thing that a person should not let go of!

P—Power, and E—Ethics

As in Thailand, there is a mental power associated with mindfulness and the ways that people use it for their own benefit and in the influencing of others. It is a power that is thought to keep one safe and sane, and that even transcends the individual life and blends with the supernatural and life after death. Sati was seen to be a clear "controller" of the person—of the healthy and powerful person. Even more than in Thailand, people reported that one can be "in" sati or "out of" sati, and when one has sati present, then things work out, and one is "in control" of oneself and one's environment. This power is very much connected to ethics. As U San La had put it, sati works to mend and heal by enabling a person to see what needs to be done. His example had been very specific—thinking of sati as "reminding" one to drink water when feeling sick—but others talked about it more broadly in relation to moral action. One monk brought in the idea of karma in mindfulness, as relating to good deeds of three kinds: behavior, speech, and thought. "Sati is the controller of these three kinds of good deeds," he said. Throughout the interviews that Tiri and I collected, ideas converged on the morality of this power of mindfulness. Mindfulness is good to have, and allows for good things to happen. If one uses what looks like mindfulness for bad ends, people said, then it isn't really mindfulness at all. "Genuine sati is good deeds, wholesome actions." This seemed very different from ideas about mindfulness as separate from the judgment of actions as good or not good. I wondered how mindfulness as a clear, penetrating, and simple noting of one's actions and environment would be necessarily connected to goodness. After all, if one simply notes things, what difference does it make in terms of the core of what mindfulness is if the things are good or not? Though some people talked about the difference between what was called *sammā sati* ("right mindfulness," the seventh point on the Eightfold Path) and *micchā sati* ("wrong mindfulness"), which suggests that even if it's wrong then it's still sati, no one stated that mindfulness is above or separate from morally good action. Instead people tended to link notation directly to moral goodness, as did a university student we talked with who said that "when

I argue and talk back to my mom I sometimes, mid-argument, notice—
sati-hta—that I'm wrong, that I shouldn't talk back to her like that, and I
tell her I'm sorry." The power of mindfulness, they implied, comes directly
from doing good. As one of the hospital workers told us plainly, "Sati is
something that controls our mind. If something happens, we will know it
is right, it is wrong. And that knowing is called sati."

S—Selfhood

Much of this moralized understanding of impermanence undergirds the
relationship that mindfulness has to memory and other temporal constructions. An understanding of impermanence is implicated too in just what a
person looks like who is healthy and full of sati. When I asked if mindfulness is connected to non-self (*anattā*), most people talked about change,
and how *anattā*'s sibling of impermanence (*anicca*) was very important for
the kind of understanding about non-self that mindfulness helps to reveal.
The connection of sati to impermanence was clear in the open-ended
interview discussions and also in the questionnaires we handed out.[12] One
of the hospital staff members outside Mandalay put it the following way,
connecting non-self to affect, impermanence, and memory:

> If we have sati we will be free of dangers. We'll have a calm mind, and
> make fewer mistakes. It is because of craving that people think there is per-
> manence, that there is a self to get things. People will never feel themselves
> that they are rich enough. They will always say they are needing something.
> It's because of impermanence and non-self. I think that sati and *asomeya*
> [memory] are related. Because we don't have sati, that's why we are want-
> ing something.

In his more abstract articulation, Sayadaw U Thilasara Bhiwuntha had
talked too about this impermanence in terms of changes—not just the
things that one encounters and can become attached to in life, but also of
the mind itself—and even of sati itself:

> Sati is the nature of mind. It is a concept of mind. That mind—*citta*—comes
> and goes. The same is true of sati; it comes and goes. The later sati is sup-
> porting the past sati. It's coming and passing; there is sati, then another sati
> that follows, and all of that is *anattā*—non-self.

From the importance of noting the impermanence of sensations that Sayadaw U Thilasara Bhiwuntha pointed out, to the farmer who described how he forgot to take care of his fields because he was drunk and without sati, people in Burma emphasized the qualities of remembering to do good things throughout their discussions about mindfulness. They couched these qualities in the explanatory contexts of their own lives and professions. Tiri in her own way as an academic and avid meditator had done so, too, explaining and elaborating each of the interview responses with reflections on her own experiences.

As the end of the period of data collection was getting closer I could tell Tiri was ready to move on to other things and complete her degree and find a long-term job, though she would first go back to the monastery for another retreat before doing so; and I was ready to move on, too. On the last day of the research in Mandalay I went to visit Tiri and her mother one last time. "I'll *sati ya* you!" Tiri's mother said as we said goodbye. As I got on the plane to return to Thailand, before turning back around for the next leg of the trip in Sri Lanka, I thought of what I had learned about mindfulness in the country. If I had gone to Yangon, I might have gotten more elaborate and even more technically sophisticated versions of mindfulness from monks and mental health professionals, but they would also be articulated in ways that were slightly different from what most people in the country felt. This was true of Mandalay, too, of course, but from the everyday lives of these nonelite or specialist practitioners I learned a great deal about how mindfulness works in the country in practice. As Jieb had observed almost immediately on arrival, the people in Burma were overwhelmingly kind, and the mindfulness practices they talked about reflected this.

From my experience in *vipassanā* meditation, and from knowing that many of its modern iterations came from Burma, I had expected Burmese mindfulness to emphasize noting the body and immediate environment. I found this to be the case, but I also found that this notation was more than just an in-the-present recognition of objects. It had as much to do with re-cognition, or "remembering" to be present, as a kind of psychological state of mind, as it did with simply a noting of the present. And I learned that this remembering is not without a moral underpinning. There was a goodness that was part of being able to see a fine mist, and avoiding missing out on spotting a giant cave in the woods.

Reflecting always-changing cultural attitudes about meditation and society (not to mention time, affect, power, ethics, and selfhood), mindfulness seemed like an idea on the move. Based on the country's reputation of spawning the regional and global interest in *vipassanā* and, with it, mindfulness, I had expected to hear about mindfulness as noting the present, and I did. But I also heard it connected with the past, and especially in remembering to do good. Thailand may be the most "modern" Theravāda Buddhist society in the sense of consumerism and economics, and Burma the most contemporarily influential, but people in both countries pointed to Sri Lanka as the traditional bastion of the religion. What, I wondered, would mindfulness look like in a place where the Theravāda tradition that developed the concept first took hold? Would mindfulness in Sri Lanka emphasize the past more than the present, nonjudgmentality more than morality? Would it pay even more attention to the Buddhist ideas of non-self, or be more or less tied to power, or emotion? People in Thailand had told me that meditation movements came from Burma, but they also pointed to Sri Lanka as being the place where Buddhism began, and many told me that it is also the place where people practice it most seriously. After returning to Thailand and arranging research assistants to help organize the large swaths of interview, questionnaire, scale, and observational data from Burma, I once again got on a plane out of Bangkok, this time to find out more about mindfulness in the contemporary social and religious practices of Sri Lanka.

5

Sri Lanka: Moral Focus and a Stalking Cat

"We're Buddhists, sure, but in Sri Lanka they're really strong in it," I had heard from a friend in Thailand. "They learn a lot from us, especially lately, but Sri Lanka is where the history is. You should go there." When she said that "they learn a lot from us," my friend was talking especially about the Siam Nikāya branch now popular as one of the three main lineages followed in the country; but in saying that people in Sri Lanka are especially strong in their practice, she was also referring to a sense of respect, and confidence that the ancient tradition was continuing especially soundly in Sri Lanka. I found the same kind of attitude about Sri Lanka in Burma too, pointing to Sri Lanka as a place with a long history and rich current culture of Buddhist practice. In a religious world where lineage and continuity are so important, this deference was no surprise. It was also a sense of shared respect in the region; many Sri Lankans, also respectful of their neighbor's practices, would say that to learn about Buddhism one should certainly also go to Thailand or Burma.

Theravāda Buddhism (literally, "The School of the Elders") is said to have begun in Sri Lanka, according to semi-mythical historical chronicles, when King Asoka was said to have sent his son Mahinda to the island a few hundred years after the Buddha's death. The idea of a single historical lineage is today being questioned by Buddhist studies scholars (see, for example, Skilling and colleagues' excellent *How Theravāda Is Theravāda?* [2012]), but most people in the region share a strong sense of religious continuity. Even as Theravāda Buddhism spread throughout mainland Southeast Asia in the years after Mahinda's travels, it grew too on the island of Sri Lanka, and through periods of waxing and waning it is still flourishing there today. Approximately 70 percent of the population of Sri Lanka is Buddhist; mostly these are lay followers, but some make up a small, visible population of ordained male and female monastic renunciates. The reverence that Sri Lankan Buddhism receives in the mainland of Southeast Asia is largely due to the religious history of the island, but it is also related to the awareness that being a monastic in Sri Lanka is considered a lifelong vocation, and that, more recently, after a revival in 1996, fully ordained female monastics were officially recognized by the Sri Lankan Buddhist sangha.

In Sri Lanka I found mindfulness to look in many ways similar to how it is conceptualized in Thailand and Burma, especially as part of its larger practical and ideological connections to temporality, affect, power, ethics, and selfhood. I also found a few differences in tone and emphasis associated with the practice there from how it is understood in Thailand and Burma, among them an attention to focus and concentration, and the ethical implications of what is considered to be correct practice as part of the *sammā sati* of the Eightfold Path. I also found many similarities to the other countries of Theravāda Asia in the meanings, purposes, and transmission of knowledge about mindfulness.

This leg of the journey began with a flight from Bangkok to the island's capital city of Colombo, followed by a train northeast to the second-largest city of Kandy. An American man named Michael, who was building a Buddhist meditation center, and a Sri Lankan Muslim woman named Rushma, an MA student at the nearby university, met me as the train pulled into the station.

"Welcome to Kandy!" they said, having been in touch with me through an activist friend in Thailand before I arrived. "Let's go have some tofu ice cream at the YMCA."

Figure 18. An airport kiosk in Sri Lanka greets those arriving and departing with an assortment of "Food for the Mind": books, figurines, and other Buddhist goods helping with meditation, fortune, and auspiciousness. Photo by J. L. Cassaniti.

Michael, Rushma, and I walked to the crowded street-side café in the middle of the city, and they told me about the town, including a good place I could stay, an old-fashioned guesthouse in the middle of the city overlooking the lake and the Sri Dalada Maligawa, the Temple of the Sacred Tooth, a temple (or literally, palace) that is said to house one of the Buddha's teeth. After the monks chant in the early mornings, visitors from Sri Lanka and abroad pour in to see the relic—when I managed to go over to it, the golden *dagaba* urn it was encased in was shining brilliantly in front of the crowds jostling for a glimpse.

As with Thailand and Burma, I had been tempted to focus my research energy on the elite universities and monasteries of the country's urban center, this time Colombo, where specialists there would be able to tell me about mindfulness in its most internationally inflected, English-language-privileging meanings. But as in Thailand and Burma, I was less interested in these elite or specialized centers and more interested in what "regular," less elite Buddhist people in Sri Lanka think. With the world-famous Temple of the Sacred Tooth, and the offices of the world-renowned Buddhist Publication Society (BPS) behind it, the old capital of Kandy is no backwater. It has gained a national and international reputation as being a center of Buddhist learning, with books published at the BPS making their way to Thailand, Burma, and around the world, and an active monastic community. But along with its many religious specialists, I would also be able to draw from it a good balance of specialist and nonspecialist, urban and rural voices.

As the three of us sat having ice cream on the busy street corner, I asked Rushma if she knew the word "sati." I knew with its Pali-language base that it appeared in Sinhalese and English-language Buddhist texts that I was sure some people in Sri Lanka read, but I wasn't sure how common it would be in vernacular speech, especially with someone who wasn't Buddhist. But even with my Thai-inflected pronunciation—saying the word quickly almost as "*sti*" rather than the "*thati*" of Burmese or the "*satiya*" I would come to associate with the Sinhalese pronunciation—Rushma recognized it right away.

"Actually, we have sati in Islam too," she told me. I was surprised by her response, becoming aware suddenly of what a different religious landscape this was from what I had been in, both in Thailand and Burma, where more than 90 percent of the people are Buddhist, and where the location of mindfulness as a Buddhist concept felt so obvious that its religious associations almost seemed to disappear into the cultural fabric of the place. "When we kneel to pay homage to Allah," she explained to me, "it's there. But, yeah," she went on, "it's mostly a Buddhist thing."

To learn more about the texture of that social and religious landscape, rather than just reading about it, I spent some time getting to know the city. After checking in to the guesthouse that my new friends had recommended, and spending a few more days talking with Michael and Rushma, I got in touch with an NGO activist named Sajeeva to help translate the interviews and questionnaire into Sinhalese, which would retain many of the same Pali-derived, colloquially Buddhist terms used in the other countries (including *sati*, *anicca*, and *anattā*). With the translations of the interview questions under way, I set out about exploring the area.

One of the first afternoons in Kandy, I went to the home of Gananath Obeyesekere, a Sri Lankan psychological anthropologist who had completed his BA at the local University of Peradeniya and was now retired after a long career as a professor at Princeton University (Obeyesekere 2014, 1985, 1990). He was certainly not a "regular Buddhist person" in a general sense, but I had followed his work since graduate school and felt that his insights into the culture here, and the study of culture more broadly, would benefit my research. In his gorgeous home outside town, with floor-to-ceiling windows overlooking the rolling mountains below, we drank tea, and I told the professor about my project. He wasn't impressed. His face crinkled up, and he laughed his wizened eighty-five-year-old laugh: "Oh, that's not interesting at all!" he told me. "I prefer the odd things, the anarchy-Buddhist things. You should do work on those things. Everyone around here knows about mindfulness, sure," he told me. "It's just basic, obvious, though they won't know much. Village people going to the monastery know it—even rich people going to escape from themselves at some meditation retreat!" He laughed again.

Making the strange familiar (and making the familiar strange) is the hallmark of anthropology. I had to remind myself that the research on what was an "obvious" part of mental life in Theravāda Asia is not so obvious to people in America, and that my job as an anthropologist was to draw out ideas and show their relevance to both. The ways that mindfulness is practiced "on the ground" in the country might be too pedestrian a subject for a local anthropological specialist like Dr. Obeyesekere (and for that matter for many of the informants I spoke with throughout Theravāda Asia), and at the same time too exotic in its local form for psychologists and scholars and followers of American Buddhism to see it as relevant for understanding the mind or the religion. But gathering perspectives on mindfulness among people who find it obvious doesn't just tell us about mindfulness. It also shows how concepts about mindfulness in their local variations reveal cultural components normally cloaked under the guise of universality. Too-near obviousness, just like too-distant exoticness, overlooks the ways that mindfulness can suggest different ways for thinking about lived experience. Dr. Obeyesekere and I talked about the strengths and weaknesses of analytic frameworks that do or don't resonate with the people they're meant to be discussing, and how theories that sensationalize activities can sometimes miss the important if more mundane parts of experience. "Mindfulness," I told him, energized by the conversation and the strangely high caffeination of the tea, "provides us a window into local realities! It challenges monolithic historical analyses. It mines for the particulars of mental practice." He argued back about magic and esoteric monks, about the importance of understanding not just the taken-for-granted but also the strange and unusual in cultural practice. After a while the sun started to set. I thanked him, we said our goodbyes, and I returned by rickshaw from the quiet of the mountains to the busy town below.

I continued to think about the meeting with Dr. Obeyesekere long after, fortified from it with both the promise and the challenge of my chosen topic of interest. I had already learned so much from Thailand and Burma, and was excited at the prospect of learning even more from Sri Lanka. One of the things I had found out about mindfulness in Theravāda Asia was that it lies at a balance of modern and ancient, developed as a "new" kind of practice in *vipassanā* that is also said to be an "old" one, one that was just now being revived. The "imagined newness" was the thing that Dr. Obeyesekere was especially laughing at when he told me about the meditation retreats gaining popularity on the island and around the world, for rich people, he had said, who have time "to escape on a vacation from themselves." People in Thailand and Burma, as well as in Sri Lanka, brought up again and again ancient texts that mindfulness was part of, and most of them had been written in Sri Lanka. The past is present everywhere, but it seemed especially present in Sri Lanka.

Theravāda Beginnings

After spending some time getting to know Kandy, and before beginning the interviews, I headed out for the ancient site of Anuradhapura
in the north of the island, where Theravāda Buddhism first took hold
almost two thousand years ago. According to the fifth-century chron-
icle the *Mahāvamsa*, it was to Anuradhapura that King Asoka sent his
son Mahinda around 220 BCE, as part of a large missionizing project he
spearheaded for the still relatively new Thera school of the religion, following a split into different schools that would later come to be called
the "Theravāda" and "Mahāyāna." At Anuradhapura, it was said,
Mahinda set up an order of monks at a monastery called the Mahavihara, the "Great Abode." Around 50 BCE the teachings of the Buddha
were said to be written down for the first time, having been orally trans-
mitted in local languages and Pali up to then for the religion's first five
hundred years.[1]

Anuradhapura is thus one of the most important historical sites in the
Buddhist world. Other, older Buddhist sites in India and Nepal may be
even more famous, among them the place of the Buddha's supposed birth
at Bodh Gaya and the site of his first teaching at Sarnath. But those sites
are general to all branches of Buddhism as a whole, rather than to the
teachings that have become known as Theravāda. I had heard about Anuradhapura from people in Thailand and Burma and in historical books
about the religion, and I was curious to see where so much had happened
so long ago.

Dr. Obeyesekere had given me the phone number of a colleague there
who would be able to show me around, but when I arrived the professor was out of town, so one of his students agreed to serve as tour
guide for the day. Twenty-year-old Moon was covered in tattoos, with
an alternative-rock-style haircut and a quiet smile. He showed my friend
and me around the ancient sites one by one, re-creating arguments about
dhamma interpretations and ritual practices as we stood by the crumbling
walls and large pits that were now empty but had once held thousands of
gallons of water for the monastics to bathe in. The friend I was traveling
with had her own share of tattoos, and the two of them bonded over the
art on their bodies and on the walls of the ruins as Moon kept up a steady
stream of comments about what had happened where and when.

Little is actually known about the social world of monastics of these early times. Scholars today work to dismantle assumptions about experience based on present-day interpretations, and instead reimagine possible contexts (see Hallisey [2015] for an excellent example of this in his *Therigatha*, a translation of ancient poetry by some of the first Buddhist women). Around 500 CE the famous Buddhaghosa wrote down the still very well-read *Visuddhimagga*, or "Path of Purification," the most important commentary on the Theravāda Buddhist Canon in Aluvihara near the town of Matale. Some textual experts claim that Buddhaghosa was the sole author of the *Visuddhimagga*, while others speculate that it was the work of many monks. But whether many or one, whether sooner or later, it was in the thriving community of the Mahavihara that many of the Buddha's words were transcribed for the first time, using the Sinhalese script to spell out the Pali words.

While my friend and Moon admired the spirally serpentine ornaments carved into the sides of the monastic sites and laughed at the monkeys that followed us everywhere, I imagined Buddhaghosa instructing his scribes as they sat at their writing desks at the corners of the now practically disappeared walls. Even in that early era there was a lot of activity and diversity in culture and opinion. At a craggy spot in the woods that was said to be his study, I imagined the famous Chinese monk Faxian arriving to offer his own interpretations, and working alongside other monks with their own input.

According to legend, at one point one of the monks at the Mahavihara temple was accused of exhibiting too much hubris by accepting donations from the queen in his name, and instead of leaving the monkhood quietly for breaking the *vinaya* rules he departed ceremoniously in a procession with his students and set up a rival monastery nearby. This rival monastery, called the Abhayagiri, was also successful for a time, incorporating interpretations from visiting Chinese monks like Faxian (and so considered more "Mahāyāna" than its Mahavihara neighbor). Like the Mahavihara, the Abhayagiri monastery produced a great deal of texts, including one called the *Vimuttimagga* (or "Path of Freedom") that is similar to the *Visuddhimagga* in its scope, but with slightly different interpretations of the teachings, including those on mindfulness. Eventually, though, the Abhayagiri lost its rivalry with the Mahavihara, and the *Vimuttimagga* became less prominent. Even today, however, some of the monks I spoke

Figure 19. Birds fly over the central stupa of the Mahavihara temple one evening in Anuradhapura, as a Buddha statue stands serenely nearby. Photo by J. L. Cassaniti.

with in Sri Lanka (and in Burma and Thailand, too) cited this lesser-known text. Mindfulness in its modern guises is often thought to be tied to a kind of general, ancient past, or else linked to a fairly contemporary (even scientific) revival, but as the influence and diversity of Anuradhapura shows, it is and was part of a dynamic multiplicity rather than a single cultural history of ideas.

The Mahavihara monastery eventually faded along with the Abhayagiri, this time (it is thought) because of the difficulty in finding water at the inland location, rather than the reality-show-type vagaries of morality connected to the Abhayagiri. But the lineage of the Mahavihara continued to thrive throughout the island. The tradition took hold especially in the twelfth-century kingdom of Polonaruwa, merging with what are sometimes called "animistic" and Hindu traditions. It was around this time that Buddhism became part of the "civilizational projects" of society in ways similar to its place in the generally contemporaneous kingdoms of Thailand's Sukhothai and Burma's Bagan. Later Buddhism continued sometimes peacefully and sometimes not so peacefully, alongside the island's more recent religious traditions. Just as people in Thailand and Burma claim a general lineage tradition to these events at Anuradhapura so long ago (and beyond them to the Buddha himself), today Buddhists in Sri Lanka continue too to follow teachings that were first written down near the Mahavihara and Aluvihara monasteries, following the ebbs and flows of Buddhist revivals and contentious connections to the politics of the country. Within these teachings came some of the commentaries and techniques of mindfulness I would hear about on the island.

After a few days of seeing the sites and drinking the never-ending cups of strong Sri Lankan tea, my friend returned to America, and I returned to Kandy to meet with Sajeeva and finalize the interview protocol. Since monks seemed like such a specialized group, I decided I would start the data collection with them, though I wasn't sure which to interview. Monks in Sri Lanka follow a general classification of what are known, according to Sagara Kusumaratne (2011, 99), as "'village dwellers' (called Grama-vasi Bhikkhus) and 'forest dwellers' (called Aranya Vaasi Bhikkhus), with 95% of the village dwellers ordaining in their teenage years or even before, and most of the significantly fewer forest dwellers ordaining after middle age and coming from the upper-middle or lower middle class." Monastics have also been, historically, generally classified as either "dhamma guides" or "meditating monks," but the categories are not exclusive, and today monks may practice both if they wish. These classification systems are similar to the social experience of monks in Thailand and Burma, though with the longer period of ordination they can become more significant personally in Sri Lanka. Because monastic ordination is open to women as well as men in Sri Lanka, there is a wider pool of possible members of the ordained sangha; but because of the much longer-term commitment that joining entails, there are far fewer of either gender who do ordain. Usually monks ordain when they are teenagers, becoming separated from their families in their residence and lifestyle, and in doing so perpetuate a more specialized and also a more socially circumscribed Buddhist scene. In Thailand I had once met a monk who had given me his business card and told me to call him to meet up for coffee after his period of ordination was over the next month; and in Burma, too, monks take an active part in their larger social world. In Sri Lanka monks are visible around town, and appear as professors and students in schools, but seemed to me relatively less accessible and less open to participating in secular life.

Michael and Rushma helped me find a university student named Shermilla who was looking for research experience. After Shermilla and two elderly aunts and an uncle carefully vetted me at a cafeteria around the corner from my guesthouse to make sure I was acceptable to work with, she agreed to help, and we were ready to start speaking with monks. Shermilla was quiet, matter-of-fact, and markedly deferential to those we interviewed, especially to the monks. She was Buddhist and interested in the project, but compared with Santi in Thailand or Tiri in Burma, she rarely spoke of her own experience, and only sometimes voiced her opinion in elaborating a point.

Monks: Focusing on the "Right Kind" of Mindfulness

It was a peaceful morning at the Sri Lankan International Buddhist Institute (SIBA) when Shermilla and I arrived, having been pointed that way by her family and my hodgepodge of research affiliates in Kandy. As they do in Thailand and Burma, monks in Sri Lanka take part in a state-sponsored, parallel system of education, many studying and living at one of the country's 561 *pirivena* monastic colleges from youth through adulthood, with some continuing to pursue higher studies at a monastic university or a secular university. SIBA was officially recognized as part of the Higher Education Institute of Sri Dalada Maligawa, the Temple of the Sacred Tooth, and was located just outside the city of Kandy. As in the monastic centers in Chiang Mai, and to a lesser extent Mandalay, the monks are mostly local but can also come from afar nationally and internationally, especially from other regional centers across Southeast Asia.

Sajeeva had recommended before going that I contact an elderly female monastic named Ven. Mawidharma at the center, who had ordained fifteen years ago and was now the director of the department of postgraduate studies. The Venerable Mawidharma (monastics in Sri Lanka are addressed with this title of "venerable") greeted us at the entrance of the institute and welcomed us inside the university grounds. The SIBA campus was beautiful, lush with greenery, with white buildings scattered around the campus and pink flowers everywhere, rolling hills in the distance and even a few elephants kept around (when not parading through town during the annual Temple of the Sacred Tooth festival). The Venerable Mawidharma was in her mid-seventies, with wrinkled dark skin, dark robes, and the bald head of a monastic. Like Phra Suphan and so many others I had met during the previous months of research, Ven. Mawidharma emitted a kind of warmth and peace that made me want to be near her, even though I couldn't exactly figure out why. She had a kind, quiet smile the whole time that Shermilla and I were there. She allowed us to use her office as a base for the interviews, and had assistants bring monks to the adjoining meeting room for interviews between their classes. She spoke with us between the interviews too, pausing only when other monastics and novice monks came in periodically to ask her a question, or when she was called away to deal with the everyday bureaucratic issues of running the program.

It was refreshing for me to see the male monks come by and speak deferentially to the venerable female *bhikkhunī*, after the religious gender inequality I had started getting used to in Thailand and Burma.

"Is it nice to have the monks come in and treat you with equal respect?" I asked Ven. Mawidharma as we sat down in her office, after a male monastic stopped by to quietly ask her to sign a piece of paper.

She smiled shyly: "Yes. When they first asked me to come here and be the director, I was a little nervous about it, but the monks have always been very polite and kind."

One of Ven. Mawidharma's assistants brought in a monk in his mid-twenties for us to interview; the young Ven. Katuwana had just finished one of his classes and was free for a while until the next one. Over the course of our time at SIBA we interviewed ten monks and surveyed thirty more. Meanwhile, a kind young Bangaladeshi monk named Bhante Chandrasana, whom I had met at the University of Peradeniya and who had agreed to help in the project, was interviewing and administering the questionnaire to another group of monks at his monastery near Kandy, to broaden our pool of monastic perspectives.[2]

Right from the first interview it became clear that the morality of mindfulness is especially marked in Sri Lanka. It is not that mindfulness is amoral in Thailand or Burma, of course—in both those places monks and laypeople alike think that mindfulness is a "good" thing to have, and that it helps one to do good. But in Sri Lanka this "goodness" is elaborated more, and is contrasted more often with the alternative possibility of "wrong" mindfulness, a concept that was fairly absent in Thailand and only sometimes brought up in Burma.

"Sati is categorized into two parts," Ven. Katuwana told us as we sat down, "the right kind [*sammā sati*] and the wrong [*micchā sati*]."

"He means there are two kinds of sati in Buddhism," Shermilla explained when I gave her a quizzical look, "right and wrong." Ven. Katuwana nodded and went on. "Yes. For example, a thief also has sati, but he has wrong intentions. Sati means paying attention to a single topic, and *sammā sati*, or right mindfulness, leads to accumulating *kusala*, skillfulness and wholesomeness. *Kusala* is the force that takes us forward to *nibbāna*. Wrong mindfulness does not."

While the Ven. Katuwana was talking, Ven. Mawidharma for the most part was busy with her own work. As we sat with her after the interview, she added a clarifying comment: "Sati can be developed either in good or bad ways," she said, "based on someone's capacity to understand. For example, a cat can have so much mindfulness as it stalks its prey, even for hours, which is also a kind of sati—yet it is a wrong kind of sati. . . . Or take the thief example he just talked about. Let's say a thief, or your enemy of some kind, is waiting very, very mindfully, even for many hours, until the opportunity comes to attack. This is mindfulness—but it's the wrong use of mindfulness. And Buddhism approves of *sammā sati*: right mindfulness."

It is right mindfulness, and not wrong mindfulness, the monastics told Shermilla and me again and again at SIBA, and told Chandrasana too, that is the way the Buddha put mindfulness into practice. "I studied how I should practice mindfulness in the proper way," one monk said. "For instance, we should utilize mindfulness to be more efficient in our actions. Right mindfulness helps us to dissolve our self-view."

"Those who don't have a good educational background in Buddhism can't understand the real purpose of sati," another monk told us, "and because of that, some have become tempted to do dangerous things, even commit murder!" In Thailand and Burma I didn't hear this kind of discussion as much. Phra Thēp and others had pointed to moral action as a way to develop mindfulness, but it seemed in Thailand that, aside from a few notable exceptions from monks, there was no such thing as "wrong mindfulness." If something is done without good intentions in Thailand, it was more likely to be seen as not mindfulness at all, rather than mindfulness in an incorrect form. This was especially true in Burma, as when I was told at one point: "When I thought wrongly about something it was because I didn't have sati, I didn't understand it." That was the typical Burmese refrain.

But what does this "right way" of mindfulness look like? Compared with "recollection" and "knowing the *tua*" in Thailand, and compared with the "noting" and "remembering to do good" of Burma, there was a greater tendency among monks and laypeople in Sri Lanka to emphasize concentration in the way that the correct form of mindfulness plays out.

"Sati is to keep the mind concentrated in one place," Ven. Mawidharma told us, when we finally sat down to conduct a formal interview with her when she had some time to spare. Her definition was similar to what we were hearing from others by that point, suggesting a definition of mindfulness as the ability to concentrate the mind and, as she said, "keep it completely straight." "Sati means doing your day-to-day work consciously, and being focused on the work while living in the present," Ven. Katuwana had told us, and Ven. Mawidharma and others agreed:

Mindfulness is maintaining full concentration in the activities one is engaged in.

It is keeping the mind fully concentrated on one aim without paying attention to anything else.

We can't concentrate and think on two subjects at the same time, so we must select one thing and concentrate on it. That's mindfulness.

Sati has two meanings. One is generally awareness, and the second is to fix your mind on something and continue doing that.

This is sati then in Sri Lanka: a general awareness and especially a kind of focused attention. In our fifty open-ended interviews in Sri Lanka, concentration was brought up forty times, in contrast to only sixteen times in Burma and twenty in Thailand. In Thailand, concentration was referred to at times as part of *samādhi*, but a separation between *samādhi* and sati was often noted with it. This separation is pointed to explicitly in Buddhadasa Bhikkhu's teaching on the *Ānāpānasati*: "*Sati* is a key term in Buddhist meditation," it says in Thanissaro Bhikkhu's English-language footnote; "it means recall, recollection, full awareness, attention: mindfulness. . . . Sati does not mean 'to concentrate or focus, which is *samādhi*." The note may reflect Buddhadasa's more modernist perspective in particular rather than broader Thai perspectives, or even may simply be a view of the American monk Thanissaro Bhikkhu who had added it, but it says clearly what others in mainland Theravāda Asia pointed to too, that sati is not typically understood centrally as concentration or focus, unlike the majority of definitions offered in Sri Lanka.[3] Of the definitional options offered for respondents to choose from in the sixty-one questionnaires we gathered from monks, "to think carefully" was the most popular, with thirty-seven (or 61 percent) of the monks surveyed choosing it, more than twice as popular as the second most common choice, "to not be careless" (at twelve monks). "To recollect," which was the most common response in the Thai and Burmese surveys, was the least chosen in Sri Lanka, where only one monk chose it.

Sammā sati, or "right sati," the monks reported, is to practice this focused attention and careful thinking, and to do so in "the right way": to practice according to mindfulness's place as the seventh of the eight factors in the Buddhist Eightfold Path. Texts that are read and referred to in Thailand and Burma also included the *sammā sati* of the seventh factor of the Eightfold Path, but the terms *sammā sati* and its opposite *micchā sati* were rarely raised in either country. The specific "right mindfulness" of *sammā sati* in the Eightfold Path was more common in Sri Lanka, as was a kind of "right mindfulness" that was referred to specifically as "the mindfulness of the four Satipaṭṭhāna." The majority (thirteen of the twenty) monks we interviewed referred often and in detail to this teaching, more than in either Thailand or Burma.

One monk talked about the *sammā sati* of the Eightfold Path in relation to the path's other components, bringing up, as did so many others, the Satipaṭṭhāna in his discussion: "Due to right view," he told us, "*sammā saṅkappa* [right thought/attitude/emotions] is developed. Due to *sammā saṅkappa, the sammā vācā* [right speech] is developed. The *nekkhamma saṅkappa* [the concept of renunciation] leads to the development of sati. All these factors of the Eightfold Path are interrelated, so sati is part of the condition for *nekkhamma saṅkappa*, as one aggregate of *sammā saṅkappa*. Through the Satipaṭṭhāna teachings, sati is acquired, which means practicing to see the real nature of the body, feeling, mind, and phenomena as they really are." Though more technically elaborated, this monk's reference to the interrelationship of mindfulness and goodness was similar to the three friends that Phra Thēp had discussed in Thailand, of morality, concentration, and wisdom referred to in the summary of the Eightfold Path, and it was similar too to Sayadaw U Thilasara Bhiwuntha's description in Burma of mindfulness as helping one to do good. It was the explicitness of the right mindfulness within the larger structure that seemed slightly different for monks in Sri Lanka.

Often the descriptions of the Satipaṭṭhāna emphasized their moral and affective aspects. A young monk named Ven. Debarawewa, whom Bhante Chandrasana roomed with in his monastic dorm at the University of Peradeniya, listed them first in a fairly typical way: "Buddhism introduced four factors that lead to the acquiring of mindfulness," he said. "They are *kayānupassanā*, which is penetrating toward the real nature of body; *vedanānupassanā*, awareness of the nature of sensation; *cittānupassanā*, being aware of the mental formations; and *dhammānupassanā*, penetrating toward the nature of phenomena relevant to the mind." In his more personal, idiosyncratic explanation, though, of these four he emphasized especially two: moral goodness and an elaborated orientation to affect:

> For *kayānupassanā*, if one is thoughtful about one's bodily action, that person will not commit bodily wrong deeds. *Vedanānupassanā* is to be able to see sensations as they are. There are three kinds of sensations [or feelings]: *sukha* [pleasant feelings], *dukkha* [unpleasant feelings], and *upekkhā* [indifferent feelings]. We must be aware of feelings, be aware if they are leading to the bondage of *samsāra* [the cycle of suffering] or to the elimination of *samsāra*. Any feelings that are *dukkha* or *sukha* that lead to *samsāra* are not good; attachments to sensual objects are not good, so Buddhism emphasizes unconditioned happiness which is acquired through practicing meditation. *Dhammānupassanā* is that we must be aware of the nature of sensual objects attached by the sensory organs. Understanding what the phenomena are exactly, through mindfulness, we neither cling to nor repulse them. *Cittānupassanā*—the mind—is the forerunner, so it must be well directed.

The affective qualities that Ven. Debarawewa spoke of, as being aware of feelings and their potential to lead to suffering, and of a kind of "unconditioned happiness" that comes from not clinging to, or rejecting, phenomena, are central to his description of the Four Foundations of Mindfulness (and thus to the performing of "right mindfulness"). His description is similar to the kind of discussion about sensation and feelings brought up at Buddhadasa's meditation retreat in Thailand, and to what Sayadaw U Thilasara Bhiwuntha was referring to when he told us that by noting *vedanā*—sensation—the "things that will trouble people will be destroyed." How this works, Ven. Debarawewa was saying, is that attending helps to create a feeling of calm detachment, leading in turn to good ends.

This general framework of affective construction and an awareness of impermanence as leading to good ends was stated in different ways by different monks. A senior monk, Ven. Weligepola, explained it through a discussion of non-self: "If I think that I am the person who is suffering, then there arises much suffering; but if I understand that 'I' is the combination of five aggregates which don't have any eternal entity to them, then the suffering can be overcome." He brought his discussion back to affect as he continued, "Here sati is related to feelings and mind. If we are conscious about how sensation and mind operate, and their nature as well, we can end the cycle of suffering. But we need to practice the relevant path that leads to complete freedom."

Not surprisingly, while mindfulness is thought to be gained through a variety of techniques, the one that these monks spoke of as a central way to gain mindfulness—and especially "right mindfulness"—is meditation. Monasteries and retreat centers are as popular in Sri Lanka as they are in Thailand and Burma, with lay meditation movements increasingly springing up in a trend that has affected even the relatively separate world of the ordained. Meditation is not always emphasized in monastic life, and some monks say that they are not particularly interested in meditation, even if they feel that they are expected to be. But for most monks, meditation, even if only in a small, practical way, is part of the same kind of regular monastic life they have known since first ordaining. As our monastic interviews continued, the monks related their own views and experiences with mindfulness in meditative practice:

When your mind is confused you can't see anything properly. If your mind is confused, it is due to the five delusions [of desire, hatred, doubt, ignorance, and confusion]. If your mind is confused, how can you see reality? In order to see reality, you have to be calm. How can you calm down your mind? Have mindfulness. And to have mindfulness you have to develop concentration by practicing meditation.

Meditation is especially connected with sati, because by practicing meditation the mind can get under control. It paves the way to the realization of the impermanence of the world. But even during meditation our mindfulness can be weak, so we need to practice gradually to retain it. If we could establish sati the very first time we meditated, we wouldn't need practice.

When the mind is conducted properly in daily activities, mindfulness can be cultivated in life. It's done through meditation—and conducting one's life properly, orderly, actually is also one kind of meditation. When we are eating, when we are sleeping, when we're studying, in silence, in all postures of our life. If we do these properly, correctly, there is mindfulness. It paves the way to understanding.

In practicing the path that leads to enlightenment, sati is necessary to get rid of obstacles. Through sati we understand the importance of giving up the concept "I," "myness," and "my soul," and the final result is the complete eradication of them, which is the eradication of all defilements.

The specific methods for gaining these realizations through mindfulness are similar to those I found elsewhere. *Ānāpānasati* sati was the most popular, with the recollection of the Buddha and his teachings (one of the kinds of *anussati*, the recollections of which one should be mindful) second. *Samatha*, concentration meditation, was also popular, tied to the relative emphasis in the country on mindfulness as *samādhi*, concentration.

One afternoon in Kandy, Bhante Chandrasana and I went over some of the textbooks on Buddhism compiled by the Sri Lankan Ministry of Buddhist Affairs, which are used in the dhamma schools that most Buddhist children in the country attend. We found instances that cited concentration (*samādhi*) and mindfulness directly: "Sati and *samādhi* in the Noble Eightfold Path are conducive to *samatha* meditation," said one, in a Pali-heavy Sinhalese section:

> An individual's mind is always covered with hindrances. It helps to eradicate those hindrances and keep the mind on one-pointedness, which is known as *samatha* meditation. Mental energy and potentiality are needed to keep the mind under control amid sensory objects. . . . The mind is a forerunner and needs to be focused on a certain object, as in breathing meditation breathing is the meditation object." (Dhamma school final examination, 2013)

While some monks did draw a direct connection between *vipassanā* and mindfulness, concentration was evoked slightly more often. It is not fully clear how much the association between *vipassanā* meditation and the mindfulness found in many global settings today is due to the popularity of the modernist meditation movements that came out of Burma in the past hundred years, and how much existed in Sri Lanka and other areas previous to them, but the connection between the recent Burmese movement's attention to *vipassanā*, compared to a relative Sri Lankan focus on concentration, seemed tied at least in some way to these relatively recent and now global trends.[4]

In our discussions, as elsewhere, monks in Sri Lanka usually spoke in the abstract about meditation rather than about their own personal experience, but sometimes they brought in preferences or events from their own lives to illustrate their larger points. Some monks offered these thoughts briefly, such as one who said simply, "We have to pay attention to meditation techniques that fit our character. For me it's *buddhanus-sati* [the recollection of the Buddha] or *ānāpānasati* [of the breath]." One *bhikkhunī* I spoke with elaborated similarly: "When worshipping the Lord Buddha and breathing in and out, I really work on sati. I do it through full consciousness. For me, when chanting, I'm fully concentrated with it." A few others spoke in more detail about their issues in meditation, based on their own experiences. A monk named Nawalapitiye told of a meditation retreat he had been on a few years previously. He didn't name the retreat, but he described the lessons he learned there about mindfulness as related to stress, clinging, and the therapeutic "right understanding" of *sammā sati* in ways that seemed to combine the kind of *vipassanā* mindfulness techniques I had learned about in Thailand and Burma with the kinds of concentrated attention to the "right mindfulness" of *sammā sati*. "I went to a meditation retreat for a week a few years ago," he told us,

and on the very first day the teacher taught us about the importance of acquiring mindfulness. From morning until we went to bed we were taught to be mindful. On waking up we were instructed to be mindful of the meditation topic we had practiced before sleeping—the mind is pure at those times, and so can remember things perfectly. The Buddha taught in the Vattūpama Sutta that as a white cloth is easily dyed, so is a pure mind. Sati is *"yoniso manasikaro"*—being aware of each task one is involved in. It is the bodily and mental concentration of eating, writing, meditating. . . . And we learned *satiyatana*—mindfulness of walking, sleeping, running, standing . . . and *dhammānupassanā*. Like when I was sitting in meditation, if there was pain, to know what it is. Awareness is acquired through mindfulness, which is derived out of practicing four *satipaṭṭhāna*, the techniques for practicing *vipassanā* meditation.

In intertwining his own personal experience with his understanding of the Buddhist teachings, Ven. Nawalapitiye spoke a bit more personally than other monks tended to. He went on:

> I used to have a lot of mental stress, and wasn't able to achieve much, but I've gotten better. Thoughts are always springing up; we must be mindful in everything. Practicing sati through right understanding, I mean the *sammā sati* of the Eightfold Path, lets us identify truth from untruth. Mindfulness leads to the realization of truth. We have clinging and attachment to sensual objects, and if we work to overcome the clinging, *upādāna*, and finally eradicate it completely, there is *nibbāna*. If I can think of how every conditioned thing is impermanent, I can acquire sati based on right understanding. Our minds must be detached from all defilements. A mindful person can eliminate craving.

Relatively few spoke even more personally than he had, but I found the stories of those who did share them to be intriguing lessons that, through example, show how mindfulness can help at difficult periods in one's life. "Mindfulness and meditation helped me be in my right mind," an older monk told us, "when my son died. It was easier for me to feel better. When my son was dying I did a lot of meditation, and from that I was able to reduce my sorrow." Another monk used a more pedestrian, though more unusual, example: "I used to work at a bank before I ordained," he said, "and one day at the end of work by mistake I got locked into the vault! I had to have a lot of mindfulness at that time so that I didn't panic. I was able to get out; mindfulness saved me."

The practices and purposes of the "right" kind of mindfulness are thought to help. This is thought to be true in the long term (even multiple-life term) of walking on the Buddhist path toward nirvana, and it is also thought to be true on the more short-term path, too, of dealing with life's more immediate experiences. After our last interview at SIBA had ended, Ven. Mawidharma shared her example of how "right mindfulness" worked in her own life, as we walked through the campus grounds one last time.

"Actually, I used to be married," Ven. Mawidharma told us, when we asked how she came to be ordained. "My husband was a really well-known man, a kind of social leader in Kandy. I've always liked to meditate, but he never liked that I was interested in that. He wanted me to go to parties, to be a socialite. He would discourage my meditation. I did that for a long time, but it wasn't fulfilling. So when I was fifty I divorced him, and now here I am!" She smiled. Ordained monastics in the Theravāda tradition, of course, can't be married. After she had gotten divorced and ordained as a *bhikkhunī*, she said, she felt more peace and happiness than she had known before. "But it's still something I struggle with," she continued. "It's not that I'm just a monastic and follow the Buddha's teachings and forget about being a human being—I'm human too."[5]

"Can you give me an example," I asked Ven. Mawidharma, "of when it's hard to be an ordained monastic?"

"Well," she said, after thinking for a moment, "a few years ago my only brother got married. It was a big wedding, on a boat off the shore in Colombo. It was going to be a big party to celebrate his life and new wife. And I wanted to go, to be part of it. But he didn't invite me. He said it would be odd to have a monastic there, that people wouldn't feel able to celebrate as much." She paused, and looked a little sad, even now. "I know he's right. And I know I shouldn't want to have gone to that. But I still feel sad about it." She smiled again, though, and said, "Mindfulness helped me to feel OK, to see it for what it was. As a passing thing. And I thought, so it goes."

It is in these real-life, work-in-progress kinds of moments that we can see how mindfulness can be put to use in everyday experience, and not simply as ideal abstractions of Buddhist teachings or in isolated scientific activity.

As Ven. Mawidharma was accompanying us around the SIBA campus after our final monastic interview, we stopped by to see the elephants, who were kept there between festival parades at the nearby Temple of the Sacred Tooth. As we were feeding the elephants, I asked why she was being so nice to us. She had gone out of her way to help us, even with her busy schedule as director of the large institute. She told us how she had once spent a year in New Jersey when she was young. "I like helping

Figure 20. Buddha images in meditation line the Dambulla Cave Temple outside Kandy, Sri Lanka. The cave complex is thought to have been established as a Buddhist monastery over two thousand years ago; it is now a World Heritage Site, reminding visitors from near and far of the religion's long history in the country. Photo by J. L. Cassaniti.

Americans when they visit," she explained. "It's nice to help. And because I have a good memory from that time."

After the leisurely stroll she showed us the gate, and we said our good-byes. As Ven. Mawidharma returned to her work, Shermilla and I headed back to town to continue the long task of transcribing and translating the interviews, and to begin to think about mindfulness in lay life.

Lay Life and the Power to Get By

With the monastic part of the research over, the two of us turned to the investigation of mindfulness outside the monastery, and with it the more everyday powers gained and practiced in mindfulness. I was a little bit worried about this final leg of the data-gathering project, after having completed the Thai, Burmese, and ordained Sinhalese section. I felt a more apparent gap between the ordained and lay communities in Sri Lanka compared with the relatively more socially interconnected Buddhists in mainland Theravāda Asia, perhaps because of my own preconceived notions of Sri Lanka, given the lifetime commitment of the monastics that kept most Sri Lankan Buddhists from trying out ordained life, or because of my perception of the more prominent religious multiplicity in Sri Lankan society that kept mainstream society from becoming as embedded in Buddhist thought, as I had found elsewhere. Besides a few assurances that regular laypeople would also have thoughts and ideas about mindfulness—as Rushma's example and others had suggested—the general view I got from people I was speaking to while out around town was that I wouldn't learn much at all about mindfulness from the general population.

This general view was reinforced especially one day while I was at the Queen's Hotel in Kandy, a kind of decadent leftover from the island's former colonial heyday in the center of town. Shermilla and I were having tea in the fancy courtyard, going over the monks' interviews, when an older expat British-Japanese couple sitting nearby joined in our conversation. The two of them were interested in Buddhism, but they didn't believe that the Buddhist people they were living among knew much about something like mindfulness. "It's a waste of your time to ask people around here," they told me when I described my plan to conduct interviews on the topic. "[Regular people] have no idea. If you really want to learn about mindfulness, and about Buddhism, you have to talk to the monks, or look outside Sri Lanka, online, at the real teachers." They offered me web links to Thich Nhat Hanh and to some Japanese Buddhist meditation masters, and gave me the phone number of a foreign monk living in Colombo who ran a mindfulness-based mental health clinic, and said I should contact him. They were adamant that it was a lost cause to talk to regular people. "But you've been living here for years and don't know the language at all," I said. "How can you know what people do or don't know if you can't even talk to them?" They were confident, however, and wished us well as they left.

I followed up on their Colombo contact, and on the more international monks, but I wanted to know what the people around me thought, too. I was in a copy center across the street from my guesthouse soon after the conversation with the expats, printing up interviews to bring to the local university to talk with the students there, when a local man paying for a copy at the cash register happened to glance at the pages coming out of the printer. He noticed the Pali word "sati" peppered throughout the Sinhalese script.

"Mindfulness!" he said to me in English. "That's a great topic! I just came back from three years in England and learned how to use it for sports. I knew about it as a Buddhist before too, and now I'm using it to coach the Kandy rowing team." I was surprised, and as a rower as much as a foreigner I was happy to hear his enthusiasm. Back in my college town in the United States, the university's crew coach Arthur also happened to be the town's meditation instructor. I was reminded that the people around me were local but not necessarily provincial, and that the global circulation of mindfulness was part of the local scene.[6] And I was reminded that evidently, contrary to what the expats had warned, "even" regular Sri Lankan people would know about mindfulness. Lay Buddhist followers in Sri Lanka typically visit their local monastery regularly, to learn to meditate on days like the full moon *poya* festivals, to pay homage to the Buddha and the monks, and to perform *puja*, a ritual of merit making connected in name to the Hindu ritual practice and the similar Buddhist activity of making merit in Thailand and Burma. Many have gone to specialized dhamma schools too, and they learn about Buddhism generally in the everyday social settings around them, making mindfulness an "obvious" part, as Dr. Obeyesekere had put it, of lay life in Sri Lanka.

Invigorated from the conversation with the man at the copy shop, I took a three-wheel trishaw out to the sprawling campus of the University of Peradeniya the next morning to begin finding laypeople to interview. Even though they weren't religious specialists, the students there would be a good place to start the lay data collection, I felt, as they would be more familiar with the social science style of audio-recording, interview, and fill-in-the-blank formats of research I was conducting. Rushma had put me in touch with her graduate professor Dr. Danesh, the University of Peradeniya's chair of the Department of Psychology, and Dr. Danesh in turn brought me to the head of the Pali Studies Department, a wizened, busy monk. He in turn assigned Mrs. Indira, one of his lecturers, to serve as my research assistant, and Mrs. Indira and I spent the next few weeks on the campus sitting with students in the courtyards and shady study areas, talking about mindfulness. The students knew a lot, we found, and had a lot to say on the subject.

The first person we approached was sitting at a large table in an otherwise empty study hall in an upstairs cafeteria, her books scattered around her in preparation for an upcoming chemistry exam. Hesitant to bother her, we tentatively explained our purpose and our goal in speaking with non-specialists about Buddhism, without a possible bias of scheduled interviews set up by the department, and she immediately agreed to help. She moved aside her piles of books and invited us to sit down, curious about what we would ask. She introduced herself as Thikshika, a third-year student at the university. She was direct and reflective as she shared her thoughts.

"Oh, yeah!" Thikshika nodded confidently when we asked her if she knew about sati, and asked her to define it. "All of Buddhism stresses sati. It's in the Satipaṭṭhāna. And in the Eightfold Path. In my opinion, mindfulness means having good attention. Like right now, studying for this test, I have to concentrate on it. I have a lot of pressure to do well. I can let that pressure get to me, and then I wouldn't have sati, but if I use sati to study I can do well."

Thikshika and the many others we would interview at the university and around town directly countered the claim made by the expats we had met that people wouldn't know about mindfulness, or that they wouldn't know much. The answers of laypeople weren't as technical as those of the monks had been, which was true in Thailand and Burma as well, yet in their different contextualization and elaborations they demonstrated a personally interpreted engagement with the concept.

Students especially discussed mindfulness as a kind of inquiry—especially as an inquiry of the right kind. "Sati is a type of investigation," one told us, after our interview with Thikshika had ended and she had returned to her work. "It is to investigate something in an intelligent manner." "Sati is seeing correctly," another said, and he paused to reflect: "By correctly, I mean seeing the things that I recognize to be correct." When we asked how one developed and improved in mindfulness, students discussed practices similar to those the monks had mentioned, especially bringing in the techniques of *ānāpānasati* (breathing), *samatha* meditation (concentration), *metta-bhāvanā* (loving-kindness meditation), and *buddhanussati-sati* (recollecting the qualities of the Buddha). The students learned these techniques, they told us, from their parents to some extent, in the general sense of "concentrating in order to do work neatly and properly," as one student put it, and also especially from the weekly lay dhamma schools (sometimes also referred to as "Buddhist Sunday schools") taught by monks, which many of them had attended as children. Unlike in Thailand and Burma, where most laypeople said they first learned about mindfulness from their parents, most laypeople in Sri Lanka said they learned about it at these more structured religious settings. The dhamma schools were raised in interviews and also by over half (65 percent, or 68) of the 105 laypeople we gathered questionnaires from, making them the most popular source for lessons on mindfulness.

To see just what kinds of lessons were being taught at these centers, Bhante Chandrasana, who was continuing to go out of his way to help me with the research, looked through more of the textbooks used in the dhamma schools. The teachings in them were similar to the ways that laypeople talked about mindfulness. In the seventh grade, for example, students are instructed to sit with a firm posture, breathe quietly as they close their eyes, and recite in a Pali chant: "I undertake the refuge to refrain from taking the life of another living being, from stealing, committing adultery, and lying." They are told to breathe normally and count the breaths in and the breaths out one at a time, and at the end to say, "May this meditation benefit me in this and the next life, and finally in the attainment of *nibbāna*," transferring the merit from their meditation to the gods. In grade eight they are taught "right mindfulness" in a lesson on the Eightfold Path, and in grade nine they learn about meditating on mindfulness in a long descriptive lesson that uses the metaphor of the body as being like an anthill, full of impure pores and orifices where little creepers "move in and out without any value."

Most of the laypeople we talked to brought up these kinds of lessons they had learned about mindfulness at these dhamma schools and at other *dhampasala* centers, which freely distribute the books at most of the monasteries around the country, and even, I was told, within the public school system. They also mentioned other books that influenced their understandings, including the canonical suttas and commentaries themselves, *jataka* stories (the stories of the Buddha's past lives), and other local and national centers, temples, and teachers. Yet even as the teachings and teachers are important, most students and other laypeople told us that they learned about mindfulness mostly through practice, rather than mainly through textual reading.

As in Thailand and Burma, when I asked people in Sri Lanka to talk about a time when they felt mindfulness to be especially absent or lacking, they talked about anger. "The mind is lost then," one student put it, "and so we can't see as clearly." Anger was the most common instance of losing sati—the clear "winner" in both surveys and interviews, with

80 (59 percent) of the 136 surveyed choosing it—but people also mentioned not having a lot of sati at times of feeling distracted ("when my
mind wanders and I lose concentration," said one, describing feeling stress
while doing his school assignments); being careless ("like one time when I
jumped off the top of a waterfall," someone else told us, "and only later
realized how dangerous it had been"); and other instances of anxiety, for-
getfulness, sadness, busyness and general feelings of preoccupation and
distraction. There is, in a sense, a similar perspective across the Theravāda
region on the negative potential for the mind to become distracted, and
the importance of training in mindfulness to help bring it back.

While moments of anger and a lost mind are not considered good experiences to have, some people we spoke with saw them as instructive incidents for training and improving in mindfulness. "Usually I try to have
more mindfulness when someone blames me for something," a thoughtful
psychology major reported, and recalled a friend who had accused him
of doing something wrong. "It's like an opportunity to test my patience."
Another talked about a time he made a bad decision and didn't have mindfulness—"it was a situation with sensitive emotions," he said, "and so
now when I have to make a decision I have more mindfulness than usual,
because of that other time." One student talked about how he got angry at
a friend and blamed the friend for something for no reason—"It happened
because of my aggressiveness," he said. "I didn't have sati then." When I
asked how he would define sati, he replied, "Calmness of mind." People
discussed mindfulness as a way to "stabilize" the mind and gain power and
control over it, especially during these difficult emotional incidents.

Though especially significant for laypeople, this attention to moments
of distraction or anger as a lesson for mindfulness had been true for
monks too. "When I'm angry," one monk had put it, "if people talk to
me roughly, I actually call myself by name and say 'Now is the time to
direct your mind! Now is the time you have to direct it and watch it and
be mindful!' It's like I give that command to my mind. My friends have
noticed that I'm often calm even when people treat me poorly. They ask
me, 'How are you able to think so calmly?' It's from mindfulness."

Meditation, not surprisingly, was cited by laypeople as the most common time when they felt a heightened sense of mindfulness, as it was by
every other group I had spoken with across all groups of informants in
all three countries. Meditation was referred to by laypeople in Sri Lanka

most often using the terms *bhāvanā* and *samatha*, pointing again to the relative attention to focus and concentration. Cleaning, spending time alone, studying, chanting, making merit, and walking were also popular times for mindfulness among the students and other laypeople who spoke with us around Kandy. Unlike in Thailand and Burma, almost no one mentioned driving as a time of feeling particularly mindful or mindless, which seemed strange to me, given driving's unusually prominent illustrative popularity—until I was riding around town in the rickshaws that are such a standard means of transportation and realized that most people don't have any experience with driving.

That people wouldn't mention driving as a time of heightened mindfulness because they didn't drive seems obvious in a sense, and even inconsequential, but it is important to think about, because it suggests that many of the qualities assumed as obvious in mindfulness practice may also be embedded in such obvious social realities, with the nuances that those particular instances reflect, as much as if not more than reflecting a kind of universal experience of what the concept looks like "underneath" the noise of particular cultural realities. Mindfulness in driving may be different from the mindfulness of reading, or even the mindfulness of meditating in one style or another; and these differences matter when some sets of behaviors are emphasized over others in a particular social context.

Ghosts, Mental Health, and Mindfulness in a Multireligious Psychiatric Setting

As in Thailand and Burma, the connection between mindfulness and mental health is very much a part of Sri Lankan ideas about the place of sati in psychological experience. And as in the other countries, for some people ghosts are part of this. The South Asian *bhūt* and dangerous *malayakā* that are said to inhabit the island look slightly different from the *phi* and *khwan* of Thailand, or the *nat* and *dta-se* in Burma, but the pan-Buddhist hungry ghosts, or *peta*, and other similar phenomena across the region share one quality: monks and laypeople alike agree that a mind with sati helps to keep them away. A person with sati is seen to have control over such negative influences, which affect those with weaker or absent mindfulness. Whether "psychologized" as animized interpretations of mental attachments, or "enchanted" as alternative ontological realities, these "spirits" of Sri Lanka draw in similar ways on theories about the balance of the mind and the unhealthy effect of a distracted mind (R. Langer 2007, 9). The concept of the *khwan* so popular in northern Thailand is absent in Sri Lanka, but people do wear similar-looking white strings (called *pirit-nula*, chanting thread) around their wrists, and use them in religious rituals in similar protective ways. Their efficacy, I was told, mostly comes from magical ritual chants rather than as reminders of mindfulness per se, but they also have emotional, mindfulness-related connections: the Satipaṭṭhāna Sutta is one of the texts used in these chants (R. Langer 2007, 10), and the experience of listening to them is thought to be "soothing, healing, and a meditation . . . the monk tying the holy thread on the wrists [is] catering to human anxieties and fears" (Wickremeratne 2006, 168).

Phra Thēp had described mindfulness similarly as like a steady hand that keeps away the blurriness of a shaken photo. This feeling of shakiness, and the steadiness that mindfulness brings, was evident too in narratives from monks and laypeople in Sri Lanka, and for a wide range of instances, especially in relation to the potentially disturbing influence of ghosts.

> As a result of the lessening of sati our body will be haunted by spirits, and we will be like the puppets of those spirits. If people are mindful in their daily activities, and have the right mindfulness as taught in Buddhism, their minds are unshaken by anything inhuman, like ghosts—and things like that.
>
> I believe individuals who are weak in mindfulness are highly vulnerable to the influence of spirits, while strong mindfulness is unshaken by any beings or objects.
>
> From my understanding, when we develop sati, our mind becomes sharpened. Much sharper than at a regular moment. Then, what we see, what we hear, and what we feel, the spirit of seeing, the spirit of hearing and feeling, becomes wider. What I can see normally is limited, and when I develop sati I can see more.

The "spirit" of feeling and hearing and seeing that the monk in the last quote above talked about in the context of meditation was his own, as part of his personal experience with sati. The beings or objects that are described as shaking a mind without mindfulness are the kinds of disturbances that are thought to lead to mental disorders. Some said that they didn't believe in the supernatural, but even they connected it to mindfulness in other ways. "I don't believe in those kinds of things," one monk had told us. "If you don't have a lot of sati you'll be distracted by those kinds of things." Though his point was different from others in saying that it was belief in the supernatural rather than the supernatural itself that was the distraction, it was similar in another sense: mindfulness was connected to not being distracted or diverted mentally.

Whether supernatural or natural, the link between mindfulness and mental health was clear for almost all whom Shermilla, Bhante Chandrasana, Mrs. Indira, and I spoke with in and around Kandy. While the doctors at the hospital would be more direct in their discussions of a connection between the two, some of the monks and laypeople had pointed to it explicitly too: "Doctors, especially psychiatrists, they have to pay attention to mindfulness," a monk had said, "because many people, those who lack sati, they're more susceptible to catch some diseases. Without sati they're very worried, and hurried, and so there is also depression, and so many stressors, and diseases. I believe that all the doctors as a basic psychological practice must teach the value of sati, or not to hurry in life." A student at the university had tied the internationally driven mindfulness-based clinical therapies put forward by Jon Kabat-Zinn to the kind of "right mindfulness" of the Four Foundations of Mindfulness in the Satipaṭṭhāna Sutta: "Doctors already use some forms of mindfulness in their jobs," he had said. "For example, in the Mindfulness Based Cognitive Therapy [MBCT] system, M stands for mindfulness. Usually doctors make patients aware of their bodies and disease. This is also a component of kayānupassanā meditation. In my view, it's better if they can learn the Buddhist approach more thoroughly." Even an old layman in a rural area near Kandy brought together science and religion in his telling of mindfulness: "Doctors can treat psychotic patients by teaching them the idea of sati in addition to giving them medicine, and by instituting meditation programs. While concentrating in meditation, mindfulness paves the way to the relinquishment of addiction." After hearing these reflections from monks and laypeople in the area, I went see how doctors themselves felt about mindfulness in Kandy, and its place and practices in their own treatments at the hospital.

The Kandy General Hospital is a busy place, located in the center of the city and packed with people, many lying on stretchers in the halls, and the rooms over capacity. Dr. Danesh had put me in touch with the main psychiatrist of the mental health ward, and after an elaborate series of official letter stamping and introductions in offices of the mazelike grounds, the doctor agreed to allow me to carry out the research, and said he would help with it. The mental health clinic occupies a ward area at the top floor of one of the hospital's buildings, as well as a housing compound in the woods at the back of the hospital complex. At the upstairs clinic outpatients can stop in to speak to the doctors and get prescriptions filled, while the compound at the back was reserved for inpatients, who stayed at the hospital for periods of a few days to a few months or longer. The doctor that met me when I showed up the first day of interviews brought me to the back compound to find Dr. Tashan, the head psychiatrist on duty, who was working in that wing for the day. The compound was constructed like a very large pavilion, open-air at the sides but with bars to keep the patients inside. I could see people lying on their beds in the darkness, with a few wandering around listlessly, and others voicing a kind of low wail into the air.

A few nurses were walking in and out of the covered area of the pavilion with their white nurse's hats, some passing through the small wooden building to the side that served as the doctor's office. This small building had a more comfortable look than the main pavilion, with books lining the shelves and piles of folders on the desk. Mrs. Indira was lecturing at the university that day, and Shermilla was busy with schoolwork, so Rushma's cousin and her friend had joined me to conduct the interviews. Dr. Tashan looked busy, but like so many others he kindly agreed to take some time from his schedule to speak with us about mindfulness. His perspectives were in many ways similar to those of the monks and laypeople I had talked with; he, like they, emphasized concentration and focus, and how that ties in to correct practice. "From my parents, and in the dhamma school, I learned that we have to focus our mind on something," he told us, "to concentrate our mind on, say, respiration, on breathing in and out. Like, we have to concentrate on a certain point, so the mind does not go [away]. This is the right way to practice sati, following the Eightfold Path."

We asked him if he uses mindfulness in his practice, as a method for his own mental well-being and as a technique to help others. He started by telling us about his own use:

"Well, I have to have mindfulness every day here. Here, I'll show you. I just got this message last night, in the middle of the night." He took out his phone: "This guy, see, an outpatient of mine, he texted me at two in the morning. 'I'm standing on the railway tracks,' he wrote, 'I think I'm going to kill myself. I don't know what to do. Help me.' I get texts like this. What am I supposed to do? I have to have mindfulness. I told him to come see me in the morning. He was here this morning. I talked to him, gave him some medicine, but I don't know what will happen next time." The psychiatrist looked tired, but it was evident that he cared deeply about his patients. "Mindfulness helps me," he said. "According to my experience, when we're in relaxed states, mentally and physically, we can find some harmony." And it wasn't just to be effective in treating his patients, he clearly was saying; mindfulness also helped him mentally to deal with the very real stresses of his job.

"What about teaching mindfulness?" I asked. "Do you do that too?"

"In this sort of unit, especially in the inpatient unit here, we do use it to teach. We don't use the word 'sati,' because of course we have people from every religion, so we tell them a bit, what we can. We tell them to find at least five or ten minutes per day just to concentrate, and that that will keep your mind relaxed. So during that period of time, even if they're not experiencing much sati exactly, they can at least think about daily things, no? Every day, during the ward rounds, we're talking with people, so during those periods of going on the rounds, when we think it's necessary we'll advise them on this."

Dr. Tashan pointed to the practical aspects of interacting with so many patients, and as he did he made reference to mindfulness's place as a Buddhist concept within a larger multireligious society, which hadn't really come up in Thailand and Burma, except in the context of international frameworks of the practice. After speaking with him for almost an hour, we thanked Dr. Tashan for his time, and as he left to check on some patients, a nurse came in to speak with us some more. We did two more interviews at this back compound of the hospital, and the rest in the main mental health ward, where the hallway was packed with people sitting on the floor waiting to be called, and the room inside was overflowing too. Everyone who worked there was busy, but they all made time to speak with us.

The hospital staff told us how they felt that mindfulness is a good Buddhist idea to have, and good for mental health, especially in the area of focus and the avoidance of distraction. "I don't know about the supernatural," one of the staff members told us when we asked if there were any connections to

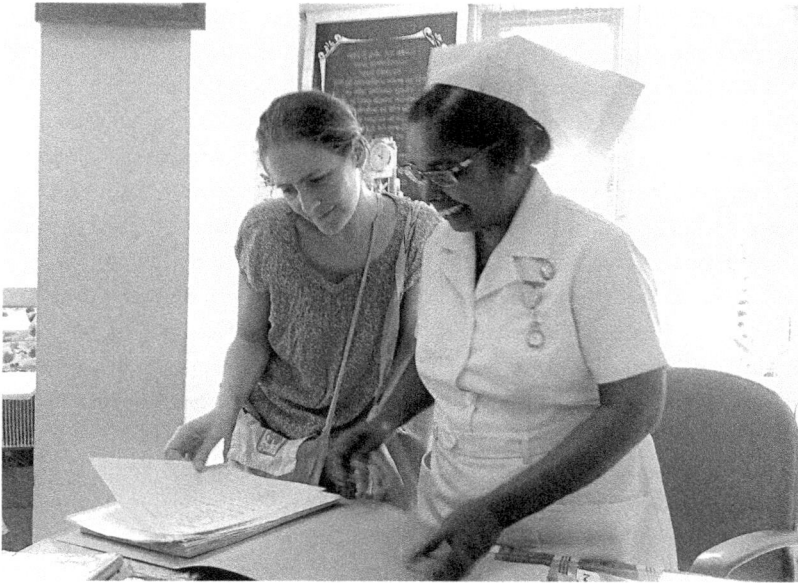

Figure 21. The author and a psychiatric nurse gather experiences with mindfulness from staff members at the Mental Health Clinic of the Kandy General Hospital in Sri Lanka. Photo by Sabrina Shafeer.

ghosts, "but if you have a lot of sati, well, I wouldn't say you're protected by anything supernatural exactly, but your mind is less vulnerable. Even clinically, we would say. It's less vulnerable to mental disorders and all of that. If you follow mindfulness, you'll avoid this negative stuff."

As a foreign researcher interested in contemporary practices of sati partly for their possible relevance to the American concept of mindfulness, a very interesting conversation I had was with two young medical residents, Ratne and Delani, who were attending Colombo University for a four-month stint at the hospital to gain professional experience, and who as part of their training had gone through a Mindfulness Based Stress Reduction seminar there for their postgraduate work in counseling and clinical psychology. They framed their understandings of mindfulness in some of the terms and meanings they learned in their internationally driven lessons, and combined them with other influences they were exposed to over their lives.

Ratne and her colleague Delani and I spoke for over two hours, with an assistant bringing in some cake and water for us after the first hour. "Mindfulness is, I suppose, to keep the mind in the present moment," Ratne said in English when I asked her to define sati. "It's being able to go back to the past with a few changes. It's being in the present." Ratne and Delani both expressed interest in the idea of incorporating mindfulness more formally into mental health treatments, even more than the other doctors or the monks and laypeople had. I asked about the course they had taken, and they said it was a little bit different from the ways they had learned about mindfulness in other places. "I mean, I learned about sati in Buddhism," Ratne said. "I'm Buddhist, so I learned about it in Buddhist school. But then, in the course we took as part of the postgrad program, I learned about it more as, like, emotion management. And for treating patients." Although particular in her own telling, Ratne invoked a present-focused, emotion-state management rhetoric of mindfulness that was very much in line with the Kabat-Zinn type of thinking of those she was learning about mindfulness from in her training.

And perhaps with a concern shared by those in other more religiously diverse settings, the main issue that Ratne and Delani found intriguing in regard to mindfulness as a mental health treatment was how to incorporate it into treatments with people who aren't necessarily Buddhist. In American settings, mindfulness's roots as a Buddhist idea are ostensibly stripped away partly to fit the practice into the meaningful framework of people following any or no religion; but Ratne and Delani didn't really believe such a move was fully using mindfulness's potential. "Right now we can talk about mindfulness," Ratne told me, taking the more active role in the conversation as Delani nodded alongside her, "but it's because you know some Buddhist words and I do too. For Buddhist patients mindfulness may be useful. But I'm not sure if I would feel as comfortable using Buddhist terms for patients who aren't." Not everyone we spoke with had the same opinion, but many had thought about the role of a Buddhist concept like mindfulness for treatments in a multireligious setting.

It is through the influence of these residents' visits to Kandy, and similar exchanges from others in the region, that different ideas about mindfulness, tied as they are to the power of the people who teach them, spread around spaces and places in Sri Lanka and the world. Ratne and Delani, like many others, were making sense of the mixture of meanings and practices of mindfulness, creating new, slightly different iterations as they transferred their ideas in practice. Awareness of the presence of people of other religions at the hospital, and training that taught them that mindfulness can help patients regardless of religion (even as in their minds it was tied so directly to Buddhism), were not unique to their own experience at the hospital. Rather than the general deference to Western science that I had found in the Thai psychiatric hospital, or the obviousness of mindfulness's Buddhist usefulness coupled with a kind of benign approval of possible new applications in Burma, in the Kandy General Hospital mindfulness was seen as especially helpful when it could be practiced as a Buddhist concept—that is, through what was considered to be "right mindfulness."

"The culture and religion someone follows is like the spectacles they wear," Ratne told me as we discussed mindfulness more. "It colors their view of the things around them." Her metaphor for the influence of religion is a classic one—it is used, for example, in a comment by the Buddhist studies scholar Richard Gombrich on the transformative process of mindfulness meditation: "In the fundamental texts of meditation, the Satipaṭṭhāna and the Maha Satipaṭṭhāna suttas," he writes in his book *How Buddhism Began*, "the meditator has to train himself to see reality as the Buddha has taught it to be. . . . The meditator moves from thinking about those teachings to thinking with them: he learns (to use an anachronistic metaphor) to see the world through Buddhist spectacles" (Gombrich 2006, 35). Ratne brought up this idea of religion as like a lens that one sees with as a way to say that she is not sure how someone from another religion, like a Muslim Sri Lankan patient, or an American (whom she takes to not be Buddhist), would think about or benefit from mindfulness as a technique of mental health. That it could be done and could be useful was certainly a possibility, she told me, but it would need to be contextualized in a different way, and the Buddhist connections that came with it might also need to be part of its package.

Others at the hospital spoke too of ways that they found they could usefully teach about mindfulness to help people—especially those, they said, "who suffer from stress and depression." They often suggested indirect teachings, made in ways that could benefit people who weren't as well versed in Buddhist ideas, or weren't Buddhist at all. They spoke of teaching "meditation" and "relaxation" as ways to indirectly teach about mindfulness. "We use mindfulness all the time in our treatments," a nurse told us, and pointed to a re-cloaking of the concept when she was treating people who had expressed curious skepticism about it, "but not always through things like worshipping the Buddha. If I explain it as deep muscle relaxation, that's not going to be as religious as something like telling them about *buddhānussati,* for example. It's the same with respiration. Respiration relaxes the muscles; anyone can use it." For most, a recognition and ability to reframe may be important, but for most the idea of mindfulness was considered to be applicable to all. Only one person at the hospital said that it would be especially difficult to teach mindfulness to someone who wasn't Buddhist:

> I wouldn't know if a person that comes in to get treatment would want to know all the religious ideas like mindfulness that could help with their issue. I suppose that the issue with the whole *anicca* situation, for example, is that we say "OK, that is the end" and you cannot die but you're always going through a cycle. When, from a Christian point of view, you don't want to end at death. You're yourself at a kind of frailty with God and judgment and all of that, so I think with *anicca* it might be worth thinking about how you might put that concept across. Because I've spoken to spiritual Muslims, and as in Christianity there are some similar components. But within Islam there's meditation, spiritualness, and I feel some mindfulness concepts involved. But you don't kind of see that in Christianity—I mean through prayer could be another way to introduce mindfulness . . . but's it's not really about mindfulness—I mean Islam, yes. But not so much Christianity.

Sri Lanka has seen a wave of recent and violent power struggles involving ethnic and religious identification. It is perhaps for this reason that Sri Lankan people seemed to be more aware of the contentiousness of religious and ethnic identity than those I had spoken with in Thailand and Burma. I didn't notice very many of what, when pointed out to me, I considered subtle differences in religion and ethnicity in the hospital, but the doctors we were interviewing did. Rushma's cousin with her Muslim head scarf who had come along to help with the interviews inadvertently illustrated this point. One of the psychiatrists I was talking with casually who knew a bit of English hit upon a word he wasn't sure how to translate into English, and sought out someone who could help. At first he called over Rushma's cousin's friend, who as a Buddhist wasn't wearing a head scarf, but she was busy talking with someone, so I motioned for Rushma's cousin to come over instead. The doctor looked at her and said to me, "No, we need someone who can write in Sinhalese." "Oh, I can!" Rushma's cousin said, a little flustered, as he nodded quickly, and motioned for her to sit down. It is this sensitivity to other religions, due as much to an awareness of wanting to both be respectful of difference and inclusive of similarity, that mostly explains why some psychiatrists and others I spoke with were particularly hopeful but also cautious in incorporating mindfulness more into their formal therapeutic practices. Even with Rushma's comment on the first day I arrived in Sri Lanka that sati is also in Islam, but that it is especially elaborated in Buddhism, the issue was not considered something to simply gloss over.

Mindfulness in Its Buddhist and Non-Buddhist Context

More than with people in Thailand and Burma, or with other laypeople or monks in Sri Lanka, my discussions with the staff members at the Kandy hospital encountered the issue that I had largely circumvented until that point: How much is mindfulness an exclusively Buddhist concept, according to the people I was doing research with in Theravāda Asia, and how would practicing it in other religions affect the kinds of findings I had been uncovering in the field? The answers seem to matter, especially because mindfulness is increasingly thought to be relevant for people who follow many different kinds of religion, and even for those who don't profess any religion at all. Mindfulness in Sri Lanka especially helps us to answer these questions. The answers speak to an issue not just about the TAPES of mindfulness, but about the relevance of these differences across them.

The overwhelming response that I got, from all groups of people and in all three countries, when I asked if one has to be Buddhist to understand and benefit from mindfulness, was that one doesn't have to be Buddhist to either understand or benefit from the concept. In Thailand and Burma, where the vast majority of people are Buddhist, the issue may not be as salient, but it was still a relevant topic to consider. In Sri Lanka, where religion and ethnicity may be even more politicized, the issue is more relevant in everyday social life. In each of the three countries, however, most people offered a very clear and confident reply of the inclusiveness of mindfulness. For the most part it was only after this positive assertion that some people articulated a few thoughts about ways that understanding Buddhism might especially help one in gaining and using mindfulness. They spoke of some of the side benefits of the practice, the indirect implications, and even the different kinds of framing that mindfulness in practice in different religious and cultural contexts might involve.

In general, in Thailand and Burma this question of the relative Buddhist distinctiveness of mindfulness was answered similarly by most people: Mindfulness is considered to be an idea that has been especially developed in Buddhist thought, but it is also considered to be one that anyone of any religion can practice and benefit from. Most people also said that understanding more about Buddhism, though, would be helpful in understanding mindfulness more thoroughly. There was also a sense that people of different religions would make use of mindfulness slightly differently—and that this was OK.

In Sri Lanka this larger pattern held, both in terms of the general feeling that mindfulness transcends any one particular religion and that Buddhism is an especially good vehicle for it. But there was a bit more discussion and variation in views on this point, which perhaps makes sense, given the relatively more politicized religious landscape of the country. People encounter a politicized religious difference every day in Sri Lanka, as compared with the practical invisibility of non-Buddhist forms of religiosity in Burma and Thailand in the areas of those countries where I collected data.

> It's really good people in America are interested in mindfulness, since they go after money and don't think about freedom, so learning and practicing sati will be very helpful for them to free their minds up to a certain point. But the problem is that there are no advanced people to educate them about correct sati, so it will be a problem for them. Without learning Buddhism, anyone can learn sati up to a certain point. But they will acquire right mindfulness only by learning Buddhism.

> In order to gain the profound understanding of sati, an individual must learn Buddhism. Buddhism is taught to all of humankind out of great compassion. Buddhism arose in India, so it is not only for Sinhalese Buddhists or whoever, but all humankind. Americans usually tend toward material development, so they expect satisfaction. . . . They must develop spirituality

out of which they could acquire the higher happiness when comparing with worldly happiness.

Sati has been included in the Upanishad tradition too, but it was not perfectly taught like Satipaṭṭhāna teachings. Teachings of sati included in other religions are only half truths. We can study about sati from Hinduism and acquire sati out of practicing yoga meditation, but to gain perfect understanding about sati one must learn the Satipaṭṭhāna teachings.

I don't know whether or not Americans use the correct methods for learning. Generally, they tend to have a preference for Tibetan Buddhism. It's not wrong. But if they ignore early Buddhism and the Theravāda tradition, it's a problem. It's better to give those traditions some priority too.

The more I learned about sati and its cultural articulations, the more I started to wonder just how much the Pali term *sati* in its Thai, Burmese, and Sinhalese permutations was similar and different from "mindfulness" as understood in English. That "mindfulness" draws from *sati* is clear, but the exact ways it does so are not. Some people relate the two as perfect translations; others separate them out as related and differently influential.

Even as I was dedicated to finding out about sati in order to broaden and strengthen the English term, rather than the other way around, I was also curious how people in Theravāda Asia saw the two as related. The two terms greatly overlap, but they do not perfectly coincide. Understanding some of the meanings of the Buddhist root was a central part of the research project I was undertaking, and through the many interviews, questionnaires, and conversations I was gathering in Theravāda Asia I felt confident I had uncovered many of these meanings. But how might sati relate to mindfulness, I wondered, keeping in mind the always on-the-move, changing meanings of each? In an essay titled "What Does Mindfulness Really Mean? A Canonical Perspective," the American Theravāda Buddhist monk Bhikkhu Bodhi raises this point in relation to larger problems of meaning and translation. "A problem in hermeneutics with intimate bearings on the actual practice of meditation," he writes,

> concerns the exact meaning of the word sati, both in general and in relation to Buddhist contemplative activity. We take the rendering "mindfulness" so much for granted that we rarely inquire into the precise nuances of the English term, let alone the meaning of the original Pali word it represents and

the adequacy of the former as a rendering for the latter. The word "mindful-ness" is itself so vague and elastic that it serves almost as a cipher into which we can read virtually anything we want. Hence we seldom recognize that the word was chosen as a rendering for sati at a particular point in time, after other terms had been tried and found inadequate. (2011, 22)

While I was in Sri Lanka I asked a few people who knew both Sinhalese and English to compare the two words explicitly. All three were monks, and each of them said clearly that "sati" and "mindfulness" are transla-tions of each other. Only one offered a slight difference in his understand-ing between the two: "Sati and mindfulness are the same," he told me, "but actually I'm not satisfied with the English term, because it doesn't encompass enough. Sometimes we can understand sati as a use of mem-ory, and sometimes as a mental function. So it can be changed according to the context." The implication, it seemed to me, was that the English word "mindfulness" may be defined too narrowly, and could benefit from being able to change according to context too.

The quality of flexibility seemed to be yet another aspect not yet devel-oped in the American mindfulness movement as I knew it. Instead of seeking to appreciate the differences in association that mindfulness may have in different places for different people in different circumstances, it seemed that most of the work I was reading about mindfulness in English-language publications sought to gloss over apparent differences in a search for what mindfulness "really is," as if it should exist as an abstract concept apart from its cultural context. Such a move is usually justified by citing the usefulness of operationalizing a concept for research and clinical ends; otherwise how can you know what you're testing and seeing? While operationalizing mindfulness may be useful for a particular research or therapeutic project, recognizing the diversity that one is choosing from in couching the concept in a certain way should be part of that project.

Happily, this tendency to objectivize the concept is now changing, as more people are appreciating the nuances of culture and context in its construction. We may not need to find one single, universal definition of mindfulness. Rather, we can understand the historical and social environ-ment that a particular working definition draws from, and its place within a wide variety of associations it may have in practice. This involves a return to the TAPES of mindfulness, through the lens of their Theravāda Asian and American associations.

CONCLUSION

Asia and the United States

The differences I have raised in this book are slight. Mindfulness in the United States looks a lot like it does in the region of the world that I have called Theravāda Asia. In both places there is an emphasis on bringing the mind to the present moment, and on being aware of one's immediate environment. In both places people who practice mindfulness find it to be a positive, useful tool for mental health. They feel that it is a powerful way to help them to be calm and accepting of things as they are, rather than what they would like or wish them to be. In these ways the TAPES of mindfulness in both places are similar: an attention to the present in time; to affective calmness; to power and mental mastery; to an ethics of practice; and to the development and realization of a self that is more connected to others and not as self-centered as in non-mindful action.

But within these overarching, general similarities are some clear differences in emphasis, which I would like to highlight here. I base this discussion on my reading of U.S. social science studies of mindfulness, as well as on the research I conducted in South and Southeast Asia. I base it also on a parallel empirical data set I gathered in the Pacific Northwestern town of Pullman, Washington, in research my students and I carried out during and after the data collection ended in Thailand, Burma, and Sri Lanka. As we did in the research in those countries, my research assistants and I spoke with a range of informants, using the same interview protocols, gathering data from 120 Buddhist religious specialists (including some meditation leaders and professors), students at Washington State University, community members, and health professionals at the university's campus mental health center. While not everyone we spoke with identified as Buddhist, they had all heard of mindfulness, and most considered it a good thing to have and develop.

This comparative perspective helps to shed light on how people understand the TAPES of mindfulness in the United States, and how these TAPES relate to those in Theravāda Asia. By drawing attention to the differences and not just the similarities in mindfulness's meanings across cultures, we can more easily recognize our own enculturated choices in practice, and expand the realm of the possible associations that mindfulness has in our journey to cultivate our minds.

T—Temporality

Mindfulness in the United States is largely about the temporal present. An emphasis on the present moment is central to virtually all the work published in English in the social sciences, with only a little bit of variation in its framing. In large part the present-moment emphasis draws from Kabat-Zinn's famous definition of mindfulness as "paying attention in a particular way: on purpose, in the present moment, and non-judgmentally" (1994), but it is common in almost all research on mindfulness. Appel and Kim-Appel (2009) refer to mindfulness as "present-moment awareness"; Brown and Ryan (2003) talk of "current experience or present reality" (822); Garland, Gaylord, and Park (2009, 37) discuss "present-centered attention to raw experience"; Marchland (2012) refers to attending to one's "moment-to-moment experience"; and so on.

I found this emphasis on present-moment awareness dominant in the discussions of mindfulness that I gathered in the Pacific Northwest too. Almost all the interviews and questionnaires collected in the area mentioned the present moment as central to mindfulness's meanings and practices, again without a lot of variation. "Mindfulness is about present moment awareness," said one student; "Mindfulness is when you are in the present moment," said another. As a third put it, "[It's about] living in the present." There was no mention at all of memory or the importance of the past on present perception.

At times social-science accounts of mindfulness acknowledge that the Sanskrit term *smṛti*, related to sati (sharing the root *smṛ*), means "memory" (Gyatso 1992), but usually this quality is glossed over in the aim of developing operational, scientific definitions that privilege the present. This glossing over is usually accomplished either by noting that the memory connotation is a relic that is downplayed in explanations of what the Buddha actually meant (just as some of his comments on karma and rebirth have been downplayed as part of his own historical context by some modern interpreters), or downplayed by suggesting that while the mindfulness of sati means in part memory, it is "just" the present-moment aspect of it that is being drawn out in the English term. Yet as we have seen from the chapters above, while there is an emphasis on present-moment awareness in Theravāda Asia, it is also augmented with a relative attention to the past, as raised in sati's connections to recollection and memory. This finding shows that memory in mindfulness is not just an archaic leftover from Buddhist texts; it is very much integrated into mindfulness's meanings today. Differing attitudes in Theravāda Asia and the U.S. about the importance of impermanence and transience (in Theravāda Asia) on the one hand, and of momentariness and stability in time (in the U.S.) on the other, may account for these differences. Judeo-Christian conceptions of idealized stability through time may influence American models of subjective experience, and while the mindfulness movement may be emphasizing a more fluid or alternative attention to time, it may also be influenced by these larger cultural orientations. The cultural relationship one has to temporality, and the many ways that we pay attention to time, are central and long-standing interests of social science researchers (Munn 1992; Gell 2001), with seemingly everyone from Émile Durkheim to Benjamin Lee Whorf to William James attending to the subject. Anthropological investigation into the cultural variation of time and temporality continues to grow (Pandian 2012; Ringel 2016; Iparraguirre 2016), and mindfulness is part of this.

A—Affect

Mindfulness in the United States is mainly about feeling happy and positive. The form that this positive happiness takes in mindfulness may be less focused on robust, excited affective states than are other (more "mainstream") practices done for mental and spiritual health in the country, yet the affective goals of mindfulness in America compared with Theravāda Asia are relatively more focused on developing a happy mind. What this happy mind looks like in mindfulness practices is often one that is relatively calm and un-riled, when viewed beside the more robust goals of exuberance in some other ideal affective approaches, but it is nevertheless usually couched as part of positive feelings (Amutio et al. 2014; Good et al. 2016; Cassaniti 2014a; Haidt 2006). Mindfulness is developed as a way to regulate one's emotions and create an optimistic, healthy affective lifestyle.

This aspirational emphasis is how people understand mindfulness in my sample of students and community members in the Pacific Northwest. "Mindfulness is about creating a higher awareness of your surroundings and yourself, and trying to get into a positive mental state," one put it. When asked if mental health doctors should use mindfulness in their treatments, a student thought for a moment and said, "Well, yeah. Being mindful means being happy, so yes, it should be, because if you think positive thoughts good things will come." A mental health professional said, "When I have patients who aren't happy with the amount of stress they have, it would be great if I could learn some tools for bringing up mindfulness." The cultivation of these positive feelings for the most part is based on the regulation of emotion, rather than its construction, though there is some of that, too. "Mindfulness helped me to control my emotions," one student said. Another, a resident mental health worker in the Pullman Hospital, discussed being "mindful of my feelings and emotions" in order to develop a sense of compassion and empathy for her patients.

Compared with the positive affect of happiness aimed at in American contexts, I found that mindfulness in Theravāda Asia was relatively more attentive to what in Buddhist terms is called "equanimity": a non-affectively charged state, which is neither happy nor sad. The difference I am drawing attention to here is very small, as American mindfulness practices also work to develop a kind of mental calmness. It may also be one of semantics; perhaps the "happiness" one gains in mindfulness in both loca-tions is "equanimity," and the difference is accounted for in the broader use of the term "happiness" in America. Yet there is a slightly different emphasis in affective goals of the practice that I think is more than just about the meaning of words. One monk in Theravāda Asia who talked about happiness told me, "If one studies sati, they can gain dispassionate happiness"; and for his part, the Dalai Lama has called the Buddhist proj-ect "the art of happiness" (Dalai Lama and Cutler 1998), but compared with American attention to happiness, talk of affect in this positive, happy way in Theravāda Asia was rare.

It is not that people in Theravāda Asia aren't happy: a book called *The Geography of Bliss* (Weiner 2008) names Thailand as one of the hap-piest places on earth. Whereas Americans might see a book titled *The King Never Smiles* (Handley 2006) as a slight, and while I do see people smiling everywhere in Thailand (the Tourism Board of Thailand has even promoted the country to foreigners as "The Land of Smiles"), in Thailand it is not considered a slight to not express the exuberance that is often considered in the West to be a part of a happy demeanor.

Psychological work on emotion across culture has in the past argued for the existence of basic universal emotions (Ekman 1992), but affec-tive and cultural psychologists have increasingly questioned these find-ings (Cassaniti 2015a, b; Cassaniti and Menon 2017; Shweder 2014). Instead of seeing emotions as things that "happen" to a person and then are dealt with (transformed, pushed down, expressed, etc.), as classic psychodynamic and contemporary folk theories of emotion suggest, the work of emotion in mindfulness practice in Theravāda Asia is about emo-tion construction as much as it is about "managing" or "regulating" fully formed emotions. Instead of the idea of being open to one's emotions and then dealing with them, as many American mindfulness studies suggest, in Theravāda Asia there is a different kind of development of affective experience. Affect theorists (Gregg and Seigworth 2010; Sedgwick 2003), phenomenological anthropologists (Hollan and Throop 2011; Csordas 2015), and cognitive psychologists (Tsai et al. 2013; Shweder 2003) are developing new theoretical and methodological approaches to engage with a richer, more culturally inclusive range of emotional experience. Not only the affective goals but also the affective construction of feeling are part of the cultural variation of mindfulness.

P—Power

Mindfulness in the United States is in large part about developing a sense of personal power and a personally efficient, effective ability to get by in everyday life. From decreasing stress to making more money in business, mindfulness in the United States is increasingly recognized as a powerful psychological practice. Compared with the power of mindfulness in Theravāda Asia, in the United States there is a relative emphasis on cultivating this power through one's mental practice for the purposes of one's own mental benefit (Tenney and Gard 2016; Bishop et al. 2004; Greeson 2009). This is understood to be done largely through the development of self-control (Black et al. 2011; Friese, Messner, and Schaffner 2012) and self-regulation (Neff and Germer 2013). Through the centering of one's self, the power of mindfulness is harnessed. This is clear in the many social science articles on mindfulness published in the United States, and it is clear too in the data I gathered in Washington, where people discussed it as a tool to use, and a muscle to be trained. "Being mindful," said a first-year student, "can help you endure a lot more than you normally could being unaware." "Being mindful of your actions can help solve conflicts," said another. A meditation teacher in the area told us about a difficult period of his life, and said, "[those kinds of challenging experiences] can help you grow the most. If you can take your mindfulness practice and apply it to those challenging times, then I think you'll get the most out of it." "Spirituality trains the mind to think about the inner self. Mindfulness," I was told by an older member of the community, "isn't a quick fix. But it's a lifestyle that can help you in the long run."

This power of self-mastery and control is also, as we have seen, a large part of what mindfulness is all about in Theravāda Asia. But as we have also seen, it is much more than this, and the spiritual, social, even supernatural foundations that it is thought to spring from are more elaborated in cultural practice. *Khwan* and other personified representations of mental energy are understood to leave and come back through mindfulness, suggesting connections to spirituality that stand in contrast to other cultural (rather than a-cultural) ideas about how power works in mindfulness in the United States. As part of the power of mindfulness, the recognition of the political and social influence of the practice is much more widespread too in Theravāda Asia, not only interpersonally or nationally but also through global exchanges of authoritative discourse of what mindfulness even is, and how it is to be understood. The power of charisma, typically associated with Christian traditions (Weber [1930] 2002; Csordas 2007; Robbins 2004), is thought to be harnessed through similar concepts of *barami* in Theravāda Asia by influential monks and politicians (Jory 2016, 2002; Tambiah 1984; Bowie 2014, Cohen, forthcoming). Laypeople develop mental strength through their own religious practices (Tannenbaum 1995) and the help of powerful others (Patton 2012; McDaniel 2010). How people exert influence on themselves and others is an intriguing topic of study, and mindfulness, at least in some regions of the world, may play a significant role in how this happens.

E—Ethics

In the United States, mindfulness is ethically good in theory, but in practice it takes a mainly nonmoral stance. Nonjudgmentality is central to experiencing and benefiting from mindfulness in American contexts. This quality of nonjudgmentality draws in large part from Kabat-Zinn's emphasis on "bare attention" as occurring without an evaluative component, but in many other American framings too mindfulness is largely about being nonjudgmental (Michal et al. 2007; Moore and Malinowski 2009; Baer 2003; Praissman 2008) and "non-evaluative" (Nauriyal, Drummond, and Lal 2006, 440) in its practice. This entails recognizing the situations one finds oneself in (including one's emotional experiences) without value judgments, and "without trying to change them" (Hall et al. 2011, 216).

This nonmoralized focus of mindfulness was also the clear case for people in Pullman, Washington. One student said, after reporting that mindfulness is about being aware of one's surroundings, "It is about being aware of the things around you, instead of having your own perspective on them." "Mindfulness is about being aware of your surroundings and the different ideas and beliefs and opinions in it," said another, "and being open-minded."

The subtle ethical thread (that it is a "good" thing to do) that is woven into the mostly nonmoral concept of mindfulness in the United States is much more elaborated and important in Theravāda Asia, where for most people ethics is a very significant part of the practice. The moral quality of mindfulness was discussed in technical terms in many different ways, but most often as part of its position as one of the items on the Eightfold Path, in the context of the Four Noble Truths of Buddhism that are thought to lead to enlightenment. (This was especially brought up in Sri Lanka.) Beyond the technical textual discussions, though, there was a wider, general sense of "remembering to do good" in Theravāda Asia that located morality within talk about mindfulness much more than in the United States. Some scholars have noticed this difference in morality, though usually by comparing a historical Buddhist philosophy to a contemporary Western science. As Gethin points out, "These ancient definitions and the Abhidhamma list of terms seem to be rather at odds with the modern clinical psychotherapeutic definition of mindfulness" (2011, 270). Most acutely, any understanding of mindfulness that insists on its nonevaluative nature might lead one to conclude that, as Gethin says, "being nonjudgmental is an end in itself, and that all states of mind are somehow of equal value, that greed is as good as non-attachment, or anger as friendliness" (273). These nonmoral perspectives were not present in Theravāda Asia.

There are increasing calls to incorporate the ethical part of mindfulness into American (and global) social science practices. Greg Murray (2015) is one advocate for this position, considering in an article on Buddhist Mindfulness Based Interventions (MBIs) that "right mindfulness is one stage of the sequential Eightfold Path, embedded in and supported by practices encouraging emergence of wisdom, ethical conduct and concentration. The aim of mindful meditation is not to decrease stress, but to foster insights into subtle concepts (or facts from the Buddhist worldview), including impermanence and emptiness. Presented outside this context, mindfulness may be weakened (is an appreciation of impermanence necessary for mindfulness' full effect?), ambiguous (does mindfulness have spiritual outcomes?) or unethical (is a sniper mindful?)" (2015, 594). These questions are important to think about in the development of mindfulness as a global concept. They also help to bring to mindfulness an increasing anthropological attention (Cassaniti and Hickman 2014; Hickman 2014; Zigon 2007; Keane 2015; Lambek 2010; Laidlaw 2002) to issues of ethics and morality across culture.

S—Selfhood

Mindfulness in the United States is largely about the cultivation of the self. The TAPES of temporality, affect, power, and ethics are tied together by common goals of developing mindfulness to improve one's life through the cultivation of and awareness of the self. But just what is this self that is cultivated? In American mindfulness studies there is a relatively greater emphasis on self-realization and self-esteem compared to how mindfulness is tied to the self in Theravāda Asia. The difference in emphasis is small, since in American settings, as in Theravāda Asia, there is a common understanding that selflessness is a positive trait developed through the practice of mindfulness, but in relative terms the self that is found in mindfulness in the United States is a more concrete and stable one. This is framed in different ways by scholars, but for most, mindfulness works through "enhancing well-being and awareness of the self" (Hamilton, Kitzman, and Guyotte 2006, 124), "self-knowledge" (Carlson 2013, 176), and more "authentic" action (Ryan and Brown 2003, 71).

This emphasis on the development of the self was clear in Pullman, Washington. "Mindfulness is about being in touch with your self and your thought processes," said one student. "It is a skill set as well as a way of being with yourself," said another. "It helps you get in touch with your spirit, your inner being," said a third. "For me," an older man who leads a Buddhist meditation program in the area told us, "for me, [mindfulness] is a spiritual path, a personal development journey."

Self-cultivation could also be seen as cultivating a "non-self" as much as a self, and so it isn't necessarily easy to tell how different this relative emphasis on the self in the United States is; but even in Pullman there was a feeling that mindfulness is a way to understand a stable, coherent self more than I found through Buddhist perspectives in Theravāda Asia. A man named Arthur, a religious specialist and leader of another local meditation group in Pullman, said that he had heard of and valued the teaching of non-self, but that it is "the hardest concept to understand. In following the Buddhist path, there are certain concepts that you can understand intellectually, and the goal is to understand them directly or truly. I feel like I can understand the concepts of the Buddhist path intellectually, but when it comes to non-self, I have a hard time understanding it intellectually, let alone directly and truly as it is. It is a different cultural way of looking at things that Western culture has a hard time trying to grasp. To me, it means there is no self, there is no entity that is a permanent me. There is a physical side to it and a mental side that are both always changing, so after an extended amount of time all of those things and ideas have passed on and been recycled."

There is a long tradition in anthropology and cross-cultural psychology of investigating variation in conceptions of the self, stemming in large part from Clifford Geertz's famous observation that "the Western conception of the person as a bounded, unique, more or less integrated motivational and cognitive universe, a dynamic center of awareness, emotion, judgment, and action organized into a distinctive whole . . . is a rather peculiar idea within the context of the world's cultures" (1983, 59).[1] In Jon Kabat-Zinn's best-selling book *Wherever You Go, There You Are* ([1994] 2005), readers are taught to recognize a particular truth about the self that is revealed through the practice of mindfulness: "Meditation," Kabat-Zinn says, "is simply about being yourself and knowing something of who that is." Through mindfulness, he tells us, "you will be in a better position to chart a course for yourself that is truer to your inner being—a soul path, a path with heart, *your* path" (xvi). But what is that "inner being," "soul path," "your path"? Whether you "are" or "aren't," wherever you go, may seem like an issue of semantics as much as science, but the concept of the person as revealed through mindfulness has important implications for how meditative practices are articulated as scientific processes.

Mindfulness-connected ideas about who the person is inform what is revealed through practice, and ideas connected to what that person looks like inform how mindfulness can usefully become incorporated into therapeutic programs for mental health. Local theories of mind, from permanent selves to non-selves to wandering mental spirits, are part of this.[2] Conceptions of the person in Theravāda Asia, about the non-self of *anattā* or the "spirits of the person in *khwan*" or others, can help to reveal related psychological, social, and political processes as they occur in cultural context.

Mindfulness in America Looks a Little Bit Different from Mindfulness in Theravāda Asia: So What?

These differences in the TAPES in Theravāda Asia and the United States point to some of the variations that are part of the larger global contemporary mindfulness tradition. But so what? Why does it matter that people in Theravāda Asia are more likely to incorporate memory and time into their mindfulness practices than are people in the United States, or emphasize in relative terms too different aspects of the affect, power, ethics, and (non-)self of the practice? Is one view right (e.g., a "Buddhist" reading, or alternatively a "scientific" reading) and the other wrong?

There are two main conclusions from what I found about mindfulness in Theravāda Asia that help answer these questions. The first is a Buddhist-centered, fairly religious conclusion, and the second is a cultural psychology-centered, fairly scientific one. They differ in emphasis, and the one that is most appealing will depend in part on one's own religious and epistemological commitments. Yet both may be useful in the ongoing development of mindfulness programs around the world, and in our understanding of the role of culture in mental life.

Conclusion 1

If we think of mindfulness as part of the larger Buddhist tradition from which it draws, then remembering the ways that people use the concept in Theravāda Asia today suggests some important subtle changes in emphasis in how mindfulness may need to be understood. Taking the Buddhist frame seriously suggests a greater emphasis on the Theravāda Buddhist TAPES in the development and practice of mindfulness programs everywhere, no matter where one is. We may all benefit, this conclusion suggests, from moving away from the American TAPES and attending more to the role of impermanence and memory in mindfulness; to nonattachment to sensations in achieving affective goals of equanimity; to social, spiritual influences and powers; to the inclusion of moral and ethical engagements; and to an understanding of the illusive and multiple nature of the self. These too may be beneficial in psychiatric contexts for better treatment outcomes. Recognizing the place of mindfulness in contemporary (and historical) Buddhist accounts also points to the need for more work on mindfulness as part of Buddhist thought in practice around the world. I have raised in this book some of the slight variations in the TAPES as they are understood in Thailand, Burma, and Sri Lanka, but the Buddhist world is large, and there are many more distinctions in this region and across Asia and elsewhere. Tibetan, Zen, Chan, and many other traditions engage with frames of mindfulness in slightly different ways, and do so differently in different places. Rather than simply seeing Buddhism as a single teaching, existing apart from historical and cultural experience, we can learn about mindfulness also as it is experienced in the always situational context of real life. Learning about these contextual uses will suggest even further elaborations of the implications of mindfulness in the diverse possibilities for living well.

Conclusion 2

If we think of mindfulness less as a Buddhist concept and more as part of a wider psychological tool kit we have at our disposal in processing the world around us, then attending to the Theravāda frames of reference I found in South and Southeast Asia also suggests some important subtle changes in emphasis in how mindfulness may need to be understood. Taking the psychological cultural frame seriously suggests that the American TAPES and the Theravāda Asian TAPES may both be valid and relevant in mindfulness's methods and results, and that we should not assume that one perspective (e.g., the American) or another (the Theravāda Asian) has any more of a universal claim to representing mindfulness's connections to temporality, affect, power, ethics, or selfhood in practice. By dislodging universal claims about mindfulness in psychological experience, this conclusion suggests that through both Buddhist and scientific perspectives we can better appreciate the reality of psychological diversity and the potential for multiple ways of living well, rather than mistaking one's own perspective for that of others. I have suggested some of these multiple ways of being by relating the variation in the TAPES across Theravāda Asia and the rest of the world, but there are more distinctions that can be made within the TAPES and mindfulness more broadly. Even more important, this attention to the pluralism in mindfulness advocates for the importance of cultural variation in not just mindfulness, but also in our understandings of medical and psychological experience.

Beyond these two main conclusions, one may still wonder why it matters to learn about Theravāda Asian perspectives in mindfulness if one isn't in that area of the world, or even wonder why it matters to learn about cultural variation in our psychological processes at all. After all, if someone is sitting in America reading about mindfulness in Theravāda Asia, maybe it's enough to say, "Well, they do their things their way, I'll do

mindfulness (or whatever) mine." Many people have this attitude, especially those who feel confident that their own way is the most efficient,
even the most rational or scientific, in working for them to lead a good life
according to their own goals and aspirations.

To this I have two final thoughts that touch on the larger implications of this project for the psychological and anthropological study of
the mind. The first implication is that as discourse about mindfulness
and mentality more broadly becomes increasingly global, we need to do
better in recognizing that this increasingly international conversation is
laden with authoritative power that can obscure the potential benefit of
its local perspectives. Rather than culture existing in spatially bounded,
atemporal locations apart from one another, as anthropologists years
ago may have tended to think, we know that the global world always
has and does incorporate movements of information that cross national
and social boundaries, and that the information in these different movements is not given equal consideration everywhere. The variation in
mindfulness around the world helps us attend to the ways that some
voices get heard over others in deciding what counts as the best or more
correct ways to practice mindfulness.

This issue returns us to my friend Sen, who continues to oscillate
between staying in his hometown of Mae Jaeng and staying at the psychiatric hospital in Chiang Mai. In the past few years it appears that he has
been getting better, but his improvements seem to be as much about taking
part in the local religious practices of his family and friends as about taking part in the more formal medical treatments of the hospital. As part of
the therapeutic treatments offered to him at the hospital, Sen has received
psychotherapy, drugs, and even electric shocks, and may soon also receive
mindfulness-based interventions.

But what will these mindfulness-based therapies look like? Sen grew
up in a Buddhist community, and stays at a hospital with Buddhist
doctors, and for these reasons alone, mindfulness seems like a relevant
concept for him to be trained in to get better there. But the American
models of mindfulness that he may be trained in may not stand to
benefit him as much as more localized versions could. Medical doctors in Theravāda Asia are only in the past few years becoming interested in incorporating mindfulness into their practice, and they have
done so largely because of the acceptability it has gained from being

seen as a global scientific technology rather than a local religious one. Yet the treatments that these doctors may employ have largely been transposed from American contexts—contexts that are considered to be a-culturally scientific but that instead, as I have shown here, include American perspectives on the TAPES of mindfulness—only to be reincorporated in different ways back into the cultural contexts from which the ideas first suggested themselves to the West. Recognizing that the TAPES of mindfulness in America are just as contextual as those of Theravāda Asia, and not a-cultural in their scientific aspirations, reminds us to keep a critical eye on universal claims to the human mind, and to the way that these claims travel over space and time. It encourages the incorporation of more locally meaningful techniques into therapeutic practices of mindfulness, as we strive for more individualized treatments in the medical fields. For Sen and others like him in Theravāda Asia, it may mean the inclusion in therapeutic settings of rituals calling back *khwan*, or letting go of affective attachments, among other locally meaningful practices. Sen's situation and the many others like it suggest the worthwhileness of resisting single versions of what mindfulness means, and what the mind looks like overall.

The second implication is even more global. The findings presented in this book suggest that even for someone reading this who may not be interested at all in other cultures, and who just wants to know about the mind and how to live well for one's self, understanding the multiplicity that exists in ways the mind works around the world may be beneficial. It may be beneficial for people everywhere, because it widens the range of possibilities to pick from in choosing how to live one's life. It may be beneficial because a recognition of psychological pluralism can open one up to greater options in what it means to flourish. Some people find living by the ocean to be healthy for them; others find solace in the woods, or by mountains or in large cities. Similarly, different ways of attending to the mind and developing one's life through intentional practice may work for some people more than others. This is part of what the global mindfulness movement offers, as an additional set of options on top of more "conventional" pop-culture, medical, and psychotherapeutic perspectives on what it means to live a good life in any one setting. Adding to the repertoire of what this movement looks like by incorporating mindfulness's meanings in Theravāda Asia opens an even more diverse mental map of possibilities. Taking seriously the lessons about mindfulness offered by monks, students, villagers, and psychiatrists in Theravāda Asia makes for a wider range of ways to live in an increasingly multicultural world.

Finally, drawing attention to the ways that mindfulness is practiced in Theravāda Asia helps to highlight, by way of contrast, some of the associations and emphases of the practice in America, emphases that point not only to attitudes about mindfulness itself but also about the mind and the good life in the two regional contexts.[3] It is in recognizing the cultural connections of these associations that we can develop mindfulness techniques that are more inclusive of cultural differences, and of different ways to live well. When American researchers recontextualize mindfulness to fit the meanings of a different cultural context (i.e. American, or Christian, or middle class), there needs to be more inclusion and awareness that this is what they are doing, rather than assuming that their perspective is objectively scientific or universal. This is increasingly being recognized in psychologically oriented mindfulness research, as cross-cultural variation is increasingly being taken into account, both around the world (e.g., Christopher, Christopher, and Charoensuk 2009) and within the United States (e.g., Hall et al. 2011). Devon Hinton and colleagues (2013) offer an excellent example of how this can be beneficial in psychiatric practice, showing how what they have called "Culturally Adapted Cognitive Behavioral Therapy" can make use of different emphases in mindfulness for different refugee populations (including Cambodians and Latinos) suffering from PTSD in the United States. Programs like these reflect a greater attention to the diversity of cultural understandings in mindfulness, and to the benefits that this diversity can bring.

These conclusions are not just confined to mindfulness: the variation in the TAPES I have pointed to here suggest the usefulness of future research into the role of culture in the workings of the mind in general, advocating for an attention to pluralism in mental processes that have too long been assumed to be universal. People sometimes think of science as located in the "West," and conflate Western perspectives with scientific ones, leading to the failure to distinguish the ways that the supposed decontextualization of mindfulness in American academic settings is very much also a contextualization in a different guise. A common trope in English-language academic research and popular culture is that the West leads the way in scientific advancement, and the rest of the world lags behind, or lives in an alternate, nonscientific present, or even a premodern past. "Mindfulness may be a Buddhist concept," such thinking goes, "but what it means for people of *today*'s global society is. . . ." Remembering the present means remembering to attend to the ways that people are living and thriving today around the world. The fact that people in Thailand, Burma, Sri Lanka, and the United States think a little bit differently about mindfulness's meanings, practices, and effects suggests that some of these meanings, practices, and effects may be intimately tied to cultural ideas and aspirations about what is true, good, and worthwhile in human experience.

NOTES

Terms

1. See the glossary at the back of the book for a full list of foreign terms.

Introduction

1. "Sen" is a pseudonym used to protect my friend's anonymity; other personal names in this book are also pseudonyms, with the exception of well-known monks and doctors, and by personal preference of informants. The town of Mae Jaeng is a pseudonym for the valley community in Northern Thailand where Sen is from, where I have been conducting ethnographic research since 2002. All other place names in this book are not pseudonyms; I preserve "Mae Jaeng" to provide a measure of anonymity for long-term research informants whom I have written about in other work.

2. Note on language and transliteration: All quotes are English translations of Thai (for the Thai half), Burmese (for the Burma chapter), and Sinhalese (for the Sri Lankan chapter). Except where different by popular precedent or the preference of an interlocutor, I follow the Royal Thai System of transliteration for Thai terms, the John Okell System for Burma, and the Sōmapāla Jayawardhana Sinhala-English Dictionary as a guide for Sinhalese. Romanization conventions vary among Thailand, Burma, and Sri Lanka in the spelling of Pali and Pali-derived words, and it has been difficult to decide how to systematically transliterate terms related to Pali in the different languages used in this research. Buddhist studies textual scholars I have spoken with have tended to suggest spelling all Pali

and Pali-influenced terms in standard Pali spelling, with local spellings in parentheses when appropriate, while anthropologists have suggested the opposite. In order to keep the local uses primary but also show their shared meanings across the region, I have chosen to foreground the regional (Thai, Burmese, or Sinhalese) spellings rather than transnational (Pali) spellings, but have included the Pali in parentheses afterward when possible. For some central terms (e.g., sati, *anicca*), I have standardized the spellings to make their similarities more apparent throughout the text, but have noted their local spellings when possible. This resolution to the problem of transliterating across language and language ideologies is imperfect, but it allows for some of the diversity as well as the commonality in ideas about mindfulness in the region. For a more thorough list of foreign terms used in the book and their local/regional spellings, see the glossary.

3. See Langer 1989 (2014); Kabat-Zinn 2003; Bishop et al. 2004; Segal, Williams, and Teasdale 2001; Garland, Gaylord, and Fredrickson 2011; Hofmann et al. 2010; Carmody and Baer 2008. A Google Scholar search with the keyword of "mindfulness" demonstrates the exponential growth of scholarly interest in the topic: between the years 1900 and 1980 there were 58 articles and books published on mindfulness; from 1980 to 1990 there were 129; from 1990 to 2000, 364; from 2001 to 2005, 816; from 2006 to 2010, 2,800; and more than 4,000 in the years since. Conferences and seminars devoted to this field of study are teeming with talks of mindfulness (including, during one of the years of research for this book, ten separate panels on mindfulness at the 2014 American Psychological Association meetings, along with extended seminars at dozens of universities and organizations, including McGill, Emory, and the Mind and Life Institute). Mindfulness-based scholarly and therapeutic programs have demonstrated mindfulness's ability to offer relief to a wide range of problems, including but not limited to those of depression (Segal, Williams, and Teasdale 2001), anxiety (Hofmann et al. 2010), and addiction (Bowen et al. 2006). See Cassaniti 2014 for an overview of mindfulness-based approaches in the field of positive psychology; for comprehensive coverage of mindfulness-based research on a range of therapeutic applications see Brown et al. 2007b, and the work of UCLA's Mindful Awareness Research Center, which includes a thorough research bibliography (http://marc.ucla.edu/workfiles/pdfs/marc_mindfulness_biblio_0609.pdf).

4. For texts and excellent English-language analysis of some of the canonical teachings mindfulness see Thanissaro Bhikkhu (2010), Shulman (2010), Kuan (2008), and Anālayo (2003).

5. Although many locations in the "West" are as heterogeneous as Asia, and this suggests a greater diversity than I am able to cover here in the "modern" or "scientific" understandings I point to, in suggesting that contemporary psychological research is not as globally inclusive or universal as is often implied I am referring to what Henrich and colleagues (2010) have termed the overrepresentation of people in "WEIRD" cultural contexts—the more Western, Educated, Industrialized, Rich, and Democratic populations that most scientific psychological studies base their work on, and who may be incorrectly seen as reflecting universal phenomena in the psychological literature. This emphasis on WEIRD-ness in psychological research has long been contested by cultural and cross-cultural psychologists (Shweder and Bourne 1984; Markus and Kitayama 1991), and now is beginning to change in the field of psychology, as cross-cultural comparative psychological anthropology research (Cassaniti and Menon 2017; Cassaniti and Luhrmann 2014) and interdisciplinary research programs (including Tanya Luhrmann's Culture and Mind Program at Stanford University, and Felix Warneken and Anni Kajanus's 2017 Radcliffe Institute Seminar on Human Social Behavior at Harvard University) continue to emerge.

1. Monks' Mindfulness

1. From Dhammathai, at http://www.dhammathai.org/watthai/watstat.php (in Thai), accessed August 3, 2017. Most formal education on mindfulness for people in Thailand comes from interactions with monks, and from the teachings and rituals practiced at the omnipresent Buddhist monasteries. While monastic ordination at the highest levels is reserved for men only, many women, in lieu of being sanctioned by the Thai sangha to officially ordain as *bhikkhunī*, or female monastics, ordain as a *mae chi*, a devout renunciate who follows the same general lifestyle as a monk, though with lower social status. Lay adherents, or "laypeople," as I refer to them here, are Buddhist followers who are not ordained. These laypeople in Thailand, Burma, and Sri Lanka (as well as in other Theravādan areas in Laos, Cambodia, and elsewhere) attend the monastery to make merit (a practice of positive karmic accrual), to support the monks, and to celebrate festivals alongside the thousands who decide to ordain at any one time. Because of a royal Thai edict in the 1930s, and a folk narrative of the *bhikkhunī* lineage dying out years earlier, those women who do ordain as full monastics in Thailand are not officially recognized by the Thai sangha, though some social movements are beginning to slowly make headway in changing this. During some time I spent working with the Thai activist Sulak Sivaraska's foundation in 2001, a group of visiting fully ordained *bhikkhunī* from Sri Lanka, Taiwan, and Indonesia were invited to walk on the traditional morning alms round in the neighborhood where they were lodged in in Nakorn Nayok, and they found that villagers overwhelmingly were more than happy to participate in making the traditional auspicious donation. Some Thai women have taken on the full ordination vows, even as they are not recognized legally as *bhikkhunī*. Such a reemergence of the female *bhikkhunī* order has in the recent past taken place in Sri Lanka (De Silva 2004; Bartholomeusz 1994) and has seen movements as well in Thailand (Seeger 2006), though the issue remains controversial. The topic of female ordination brings up larger questions about the politics of equality and gender categories in Thailand, including that of transexuality, as what counts as "male" and thus open to being a monk is itself a flexible and contested category in Thai practice (Chladek 2017; Jackson 2002). There is no doubt that the social space of Buddhism is biased in favor of males, but males usually ordain for short periods, and those that ordain are the husbands, sons, brothers, and friends of women who often take charge of their ordinations (Eberhardt 2006) and with whom they share what they have learned. The Thai Buddhist monastery is the social center for many of the activities of everyday life, especially in rural areas, and both women and men are very much immersed in monastic practices in the country. Cassaniti (2015), Seeger (2006 and forthcoming), Collins and McDaniel (2010), and others discuss some of the attitudes and politics surrounding the contentious issue of *bhikkhunī* ordination and women's roles in Thai society. While in some ways the monastery is a cloistered space for monks and *mae chi*, over the past hundred years the domain of the monastery and its teachings have become more and more accessible to lay followers through periods of modernization and reform. While my focus in this chapter is on monks, many of its points are relevant for laypeople too. Over the past ten or twenty years there has been a shift in popular perceptions of religious engagement, as practices that laypeople can take increasing parts in through meditation retreats become more common, as well as multimedia dhamma studies, and even individual readings of the Tipiṭaka, the compendium of the main teachings in all its forty-five Thai and Pali-language volumes in the popular Tipiṭaka Chulalongkon Ratchawitthayalai edition. Zeamer (2008) traces these changes in increased personal engagements with spirituality in Thailand's urban middle class. The turn toward personal, direct engagement with religious experience is found not only in Thailand: Luhrmann (2012) points to what may be a more global trend, in an analysis of personal rather than authoritatively based experiences of evangelical Christians in America.

2. There was some variation in the popularity of different definitions among different groups of people, but *raluk dai* and *ru tua* were across-the-board the most common and popular definitions. Forty-two of the sixty-six monks surveyed (63 percent) chose "to recollect," and twenty-eight of them (42 percent) chose "to know the body and mind" as a definition of *sati* (in the questionnaires participants were encouraged to choose more than one option if they wanted to, though most chose just one); while on the other end of the spectrum, at the psychiatric hospital, of the thirty-one asked, nine (29 percent) and twenty-six (83 percent) chose these, respectively. The other most common definitions offered by people in Thailand were "to not be careless," "to think carefully," and, less often, "to know the present."

3. Many of these analogies are common to descriptions of Buddhism in Thailand and elsewhere. The analogy of mindfulness as being like the work of tying an animal (here, the mind) to a post is a familiar one and draws from well-known Buddhist teachings, such as a passage in the famous fifth-century text the *Visuddhimagga* which reads, "Just as a man who takes a calf would tie it to a post, so here should his own mind by mindfulness be firmly to the object tied" (*Buddhaghoṣa*, trans. Nanamoli, 1977, 262). The analogy of the mind being like that of a monkey is even more common. I heard other analogies for mindfulness in Thailand, too: of it being like caring for a baby, who is weak and must be taken care of (Prawet Wai 1984), or like a doorman, who watches people enter and leave (Payutto [1971] 1985), and many more.

4. There are some disagreements on the specifics of these Noble Truths in the many different Buddhist traditions around the world, but in general they are thought to state that (1) life is unsatisfactory, (2) the reason for this unsatisfactoriness is that we crave and cling to things that are necessarily impermanent, and (3) there is a way out of this suffering, which is to follow (4) the Eightfold Path. For more on the Four Noble Truths and on Buddhist teachings more generally see also Bodhi (2000), Harvey (1990), Gethin (2001) and Rahula's excellent, accessible book *What the Buddha Taught* (1974).

5. Steven Collins (1990) offers a compelling critique of the idea of the Theravāda canon as a set or unalterable, full compendium of Buddhist teaching. I use the term "the Buddhist canon" for convenience to refer to the body of extant works in the *Vinaya Piṭaka, Sutta Piṭaka,* and *Abhidhamma Piṭaka* used in Theravāda Buddhist contexts, but have kept the qualifying notion of "canonical flexibility" in mind.

6. As cited in the *Navakovada*, the *Satipaṭṭhāna Sutta* can be found in the Pali canon in the Majjhima Nikāya 10; i, 55, and in an almost identical version in the Dīgha Nikāya 22; ii, 290–315. (The difference is only that in the *Dīgha*, the dhamma section contains more doctrinal items.) The translations for this overview of the Buddhist teachings on mindfulness as represented in the *Navakovada* use standard Romanized Pali spellings (following Collins 2006). Following the Royal Institute system of transliteration they can be spelled as *sati* and *sampachanya*. Translations into English of the entries on mindfulness in the *Navakovada* are a combination of my own translation work, the translation by Piyawit Moonkham (based in turn on a Thai version available at http://www.baanjomyut.com/pratripidok/navakovard/01. html), and a translation from the Thai done by the Pali Text Society of the Royal Thai Pali edition. The *Navakovada* cited the Aṅguttara Nikāya (v.1:95) and the Dighā Nikāya (III:273) as sources for the section of Dhamma-s of Very Great Assistance.

7. In Thai, these Four Foundations of Mindfulness are called *kayanupatsana, wetthananupatsana, chittanupatsana,* and *thammanupatsana*. For textual analyses on variations in the rendering of the different versions of the Satipaṭṭhāna Sutta see Kuan's (2008) analysis of three Pali versions from Sri Lanka and southern China, and Mahāsī Sayādaw's introduction to his Burmese translation and his *Satipaṭṭhāna Vipassanā Meditation: Criticisms and Replies* (1979). "Paṭṭhāna" is usually translated into English as "foundations" but has also been

translated as "arousings" (Anālayo 2006) and "establishment" (Bodhi 2000). Soma Thera's English translation of the Satipaṭṭhāna Sutta can be found at http://www.accesstoinsight.org/lib/authors/soma/wayof.html.

8. For more on theories of enlightenment in Buddhist traditions see Collins's *Nirvana and Other Buddhist Felicities: Utopias of the Pāli Imaginaire* (1998).

9. *Dhamma* is a word that is notoriously tricky to translate. It can have different shades of meanings in different contexts. Here it is raised as a Pali-influenced Thai word that everyone in Thailand knows (as *tham* in Thai, as in *thammachat*, or "nature"), but it is not easy to represent simply in English. Dhamma is related to the Sanskrit word "dharma," sometimes represented as "dogma," but while dogma has come to mean "facts" or truths to be accepted, in its Buddhist interpretation it means a series of particular truths about the world that the Buddha taught. It can mean slightly different things at different times, from "thoughts" to specific teachings to the religion as a whole. In his analysis of the Satipaṭṭhāna Sutta, Richard Gombrich says this about the meaning of the term "dhammā": "Dhammā has been rendered as '[one's own] thoughts,' but the dhammā that the text spells out are in fact the teaching of the Buddha," and uses the whole of the Four Noble Truths to illustrate ([1996] 2006, 35). As Pali expert Steven Collins has told me (personal communication), "The word dhammā is plural, and is only used in the context of the fourth satipaṭṭhāna (where the translation is very difficult) and in such phrases as *bodhipakkhiya-dhammā*, 'things' conducive to enlightenment. This plural is rare elsewhere, apart from within *Abhidhamma* texts."

10. The number of *anussati* vary in different texts; the *Visuddhimagga* lists six. Different factors are discussed in other teachings as well, such as the *ānāpānasati* or "mindfulness of the breath," which is elaborated in the Ānāpānasati Sutta. For more on the *anussati* in Buddhist meditation see Punnaji Thero (2017).

11. The *Navakovada* cites the Saṃyutta Nikāya (V:63) for the section on the Factors of Enlightenment.

12. The *Navakovada* cites the Aṅguttara Nikāya (V:25) for the section on the Dhammas for Help and Protection.

13. The *Navakovada* cites the Majjhima Nikāya (I:15) and the *Vibhariga* (235, 486).

14. The different ways that one can navigate the philosophic and administrative system of Thailand's state-sponsored Buddhist education are elaborate; a simple schematic overview of the system can be found at https://www.eduzones.com/knowledge-2-1-29806.html.

15. Wat Chedi Luang and Wat Suan Dok each follow one of the two main *nikayas*, or sects of Buddhism, that are predominant in Thailand, the Thammayut and the Mahanikai, respectively. The Thammayut sect was founded by Thailand's King Mongkut in 1830, and emphasizes strict attention to Pali studies, and to what was considered a more rational approach to the religion than the other traditions, in large part as a move to nationalize the country and keep away foreign colonial powers. Thailand is one of the few countries in Southern Asia that has never been colonized by European powers (though see Herzfeld's [2002] and Loos's [2006] discussions of "cryptocolonialism" and "semi-colonialism," and Winitchakul's [1994] arguments about internal semi-colonialism in the country). In establishing the Thammayut sect, King Mongkut then lumped together the rest of the country's heterogeneous traditions, in what he called the sect of the Mahanikai, a more open approach to Buddhist interpretation. The theoretical and practical divisions between these two major sects were very contentious in the early years of their formation (see Cook 2010, 30; Tambiah 1984; Bowie 2017), and although Thammayut monasteries are thought to emphasize language study and meditation, today there does not appear to be much of a systematic differentiation between the two. Only one monk I spoke with offered a rare though indirect critique

of the division, referring to the kings Rama IV and V and the establishment of the sects, saying that "the one who separates the sangha will be in great sin." For most people, though, the differences between the Thammayut and the Mahanikai, and hence between Wat Chedi Luang and Wat Suan Dok, are seen as minor, with the head monk and his particular lineage of teachings much more important. Monks from Mae Jaeng and other areas in the Chiang Mai region who continue past the high school level of education and want to continue learning as monks would most likely go to one of these two monasteries, or to one of the other university monasteries in the country, as would some of the adult monks who ordained after the age of twenty. Lay Buddhists and international Theravāda monks are also permitted to enroll in the monasteries' MA or PhD programs.

16. As part of the project, I administered a mindfulness scale to 705 research participants in Thailand, Burma, Sri Lanka, and the United States. Mindfulness scales are used often in the United States to assess trait and state mindfulness (e.g., Cardaciotto et al. 2008) and are increasingly being incorporated into transnational research (e.g., Deng et al. 2011 and Silpakit, Silpakit, and Wisajun 2001, who analyze the applicability of the scale used in Cardaciotto et al. for a Thai population). The scale I used was adapted from the Mindful Attention Awareness Scale (MAAS) (Brown and Ryan 2003); the Thai version was taken from Christopher et al. (2009); and the Burmese and Sri Lankan ones I created with the help of research assistants in the two countries, who translated and back-translated each item. Although our findings showed similar patterns to those found in other American studies (Brown and Ryan 2003) and cross-cultural studies (Christopher et al. 2009; Christopher, Christopher, and Charoensuk 2009; Black et al. 2012), because of the multiple social factors involved in filling in scales of this kind I have not included the results of this scale in *Remembering the Present*. I plan to write about these results and the strengths and weaknesses of using scales in mindfulness research in upcoming work.

2. The Feeling of Mindfulness in Meditation

1. This list is from the English-language version of the manual. The two language versions are similar but have a few differences based on the expected knowledge and interest of the visitor. The Thai version highlights the lineage history and royal patronage of the center, while the English version attends more to the etiquette expected of people visiting the monastery (for example, not to point one's feet at a Buddha image), and foregrounds mindfulness a bit more than the Thai one. These slight differences point even more to the importance of understanding the contextual variation of mindfulness, even at a single monastery that emphasizes the same general technique of meditation.

2. The relationship between *samatha* and *samādhi* is an ongoing topic of investigation in scholarly engagements with classical texts, but it rarely if ever comes up in regular conversation in Thailand. For detailed discussions of the relationship between *samatha*, *samādhi*, and *vipassanā* in the Pali canon see Thanissaro Bhikkhu 2011a, 2011b.

3. Lists very similar to this one can be found in slight variations in commentaries across the Theravāda world: the one I offer here is an amalgamation of different versions I came across during my fieldwork but draws especially from a version by the Thai monk Buddhadasa Bhikkhu, who in turn cites the *Visuddhimagga* (iii, 104–33).

4. Counts of these centers are from Vipassanā Meditation Center—Dhamma Dharā, Dhara.dhamma.org.

5. See Braun (2013) and Stuart (forthcoming) for more on the historical emergence of this movement.

6. The original has the Buddha saying he is not a "close-fisted" teacher, meaning he has nothing in his (metaphorical) hand to hide.

7. Many of the stories from these evening dhamma talks can be found in meditation booklets and online. The best-known English summary of Goenka's teaching is *The Art of Living* (1997), a compendium of teachings and explanations compiled by William Hart. Goenka has also written a commentary on the Satipaṭṭhāna Sutta itself (available at http://www.vridhamma.org/Discourses-on-Satipatthana-Sutta [in English] and http://store.pariyatti.org/Discourses-on-Satipatthana-Sutta-Thai--365236073618_p_4320.html [in Thai]). In his translation/interpretation of the Satipaṭṭhāna Sutta one can see a slightly higher degree of emphasis on feelings (Pali: *vedanā*, the second of the Four Foundations of Mindfulness in the Satipaṭṭhāna Sutta) and on observation: "In the Satipaṭṭhāna Sutta," he suggests, "the Buddha presented a practical method for developing self-knowledge through self-observation" (147).

8. Schedneck 2015; see also Jackson's (2003) biography of Buddhadasa, and Swearer's (1989) translation of his teaching on attachment and personhood *Me and Mine*. Other well-known works by Buddhadasa Bhikkhu that have been translated into English include his *Handbook for Mankind* (2005), *The A, B, Cs of Buddhism* (1982), *No Religion* ([1967] 1996), and *Mindfulness with Breathing* ([1989] 2006).

9. Buddhadasa has published a description of his interpretation of the teaching of the *Paṭiccasamuppāda*, the "Wheel of Dependent Origination" (Buddhadasa 1992). I discuss the example of the bee sting more in my book *Living Buddhism* (Cassaniti 2015c) and in "Unsettling Basic States: New Directions in the Cross-Cultural Study of Emotion" (Cassaniti 2017a).

10. Some versions of the Satipaṭṭhāna Sutta (including Soma Thera's English version) include a section heading of *ānāpānasati*, while others do not. The relative importance or integration of the Ānāpānasati Sutta is debated by Buddhist studies scholars. There are online discussion forums about how and whether the technique of *ānāpāna* could be considered part of the *kayānupassanā* (e.g., http://www.buddhismwithoutboundaries.com/showthread.php?3204-Sati-patthana-Sutta-vs-Anapanasati-Sutta-how-they-differ/page2, and http://www.vipassana.com/meditation/foundations_of_mindfulness.php). Mindfulness of the breath is also discussed in other suttas, as well as in the *Visuddhimagga*, the *Vimuddhimagga*, sections of the *Abhidhamma*, and later commentaries. Thanissaro Bhikkhu's English version of the Ānāpānasati Sutta is quoted here; for a thorough anthology of canonical and commentarial texts on the Ānāpānasati Sutta see Ñāṇamoli (1964).

11. A video of this practice of *poet kam* at Wat Tham Thong can be found at youtube.com/watch?v_fermTH2lllbk. As with many other techniques in the region, it accesses ideas about power and potency in meditative practices with long histories in the region.

12. This passage is excerpted from *Botsuatmon Wham Wat Chao-yen "Wat Mae Long"* (Book of chants for morning and evening at Wat Mae Long).

3. Power and the Ghosts of Insanity in Lay Thai Life

1. A recent popular Thai song called "Rai Sati" by the band Soundlanding tells about one such moment of losing sati: see https://www.youtube.com/watch?v=Og5uUov9QIk (in Thai).

2. These quotes are samples of the most common perspectives on mindfulness's lessons from parents across the two hundred interviews and questionnaires conducted in Thailand. Less commonly than remembering some basic lesson, some people talked about learning either a lot or nothing about mindfulness from their parents, depending on their own parents' exposure and interest. Two monks I met at a monastery in Chiang Mai had very different experiences with mindfulness when they were young: "This is my personal story," said one. "I was born into a very strict Buddhist family. They taught me to pray, and to chant, and to make merit when offering food to the monks. They taught me while making merit that I should make a wish and recollect good things in my life. They taught me to meditate for one or two

minutes each day to practice sati." The second reported almost the opposite: "I was born into a family that had very little schooling, so I didn't learn sati at home. I learned it only after I ordained as a monk." For most people, however, mindfulness was taught in a general sense of learning to be careful as part of growing up.

3. Similar kinds of lessons are repeated and reiterated each year with increasing levels of detail; for example, a lesson from the third year of elementary school teaches mindfulness of the breath as follows: "To meditate, you should concentrate sati at the stomach, by using sati to realize bodily movement as the stomach goes up and down while you are breathing" (bor 3, 114). And a few years later, in middle school, a similar lesson on mindfulness of the breath reads: "Students will practice meditation according to the principle of ānāpānasati which is categorized in Satipaṭṭhāna number one, which is the body or āyaupaṭ ṭhāna, and which uses sati to condition the bodily movement or the breath going in and out" (mor 3, 99).

4. The ad can be seen on YouTube (in Thai) at https://www.youtube.com/watch?v= sumok2A8PFE.

5. For more on the notoriously complicated political context of contemporary Thai society see Ferrara's The Political Development of Modern Thailand (2015) and Haberkorn's Revolution Interrupted: Farmers, Students, Law, and Violence in Northern Thailand (2011). To put recent events into their larger historical context see also Wyatt's Thailand: A Short History (2003) and Reynolds's National Identity and Its Defenders (1991).

6. The speech can be found (in Thai) at http://morning-news.bectero.com/political/28-Oct-2013/4489.

7. For more on Buddhist textual perspectives on the self see Collins 1982. See Collins 2014 for perspectives on madness in Pali texts.

8. Justin McDaniel offers a layered analysis of this very well-known ghost story in The Lovelorn Ghost and the Magical Monk (2011).

9. I discuss these ghost stories and others more thoroughly in Cassaniti 2015b and Cassaniti and Luhrmann 2014, 2011.

10. Among other topics, Dr. Pari also talked about the influence of China in Chinese Thai Buddhist practices, and the difficulties of meditation: "During the time of King Rama V there were Chinese people and they brought the shrine. Which is like a kind of Chinese god. The God of the sea, the God of the mountain. They have ceremonies to worship their God. Have you ever noticed a Chinese-Thai person, they like to offer things to the monastery, because many Chinese have a lot of money, they're rich, they want to have a lot of merit, but they don't have time so they offer things. I mean, they're good people, but they didn't train about sati. And when we talk about sati, and when the monks teach about sati, they teach in the monks' way, which is very strict, and people who don't go to the monastery often will have difficulty [presumably pointing to the difficulty of meditation]. Because people aren't used to that kind of environment, the environment that's very quiet. The environment that people are used to is a working environment. When they practice sati they go to the temple instead of practicing at home."

4. Burma: A Fine Mist, or a Cave in the Woods

1. As in Thailand, Theravāda Buddhism is the dominant religion in Burma, followed by the overwhelming majority of its people. As in Thailand, there are some relatively small numbers of people following other religions, however, and in recent years long-brewing issues linked to the oppression of religious minority groups have come more into the open, including treatment of the mostly Christian Karen people and the Muslim Rohingya population. As in Thailand, this diversity of religious practice is usually treated with tolerance but has

sometimes sparked controversy, violence, silencing, and the covering up of oppression by the people in power in the majority. For more on the representation of ethnic and religious diversity in Burma see Salem-Gervais and Metro 2012 and Ferguson 2015.

2. For more on these monks and monastic traditions see writings of these monks themselves (e.g., Mahāsī's "Lessons of Practical Basic Exercises in Satipaṭṭhāna Vipassanā Meditation" [1955] and *Discourse on the Basic Practice of the Satipaṭṭhāna Vipassanā* [1958]); see Braun (2013) for a biographical analysis of Ledi Sayadaw; see Silanandabhivumsa (1982) and Kornfield ([1977] 1996) for biographies of Mahāsī Sayādaw. Cook (2010) and Schedneck (2015) relate some of the influences of Mahāsī Sayādaw's lineage and other famous Burmese traditions in contemporary Thailand.

3. *Bhāvanā* means "bringing into being" in Pali, and can refer to many aspects of mentality in Buddhist thought. In Thailand, Burma, and Sri Lanka, some people used the term to refer specifically to meditation, a practice followed in at least some commentarial accounts; Gethin describes *bhāvanā* as one of the closest translations in Buddhism of the English term "meditation," calling it "mental or spiritual exercises aimed at developing and cultivating wholesome mental states that conduce to the realization of the Buddhist path" (Gethin 1994, 174).

4. In *Burma's Mass Lay Meditation Movement: Buddhism and the Cultural Construction of Power* (2007) Ingrid Jordt has written about the complex issues of monks' role in social activism in recent Burmese history.

5. For discussions of female renunciates in Burma see Patton 2015 and Kawanami 2013.

6. There are five kinds of *khandha*, U San La went on, repeating the list I had heard in Thailand but offering his own definitions of them: *rupa khandha* (body), *vedanā khandha* (feeling), *saññā khandha* ("conception" or "perception," processing sensory and mental objects to label and classify them; interpretation), *saṅkhāra khandha* (constructing activities like emotions and motivations), and *viññāṇa khandha* (discriminating processes, awareness of these objects; knowing). These aggregates are thought to create the illusion of a self that isn't really there (*anattā*); there are many interpretations of each of them in practice. They are discussed especially in the *Abhidhamma*, but are found in the *Visuddhimagga* and throughout the Buddhist canon.

7. That driving was brought up so often continued to surprise me, because it seemed to be just one possible example among many. But it was a meaningful illustration for many, even for monks who didn't drive and even for questions that had nothing to do with driving. One monk, when asked if and how he thought doctors and especially psychologists might want to incorporate mindfulness into their therapeutic practices, said, "It would be good if doctors and psychologists could teach about mindfulness in their work. If a person is learning how to drive, and without having the instruction of the teacher, he may cause a lot of accidents. The teacher has to teach him to put all his mind into mindfulness, as only at that time can they drive."

8. In the questionnaires that Tiri and I were handing out, the options (translated into Burmese) were "when I'm angry," "when someone died," "at difficult times," "when I'm having too much fun with friends," "when people aren't listening to me," "when I really want something," and "other," and the most commonly checked option by far was "when I'm angry," which was picked by 104 (62 percent) of the 168 questionnaire participants. It was also the most chosen option in the Thai questionnaires, at 85 (49 percent) of 175. This points in many ways to the importance of emotion in mindfulness—it might suggest "anger" as an affective state that isn't conducive to mindfulness, but it might also suggest a theory of emotion altogether different from the kind of focused anger often understood by state theories. It may suggest a model of emotion in which anger is understood to be a riled, muddled, and foggy mind.

9. *Bala* is a Pali term connected to the Thai word *phalang*, for energy, including supernatural energies.

10. The role of mindfulness in these kinds of practices has been noticed by more than just this monk and me: Ellen Langer, one of the authors of the early nursing home studies, is today one of the world leaders of mindfulness-based therapeutic interventions (Langer [1994] 2014).

11. Tiri showed me the website http://static.sirimangalo.org/mahasi/Lokadhamma.htm when we were going over Dr. Soe's interview to explain what she called the eight *loka dhamma*. "Whenever we meet with *loka dhamma* we feel *anattā*, non-self," she said.

12. In preliminary research we had gathered the following responses that participants could choose from in answering the questions "Do you think that sati is related to non-self? How?" They were: "Sati helps you to understand non-self"; "It is related to the three characteristics of *dukkha, anicca,* and *anattā*"; "It helps at the point of death"; "They're related, but I'm not sure how or how to explain"; "I don't know what *anattā* is"; "It's not related to *anattā*"; and "Other." The number-one response was that sati is related to *dukkha, anicca,* and *anattā* (with 83, or 49 percent of the 168 respondents, choosing it). That sati helps one understand *anattā* in a general sense came in second, with half as many responses at 40 (24 percent). In Thailand, 51 (29 percent) and 52 (30 percent) of the 175 respondents chose them, respectively, for a slightly more even distribution among these most common responses.

5. Sri Lanka: Moral Focus and a Stalking Cat

1. As noted in Geiger's standard translation (1912), while far from being a historical document in a contemporary sense of the term, the *Mahāvamsa* is one of the few records of the early years of Theravāda Buddhism. See also Skilling et al. (2012), along with Almond's (1988) critique of the Orientalizing tendency of Western scholars in representing Buddhism, and Hallisey's (2016) critique of this critique.

2. All interviews in Sri Lanka with the exception of two done in English were conducted in the Sinhalese language; as with the others, they were audio recorded in the language they were spoken in, transcribed in that language, and then translated into English. As in the Thai and Burmese samples, this method of data collection in the local language and transcribed audio recordings was more elaborate than seeking out only English speakers or writing answers directly into notes, but it allowed my research assistants and me to be sure that the people being interviewed were not starting out with English-language categories in their minds, or that we didn't lose nuances of language that would have gone unnoticed if the interviews were just recorded in the interviewer's notes instead of audio.

3. The general definition offered in Sri Lanka of mindfulness as concentration comes from the open-ended interviews rather than the questionnaires, where "concentration" was not an option, because of its not being mentioned as significant in the preliminary research I carried out in Thailand the previous year. Rather than gathering the most common Sri Lankan responses to the definition question and then making the Sri Lankan survey options from that, as in Burma I chose methodological consistency of the research and translated the options from the Thai surveys. This did not allow me to see exactly how many people in the Sri Lankan questionnaires might have chosen options that were especially prominent in the interviews there but not in Thailand, but it did allow me to see how particular popular Thai definitions like "recollection" were not chosen in Sri Lanka. Since differences between countries in these counts may be as much an issue of differences in translation as in conceptual understandings, I have not emphasized the results of the questionnaires in this book, and focus instead on the interview data, where "concentration" and "focus" were offered most often in Sri Lanka.

4. Mahāsī Sayādaw, who is said to be one of the proponents, if not the main proponent, of modern global *vipassanā* meditation, visited Sri Lanka in 1955, when representatives from Thailand, Burma, and Sri Lanka were gathering for the twenty-five-hundred-year anniversary of the Buddha's death. This visit may have been influential in drawing broader attention to lay meditation and mindfulness on the island (Cook 2010, citing Gombrich and Obeyesekere 1988).

5. Jeffrey Samuels has richly pointed out in his ethnographic book *Attracting the Heart* (2010) similar types of issues to those discussed here, showing how even those who have been monks for years struggle with personal attachments. If it is simple to detach, the logic of the teaching suggests, ideal mental attainments like those of nonattachment would not have become part of such a large religion followed by so many people, for such a long period of time.

6. Social reformers in the late nineteenth and early twentieth centuries helped to strengthen the Sri Lankan sangha, and in doing so helped make the religion more available to lay followers (like the international Sri Lankan rowing coach) in ways that may not have been possible before. Anagārika Dharmapāla is arguably the most famous of these reformers, and from his studies with both S. N. Goenka and Mahāsī Sayādaw he no doubt incorporated into his reforms some of the *vipassanā* meditation (including that of mindfulness) being advocated in Burma. For more on the Buddhist revivals that influenced the contemporary religious landscape in Sri Lanka see also Samaranayake 2010; Kemper 2015; Bond 1992; and Carrithers 1983. Anne Blackburn rightfully critiques an essentialized narrative of "Protestant Buddhism" or the "Buddhist revival" of this period that suggests such movements to be solely a reflection of colonial rule. As Blackburn points out, the "laicization" that resulted from these Buddhist revivals did not mean a lessening of monastic power, but rather the "continued collaboration between laypeople and monastics" (Blackburn 2010, 200).

Conclusion

1. E.g., Markus and Kitayama 1991; Shweder 2003; Kondo 1990; Mageo 2003.

2. I discuss these issues further in "'Wherever You Go, There You . . . Aren't?'" (Cassaniti 2017b).

3. Overwhelmingly I found that mindfulness offers similar lessons in Theravāda Asia and the United States. One lesson I learned from both the Theravāda Asia and U.S. parts of the research was that mindfulness is very much about how we pay attention, regardless of what we may be paying attention to. The potential for mindfulness training to alter our ways of perceiving suggests a new avenue for research into a psychological field increasingly aware of a relationship between attention and experience (Lindsay and Creswell 2015; Kahneman 2011; Kahneman and Tversky 1979). I have attended to the differences more than the similarities between them in this conclusion in part because so much research has emphasized similarities (e.g., Wallace and Shapiro 2006), but the similarities in mindfulness are also important, not because they necessarily suggest a real "core" of mindfulness under the guise of culture, but because they offer some shared approaches to experience in different contexts. Within the broader similarity there is a great deal of variation in mindfulness's associations in both places, and the general differences that I found are for the most part in relative terms. While the project for *Remembering the Present* was not a longitudinal one, the differences I found, of course, are also susceptible to moving and changing across time and space. This holds true for the differences within the region as much as between the two larger parts of the world that are the focus of this chapter. I have pointed to some of the regional differences in mindfulness in Theravāda Asia in the chapters above, but there are more differences emerging and still waiting to be found, within them (e.g., Christopher et al. 2009), across other Buddhist cultural contexts in Asia (e.g., Dunne 2015), and around the world. Within Western perspectives in particular on mindfulness there is also a great deal of variation, from acceptance-based

mindfulness therapies to cognitive ones, and from explicitly secular to explicitly religious frames. I have raised some of the variation in American perspectives in this chapter, but emphasize regional similarities over differences to show larger trends. For some excellent work on some of the many different approaches to mindfulness in the United States see Wilson 2013 and McMahan and Braun 2017.

Glossary

1. The definitions offered here are general glosses of much more complex concepts; many are extensively elaborated and debated in Buddhist studies. For more definitions and canonical references on many of the terms in this glossary see Nyanatiloka's *Buddhist Dictionary: Manual of Buddhist Terms and Doctrines* (1972). I would like to thank Steven Collins for helping with the Romanized spellings of Pali terms, and recommend his book, *A Pali Grammar for Students* (2006). All mistakes are my own.

GLOSSARY

The terms are Pali-language terms unless noted otherwise. I have listed the terms in the language spellings they are raised in in the text; many have alternate spellings in related languages, some of which are noted here.[1]

ajarn—Professor or teacher (Thai. From the Pali word *ācariya*).

ānāpānasati—Mindfulness of the breath.

anattā—Non-self. One of the "Three Characteristics" of existence.

anicca—Impermanence (Thai: *anicca/aniccang*). One of the "Three Characteristics" of existence.

anussati—Recollection, or activity of which one should be mindful.

arahat—"Noble One" (Burmese *arya*).

arom—Mood (Thai).

asomaya—Memory (Burmese).

asweya—Attachment (Burmese).

ba—Crazy (Thai).

bala—Powers of the mind.

barami—Power, energy, a kind of charisma (Thai).

bhāvanā—Mental development; sometimes referred to more broadly as "meditation" (Thai *phawana*).

bhikkhu—Monk (Thai *phiksu*).

bhikkhunī—Female monastic (Thai *phiksuni*).

bojjhaṅga—The Seven Factors of Enlightenment; related to the *bodhipak-khiya*, the Thirty-Seven Things Pertaining to Enlightenment.

buddhānussati—Recollection of the Buddha (Thai *phutthanutsati*). One of the *anussati*.

byahma—Burmese spirits (Burmese).

cāgānussati—Recollecting generosity (Thai *chakhanutsati*). One of the *anussati*.

citta—Mind (Thai *jit*).

cittānupassanā—Contemplation of consciousness. One of the Four Foundations of Mindfulness.

citta-tikha—Mental sense object (Burmese).

dāna—Almsgiving, donations.

deva-s—Heavenly beings, deities (Thai *thep, thewa, thewada*).

devatānussati—Recollecting devas (Thai *thewatanutsati*). One of the *anussati*.

dhamma—Buddhist teaching, truth about the world, mental concept (Thai *thama/tham*; Sanskrit **dharma**). The plural form is dhammā, used only in the context of the fourth satipaṭṭhāna, or dhamma-s, in the sense of multiple teachings/truths.

dhammānupassanā—Contemplation of mental formations or truths about the world (Thai *thammanupatsana*). One of the Four Foundations of Mindfulness.

dhammānussati—Recollecting the dhamma (Thai *thammanutsati*). One of the *anussati*.

dhampasala centers—Buddhist "Sunday schools" and other monastery centers (Sinhalese).

dukkha—Dissatisfaction, suffering. (Thai *thuk/thukka*, Burmese *douqkha*). One of the "Three Characteristics" of existence.

hmet hta—Noting (Burmese).

hong khwan—Calling back the *khwan* (spirits) of the self (Thai); also called *riak khwan*.

kamma—Volitional action (Thai **kam**, Sanskrit **karma**).

karunā—Loving kindness.

kasina-s—Meditation objects.

kāyagatāsati—Recollecting the body so that one sees that it is ugly (one of the *anussati.*

kayānupassanā—Mindfulness of the body. One of the Four Foundations of Mindfulness.

khandha—Five groups of existence; aggregates.

khat sati—"Cut one's sati" (Thai, colloquial).

khriat—Stressed (Thai).

khwan—Spirits of the self (Thai).

kilesa—Defilements; mind-defiling, unwholesome qualities.

kreng-jai—Deferential (Thai; lit., awe-hearted).

kuti—A monastic residence hall.

mae chi—Nun (Thai).

malayakā—Dangerous Sri Lankan spirits (Sinhalese).

maraṇānussati—Recollection of death. One of the *anussati.*

mettā—Loving kindness, compassion.

micchā sati—Wrong mindfulness.

moha—Delusion, ignorance.

mo phi—Spirit doctor (Thai).

nak-naga—Mythical serpents.

nats—Traditional Burmese spirits (Burmese).

Navakovada—A small text of Buddhist teachings, read by most monks and many laypeople in Thailand (Thai).

nibbāna—Nirvana, enlightenment; freedom from desire (Thai *nippan*).

Pali—The religious language of Theravāda Buddhism.

paññā—Wisdom (Thai *panya*).

paraloka—Another world.

paṭiccasamuppāda—Doctrine of dependent origination.

phalang—Energy (Thai).

phi—Spirit, ghost (Thai).

phra—Monk (Thai).

phut-tho—Buddha; a breath meditation technique using the sound of the name of the Buddha (Thai).

piṇ ḍapāta—Morning alms rounds for monastics (Thai *binthabat*).

pirit-nula—Protective chanting threads (Sinhalese).

pit waja—To keep silent (Thai; lit., to close the external distractions).

pom peng—A breathing meditation technique focused on the stomach (Burmese).

poya—Full-moon celebrations (Sinhalese).

puja—Ritual acts of offerings (Hindi).

put kham—To open up one's karma (Thai).

rai sati—Mad, or crazy (Thai, colloquial).

raluk dai—Recollection (Thai; lit., the ability to recall).

rūpa—The body; corporeality.

ru tua—To know the body, self (Thai).

sai sin—White string bracelet given out by monks and elders for good luck, and to keep in one's *khwan* (Thai).

samādhi—Concentration.

samatha—Concentration meditation; tranquillity. (Nyanatiloka says "a synonym of *samādhi*, though there are many interpretations of the difference between the two.)

sammā sati—Right mindfulness. One of the factors on the Eightfold Path.

sampajañña—Clarity of consciousness; awareness (Thai *sampachanya*).

samsāra—Round of rebirth; wheel of continual existence.

sangha—The monastic order. Sometimes used to refer more broadly to the community of Buddhist followers.

sanghānussati—Recollection of the sangha (Thai *sangkhanutsati*). One of the *anussati*.

sankhāra-s—(Mental) formations.

saññā—Perception (Thai *sanya*).

sati—Mindfulness (Thai *sati*; Burmese *thati*; Sinhalese *satiya*).

sati hlut—To forget (Burmese).

sati-lok—Sati of the world (Thai).

sati ne thaw—Remind someone to go with mindfulness (Burmese).

Satipaṭṭhāna Sutta—The Discourse on the Four Foundations of Mindfulness (Thai **Sati Paṭṭhāna Si**).

sati taek—Losing one's sati (Thai).

sati-thamm—"Dharma sati" (Thai).

sati ya—To remind (Burmese).

sayadaw—Monk (Burmese).

Siam—The old name for the kingdom now encompassed by Thailand.

sia sati—To lose one's sati.

sīla—Moral action (Thai *sin*).

sīlānussati—Recollecting one's own moral action (Thai *silanutsati*). One of the *anussati*.

sup arom—A kind of "mood exam" (Thai).

sutta—Sayings of the Buddha (Sanskrit *sutra*).

tang sati—Remember sati (Thai).

taṅhā—Craving.

tham jai—To come to terms with something, to accept (Thai; lit., to make the heart); *thamchai tam wat chao/yen*—cleaning the monastery grounds in the morning/evening (Thai).

Theravāda—A term with multiple meanings, usually used in reference to Buddhism followed especially in Thailand, Burma, Cambodia, Laos, and Sri Lanka, which most likely began as a monastic order and textual transmission in Sri Lanka and only recently has come to take on the sense of a consolidated school of thought. For more on the many meanings of Theravāda Buddhism see Skilling et al., *How Theravāda Is Theravāda?* (2012).

thudong monk—Wandering forest monk; one who practices the *dhutaṅga-s*.

Tipiṭaka—Compendium of Buddhist teachings; the Three Baskets of the Pali canon: the *Vinaya piṭaka* (basket of discipline), *Suttapiṭaka* (basket of discourses), and *Abhidhamma piṭaka* (Thai *phratraipidok*).

tua—Body, corporeal sense of self (Thai).

upasamānussati—Recollection of peace (Thai *upasamanutsati*). One of the *anussati*.

upekkhā—Equanimity.

vedanā—Feeling, sensation.

vedanānupassanā—Mindfulness of feelings (Thai *wethananupatsana*).

viññāṇa—Consciousness, one of the five aggregates said to make up the human being (Thai *winyan*).

Visuddhimagga—The *Path of Purification*, a treatise on Buddhist doctrine said to have been written by Buddhaghosa approximately in the fifth century in Sri Lanka.

wat—A Buddhist monastery (Thai).

yom—To accept (Thai).

yoniso manasikaro—Being mindful of each task (Sinhalese).

yup no phong no—A walking meditation technique (Thai; lit., raising and lowering the foot).

References

Almond, Philip C. 1988. *The British Discovery of Buddhism*. New York: Cambridge University Press.

Amutio, Alberto, Cristina Martínez-Taboada, Daniel Hermosilla, and Luis Carlos Delgado. 2014. "Enhancing Relaxation States and Positive Emotions in Physicians through a Mindfulness Training Program: A One-Year Study." *Psychology, Health & Medicine* 20, no. 6: 1–12.

Anālayo. 2003. *Satipaṭṭhana: The Direct Path to Realization*. Birmingham, UK: Windhorse.

Anderson, Benedict. (1983) 2006. *Imagined Communities: Reflections on the Origin and Spread of Nationalism*. London: Verso.

Appel, Jonathan, and Dohee Kim-Appel. 2009. "Mindfulness: Implications for Substance Abuse and Addiction." *International Journal of Mental Health and Addiction* 7, no. 4: 506–12.

Aulino, Felicity. 2014. "Perceiving the Social Body: A Phenomenological Perspective on Ethical Practice in Buddhist Thailand." *Journal of Religious Ethics* 42, no. 3: 415–41.

Baer, R. A. 2003. "Mindfulness Training as a Clinical Intervention: A Conceptual and Empirical Review." *Clinical Psychology: Science and Practice* 10:125–43.

Barker, J., E. Harms, and J. Lindquist, eds. 2013. *Figures of Southeast Asian Modernity*. Honolulu: University of Hawai'i Press: 123–25.

Bartholomeusz, Tessa J. 1994. *Women under the Bō Tree: Buddhist Nuns in Sri Lanka.* Cambridge: Cambridge University Press.

Batchelor, Stephen. 1998. *Buddhism without Beliefs: A Contemporary Guide to Awakening.* New York: Penguin.

Bishop, S. R., M. Lau, S. Shapiro, L. E. Carlson, N. D. Anderson, J. Carmody, and G. Devins. 2004. "Mindfulness: A Proposed Operational Definition." *Clinical Psychology: Science and Practice* 11:230–41.

Black, D. S. 2011. "A Brief Definition of Mindfulness." Mindfulness Research Guide. http://www.mindfulexperience.org.

Black, David S., Randye J. Semple, Pallav Pokhrel, and Jerry L. Grenard. 2011. "Component Processes of Executive Function—Mindfulness, Self-Control, and Working Memory—and Their Relationships with Mental and Behavioral Health." *Mindfulness* 2:179–85.

Black, David S., S. Sussman, C. A. Johnson, and J. Milam. 2012. "Psychometric Assessment of the Mindful Attention Awareness Scale (MAAS) among Chinese Adolescents." *Assessment* 19, no. 1: 42–52.

Blackburn, Anne. 2010. *Locations of Buddhism: Colonialism and Modernity in Sri Lanka.* Chicago: University of Chicago Press.

Bodhi, Bhikkhu, trans. 2000. *The Connected Discourses of the Buddha: A Translation of the Saṃyutta Nikāya.* Somerville, MA: Wisdom.

———. 2011. "What Does Mindfulness Really Mean? A Canonical Perspective." *Contemporary Buddhism* 12, no. 1: 19–39.

Bond, George. 1992. *The Buddhist Revival in Sri Lanka: Religious Tradition, Reinterpretation and Response.* Delhi: Motilal Banarsidass.

Borchert, Thomas. 2017. Educating Monks: Minority Buddhism on China's Southwest Border. Honolulu: University of Hawai'i Press.

Bourdieu, Pierre. 1984. *Distinction: A Social Critique of the Judgment of Taste.* Cambridge, MA: Harvard University Press.

———. 1986. "The Forms of Capital." In *Handbook of Theory and Research for the Sociology of Education,* edited by J. Richardson, 241–58. New York: Greenwood.

Bowen, S., K. Witkiewitz, T. M. Dillworth, N. Chawla, T. L. Simpson, B. D. Ostafin, M. E. Larimer, A. W. Blume, G. A. Parks, and G. A. Marlatt. 2006. "Mindfulness Meditation and Substance Use in an Incarcerated Population." *Psychology of Addictive Behaviors* 20:343–47.

Bowie, Katherine. 2014. "The Saint with Indra's Sword: Kruubaa Srivichai and Buddhist Millenarianism in Northern Thailand." *Comparative Studies in Society and History* 56, no. 3: 681–713.

———. 2017. "Khruba Siwichai: The Charismatic Saint and the Northern Sangha." In *Charismatic Monks of Lanna Buddhism,* edited by Paul Cohen, 27–58. Chiang Mai, Thailand: Silkworm.

Braun, Erik. C. 2009. "Local and Translocal in the Study of Theravada Buddhism and Modernity." *Religion Compass* 3, no. 6: 944.

———. 2013. *The Birth of Insight: Meditation, Modern Buddhism, and the Burmese Monk Ledi Sayadaw.* Chicago: University of Chicago Press.

Brown, Kirk Warren, and Richard M. Ryan. 2003. "The Benefits of Being Present: Mindfulness and Its Role in Psychological Well-Being." *Journal of Personality and Social Psychology* 84, no. 4: 822–48.

Brown, Kirk Warren, Richard M. Ryan, and J. David Creswell. 2007a. "Addressing Fundamental Questions about Mindfulness." *Psychological Inquiry* 18, no. 4: 272–81.

———. 2007b. "Mindfulness: Theoretical Foundations and Evidence for Its Salutary Effects." *Psychological Inquiry* 4, no. 11: 211–37.

Buddhadasa Bhikkhu. (1967) 1996. *No Religion*. Translated from the Thai by Bhikkhu Punno. Suan Mokkh, Thailand.

———. (1989) 2006. *Mindfulness with Breathing: Getting Started*. Adapted and translated by Santikaro Bhikkhu. Woodinville, WA: Atammayatarama Buddhist Monastery.

———. 1990. *The Buddha's Doctrine of Anattā*. Bangkok: Vuddhidamma Fund.

———. 1992. *Paticcasamuppada: Practical Dependent Origination*. Nonthaburi, Thailand: Vuddhidamma Fund.

Cardaciotto, L., J. D. Herbert, E. M. Forman, E. Moitra, and V. Farrow. 2008. "The Assessment of Present Moment Awareness and Acceptance: The Philadelphia Mindfulness Scale." *Assessment* 15, no. 2: 204–23.

Carlson, Erika N. 2013. "Overcoming the Barriers to Self-Knowledge: Mindfulness as a Path to Seeing Yourself as You Really Are." *Perspectives on Psychological Science* 8:173–86.

Carmody, J., and R. A. Baer. 2008. "Relationships between Mindfulness Practice and Levels of Mindfulness, Medical and Psychological Symptoms and Well-Being in a Mindfulness-Based Stress Reduction Program." *Journal of Behavioral Medicine* 31:23–33.

Carrithers, Michael. 1983. *The Forest Monks of Sri Lanka*. London: Oxford University Press.

Cassaniti, Julia. 2006. "Toward a Cultural Psychology of Impermanence in Thailand." *Ethos: The Journal of Psychological Anthropology* 34:58–88.

———. 2013. "Rural DJ." In *Figures of Southeast Asian Modernity*, edited by J. Barker, E. Harms, and J. Lindquist, 123–25. Honolulu: University of Hawai'i Press.

———. 2014a. "Buddhism and Positive Psychology." In *Positive Psychology of Religion and Spirituality across Cultures*, edited by Chu Kim-Prieto, 101–24. New York: Springer.

———. 2014b. "Meditation and the Mind: Neurological and Clinical Implications of Buddhist Practice." *Pratcha: Chiang Mai University Journal of Philosophy and Religion*. Spring.

———. 2015a. "Asanha Bucha Day: Boring, Subversive, or Subversively Boring?" *Contemporary Buddhism* 16, no. 1 (May): 224–43.

———. 2015b. "Intersubjective Affect and Embodied Emotion: Feeling the Supernatural in Thailand." *Anthropology of Consciousness* 26, no. 2: 135–46.

———. 2015c. *Living Buddhism: Mind, Self, and Emotion in a Thai Community*. Ithaca, NY: Cornell University Press.

———. 2016. "Return to Baseline: A Woman with Non-acute, Remitting Psychosis in Thailand." In *Our Most Troubling Madness: Case Studies in Schizophrenia across Cultures*, edited by Tanya Luhrmann and Jocelyn Marrow, 167–79. Oakland: University of California Press.

———. 2017a. "Unsettling Basic States: New Directions in the Cross-Cultural Study of Emotion." In *Universalism without Uniformity: Explorations in Mind and Culture*, edited by Julia Cassaniti and Usha Menon, 101–14. Chicago: University of Chicago Press.

——. 2017b. "'Wherever You Go, There You . . . Aren't?' Non-self, Spirits, and the Concept of the Person in Thai Buddhist Mindfulness." In *Meditation, Buddhism, and Science*, edited by David McMahan and Erik Braun, 133–51. New York: Oxford University Press.

Cassaniti, Julia, and Jacob Hickman. 2014. "New Directions in the Anthropology of Morality." *Anthropological Theory* 14, no. 3: 251–62.

Cassaniti, Julia, and Tanya Luhrmann. 2011. "Encountering the Supernatural: A Phenomenological Account of Mind." *Religion and Society* 2:37–53.

——. 2014. "The Cultural Kindling of Spiritual Experiences." *Current Anthropology* 55, no. 10: 333–43.

Cassaniti, Julia, and Usha Menon. 2017. *Universalism without Uniformity: Explorations in Mind and Culture*. Chicago: University of Chicago Press.

Chiesa, A., and A. Serretti. 2009. "Mindfulness-Based Stress Reduction for Stress Management in Healthy People: A Review and Metaanalysis." *Journal of Alternative and Complementary Medicine* 15:593–600.

Chladek, Michael. 2017. "Making Monks, Making Men: The Role of Buddhist Monasticism in Shaping Northern Thai Identities." PhD diss., University of Chicago.

Christopher, M. S., S. Charoensuk, B. D. Gilbert, T. J. Neary, and K. L. Pearce. 2009. "Mindfulness in Thailand and the United States: A Case of Apples versus Oranges?" *Journal of Clinical Psychology* 65, no. 6: 590–612.

Christopher, Michael, Varinthorn Christopher, and Sukjai Charoensuk. 2009. "Assessing 'Western' Mindfulness among Thai Theravāda Buddhist Monks." *Mental Health, Religion & Culture* 12, no. 3: 303–14.

Chung, Jason. 2015. "How Can I Become a Person? The Paradoxical Nature of the Ideal Self within Whoonga Addiction in South Africa." Department of Anthropology, Washington State University.

Cohen, Paul. Forthcoming. *Charismatic Monks of Lanna Buddhism*. Chiang Mai, Thailand: Silkworm.

Collins, Steven. 1982. *Selfless Persons: Imagery and Thought in Theravāda Buddhism*. Cambridge: Cambridge University Press.

——. 1990. "On the Very Idea of the Pāli Canon." *Journal of the Pāli Text Society* 15:89–126.

——. 1998. *Nirvana and Other Buddhist Felicities: Utopias of the Pāli Imaginaire*. New York: Cambridge University Press.

——. 2006. *A Pali Grammar for Students*. Chiang Mai, Thailand: Silkworm.

——. 2014. "Madness and Possession in the Pāli Texts." *Buddhist Studies Review* 31, no. 2: 195–214.

Collins, Steven, and Justin McDaniel. 2010. "Buddhist 'Nuns' (*Mae Chi*) and the Teaching of Pāli in Contemporary Thailand." *Modern Asian Studies* 44:1373–1408.

Cook, Joanna. 2010. *Meditation in Modern Buddhism: Renunciation and Change in Thai Monastic Life*. New York: Cambridge University Press.

Crosby, Kate, and Jotika Khur-Yearn. 2010. "Poetic Dhamma and the Zare: Traditional Styles of Teaching Theravāda amongst the Shan of Northern Thailand." *Contemporary Buddhism* 11, no. 1: 1–26.

Csordas, Thomas. J. 1990. "Embodiment as a Paradigm for Anthropology." *Ethos* 18, no. 1: 5–47.

———. 1997. *The Sacred Self: A Cultural Phenomenology of Charismatic Healing*. Berkeley: University of California Press.

———. 2007. "Global Religion and the Re-enchantment of the World: The Case of the Catholic Charismatic Renewal." *Anthropological Theory* 7, no. 3: 295–314.

———. 2015. "Cultural Phenomenology and Psychiatric Illness." In *Re-visioning Psychiatry: Cultural Phenomenology, Critical Neuroscience, and Global Mental Health*, edited by Laurence J. Kirmayer, Robert Lemelson, and Constance A. Cummings, 117–40. New York: Cambridge University Press.

Dalai Lama and H. C. Cutler. 1998. *The Art of Happiness: A Handbook for Living*. New York: Riverhead Books.

D'Andrade, Roy. 2001. "A Cognitivist's View of the Units Debate in Cultural Anthropology." *Cross-Cultural Research* 35, no. 2: 242–57.

Deng, Y. Q., X. H. Liu, M. A. Rodriguez, and C. Y. Xia. 2011. "The Five Facet Mindfulness Questionnaire: Psychometric Properties of the Chinese Version." *Mindfulness* 2, no. 2: 123–28.

De Silva, Ranjani. 2004. "Reclaiming the Robe: Reviving the Bhikkhunī Order in Sri Lanka." In *Buddhist Women and Social Justice*, edited by Karma Lekshe Tsomo, 119–35. Albany: SUNY Press.

Devendra, Kusuma. 1985. *Sati in Theravada Buddhist Meditation: A Mental Therapy, Development of Mindfulness*. Colombo, Sri Lanka: Satara Prakasakayo.

Dicks, Andrew. 2015. "Enlightening the Bats: Sound and Place Making in Burmese Buddhist Practice." Theses and Dissertations, Paper 803.

Dunne, John. 2015. "Buddhist Styles of Mindfulness: A Heuristic Approach." In *Handbook of Mindfulness and Self-Regulation*, edited by B. D. Ostafin, M. D. Robinson, and B. P. Meier, 249–70. New York: Springer.

Eberhardt, Nancy. 2006. *Imagining the Course of Life: Self-Transformation in a Shan Buddhist Community*. Honolulu: University of Hawai'i Press.

Eberth, Juliane, and Peter Sedlmeier. 2012. "The Effects of Mindfulness Meditation: A Meta-analysis." *Mindfulness* 3, no. 3: 174–89

Ekman, Paul. 1992. "An Argument for Basic Emotions." *Cognition & Emotion* 6, nos. 3–4: 169–200.

Engel, David, and Jaruwan Engel. 2010. *Tort, Custom, and Karma: Globalization and Legal Consciousness in Thailand*. Stanford, CA: Stanford University Press.

Ferguson, Jane. 2015. "Who's Counting? Ethnicity, Belonging, and the National Census in Burma/Myanmar." *Bijdragen tot de Taal- Land- en Volkenkunde* (*Journal of the Humanities and Social Sciences of Theravāda Asia*) 171, no. 1: 1–28.

Ferrara, Feberico. 2015. *The Political Development of Modern Thailand*. London: Cambridge University Press.

Formoso, Bernard. 1998. "Bad Death and Malevolent Spirits among the Tai Peoples." *Anthropos* 93, H. 1./3.: 3–17.

Foucault, Michel. 1988. "Technologies of the Self." In *Technologies of the Self: A Seminar with Michel Foucault*, edited by Luther H. Martin, Huck Gutman, and Patrick H. Hutton, 16–49. Amherst: University of Massachusetts Press.

Friese, Malte, Claude Messner, and Yves Schaffner. 2012. "Mindfulness Meditation Counteracts Self-Control Depletion." *Consciousness and Cognition* 21 (February): 1016–22.

274   References

Fuhrmann, Arnika. 2009. "Nang Nak Ghost Wife: Desire, Embodiment, and Buddhist Melancholia in a Contemporary Thai Ghost Film." *Discourse* 31, no. 3: 220–47.
———. 2016. *Ghostly Desires: Queer Sexuality and Vernacular Buddhism in Contemporary Thai Cinema.* Durham, NC: Duke University Press.
Garland, E. L., S. A. Gaylord, and B. L. Fredrickson. 2011. "Positive Reappraisal Mediates the Stress-Reductive Effects of Mindfulness: An Upward Spiral Process." *Mindfulness* 2, no. 1: 59–67.
Garland, Eric, Susan Gaylord, and Jongbae Park. 2009. "The Role of Mindfulness in Positive Reappraisal." *Explore: The Journal of Science and Healing* 5, no. 1 (January): 37–44.
Geertz, Clifford. 1983. *Local Knowledge: Further Essays in Interpretive Anthropology.* New York: Basic Books.
Gell, Alfred. 2001. *The Anthropology of Time: Cultural Constructions of Temporal Maps and Images.* New York: Bloomsbury.
Gethin, Rupert. 1998. *The Foundations of Buddhism.* London: Oxford University Press.
———. 2001. *The Buddhist Path to Awakening.* Oxford: Oneworld.
Goenka, S. N. 1998. *Satipaṭṭhāna Sutta Discourses: Talks from a Course in Mahāsatipaṭṭhāna Sutta.* Condensed by Patrick Given-Wilson. Onalaska, WA: Pariyatti.
Gombrich, Richard F. (1988) 2006. *Theravāda Buddhism: A Social History from Ancient Benares to Modern Colombo.* New York: Routledge & Kegan Paul.
———. (1996) 2006. *How Buddhism Began.* New York: Routledge.
Gombrich, R. F., and G. Obeyesekere. 1988. *Buddhism Transformed: Religious Change in Sri Lanka.* Vol. 8. Delhi: Motilal Banarsidass.
Good, Darren J., Christopher J. Lyddy, Theresa M. Glomb, Joyce E. Bono, Kirk Warren Brown, Michelle K. Duffy, Ruth A. Baer, Judson A. Brewer, and Sara W. Lazar. 2016. "Contemplating Mindfulness at Work: An Integrative Review." *Journal of Management* 42, no. 1 (January): 114–42.
Greeson, Jeffrey. 2009. "Mindfulness Research Update." *Complementary Health Practice Review* 14:10–18.
Gregg, Melissa, and Gregory Seigworth. 2010. *The Affect Theory Reader.* Durham, NC: Duke University Press.
Grossman, Paul, Ludger Niemann, Stefan Schmidt, and Harald Walach. 2004. "Mindfulness-Based Stress Reduction and Health Benefits: A Meta-analysis." *Journal of Psychosomatic Research* 57, no. 1: 35–43.
Grossman, P., U. Tiefenthaler-Gilmer, A. Raysz, and U. Kesper. 2007. "Mindfulness Training as an Intervention for Fibromyalgia: Evidence of Postintervention and 3-Year Follow-Up Benefits in Well-Being." *Psychotherapy and Psychosomatics* 76:226–33.
Grossman, Paul, and Nicholas Van Dam. 2011. "Mindfulness, by Any Other Name . . . : Trials and Tribulations of *Sati* in Western Psychology and Science." *Contemporary Buddhism* 12, no. 1: 219–39.
Gyatso, Janet, ed. 1992. *In the Mirror of Memory: Reflections on Mindfulness and Remembrance in Indian and Tibetan Buddhism.* Albany: SUNY Press.
Haberkorn, Tyrell. 2011. *Revolution Interrupted: Farmers, Students, Law, and Violence in Northern Thailand.* Madison: University of Wisconsin Press.
Haidt, Jonathan. 2006. *The Happiness Hypothesis: Finding Modern Truth in Ancient Wisdom.* New York: Basic Books.

Hall, Gordon C. N., Janie J. Hong, Nolan W. S. Zane, and Oanh L. Meyer. 2011. "Culturally Competent Treatments for Asian Americans: The Relevance of Mindfulness and Acceptance-Based Psychotherapies." *Clinical Psychology: Science and Practice* 18, no. 3: 215–31.

Hallisey, Charles. 2015. *Therigatha: Poems of the First Buddhist Women.* Murti Classical Library of India. Cambridge, MA: Harvard University Press.

——. 2016. "Roads Taken and Not Taken in the Study of Theravāda Buddhism." In *Defining Buddhism(s): A Reader,* edited by Karen Derris and Natalie Gummer, 92–116. New York: Routledge.

Hamilton, Nancy, Heather Kitzman, and Stephanie Guyotte. 2006. "Enhancing Health and Emotion: Mindfulness as a Missing Link between Cognitive Therapy and Positive Psychology." *Journal of Cognitive Psychotherapy: An International Quarterly* 20, no. 2: 123–34.

Hanh, Thich Nhat. 1998. *The Heart of the Buddha's Teaching: Transforming Suffering into Peace, Joy, and Liberation.* New York: Broadway Books.

——. 2010. *Keeping the Peace: Mindfulness and Public Service.* Bangkok: DMG Books.

Hart, W. 2011. *The Art of Living: Vipassanā Meditation as Taught by S. N. Goenka.* Onalaska, WA: Pariyatti.

Harvey, P. 1990. *An Introduction to Buddhism: Teachings, History and Practices.* Cambridge: Cambridge University Press.

Hayes, S. C. 2002. "Acceptance, Mindfulness, and Science." *American Psychological Association* 9, no. 1: 101–6.

Hayes, S. C., K. Strosahl, and K. G. Wilson. 1999. *Acceptance and Commitment Therapy: An Experiential Approach to Behavior Change.* New York: Guilford.

Heeren, A., C. Douilliez, V. Peschard, L. Debrauwere, and P. Philippot. 2011. "Cross-Cultural Validity of the Five Facets Mindfulness Questionnaire: Adaptation and Validation in a French-Speaking Sample." *Revue Européenne de Psychologie Appliquée / European Review of Applied Psychology* 61, no. 3: 147–51.

Heffernan, Virginia. 2015. "The Muddied Meaning of 'Mindfulness.'" *New York Times Magazine,* April 15, 2015. http://www.nytimes.com/2015/04/19/magazine/the-muddied-meaning-of-mindfulness.html?_r=0.

Henrich, J., S. J. Heine, and A. Norenzayan. 2010. "Most People are not WEIRD." *Nature* 466, no. 29 (July 1). http://www.nature.com/nature/journal/v466/n7302/full/466029a.html?foxtrotcallback=true.

Herzfeld, Michael. 2002. "The Absence Presence: Discourses of Crypto-colonialism." *South Atlantic Quarterly* 101, no. 4: 899–926.

——. 2016. *Siege of the Spirits: Community and Polity in Bangkok.* Chicago: University of Chicago Press.

Hickman, Jacob. 2014. "Ancestral Personhood and Moral Justification." *Anthropological Theory* 14, no. 3: 317–35.

Hinton, Devon, Vuth Pich, Stefan Hofmann, and Micael Otto. 2013. "Acceptance and Mindfulness Techniques as Applied to Refugee and Ethnic Minority Populations with PTSD: Examples from 'Culturally Adapted CBT.'" *Cognitive and Behavioral Practice* 20:33–46.

Hirschkind, Charles. 2009. *The Ethical Soundscape: Cassette Sermons and Islamic Counterpublics.* New York: Columbia University Press.

Hofmann, S. G., A. T. Sawyer, A. A. Witt, and D. Oh. 2010. "The Effect of Mindfulness-Based Therapy on Anxiety and Depression: A Meta-analytic Review." *Journal of Consulting and Clinical Psychology* 78:169–83.

Hollan, D. W., and C. J. Throop, eds. 2011. *The Anthropology of Empathy: Experiencing the Lives of Others in Pacific Societies.* Vol. 1. New York: Berghahn.

Iparraguirre, Gonzala. 2016. "Time, Temporality and Cultural Rhythmics: An Anthropological Case Study." *Time & Society* 25, no. 3: 613–33.

Ives-Deliperi, V. L., M. Solms, and E. M. Meintjes. 2011. "The Neural Substrates of Mindfulness: An fMRI Investigation." *Social Neuroscience* 6:231–42.

Jackson, Peter. 1989. *Buddhism, Legitimization, and Conflict: The Political Functions of Urban Thai Buddhism.* Singapore: Institute of Theravāda Asian Studies.

——. 2002. "Offending Images: Gender and Sexual Minorities, and State Control of the Media in Thailand." In *Media Fortunes, Changing Times: ASEAN States in Transition,* edited by Russel Heng, 201–30. Singapore: Institute of Theravāda Asian Studies.

——. 2003. *Buddhadasa: Theravāda Buddhism and Modernist Reform in Thailand.* Bangkok: Silkworm.

Janakābhivaṁsa, Ashin. 2009. *Abhidhamma in Daily Life.* Corporate Body of the Buddha Educational Foundation.

Jessor, Richard, Anne Colby, and Richard Shweder. 1996. *Ethnography and Human Development: Context and Meaning in Social Inquiry.* Chicago: University of Chicago Press.

Jha, A. P., J. Krompinger, and M. J. Baime. 2007. "Mindfulness Training Modifies Subsystems of Attention." *Cognitive, Affective, & Behavioral Neuroscience* 7:109–19.

Jirattikorn, Amporn. 2016. "Buddhist Holy Man Khruba Bunchum: The Shift in a Millenarian Movement at the Thailand–Myanmar Border." *SOJOURN: Journal of Social Issues in Southeast Asia* 31, no. 2: 377–412.

Johnson, Andrew. 2014. *Ghosts of the New City: Spirits, Urbanity, and the Ruins of Progress in Chiang Mai.* Honolulu: University of Hawai'i Press.

Jordt, Ingrid. 2007. *Burma's Mass Lay Meditation Movement: Buddhism and the Cultural Construction of Power.* Vol. 115. Athens: Ohio University Press.

Jory, Patrick. 2002. "The Vessantara Jataka, Barami, and the Bodhisatta-Kings: The Origin and Spread of a Thai Concept of Power." *Crossroads: An Interdisciplinary Journal of Theravāda Asian Studies* 16, no. 2: 36–78.

——. 2016. *Thailand's Theory of Monarchy: The Vessantara Jataka and the Idea of the Perfect Man.* Albany: SUNY Press.

Jung, Carl. (1914–1930) 1999. The Red Book. W. W. Norton.

Kabat-Zinn, J. 1982. "An Outpatient Program in Behavioral Medicine for Chronic Pain Patients Based on the Practice of Mindfulness Meditation: Theoretical Considerations and Preliminary Results." *General Hospital Psychiatry* 4, no. 1: 33–47.

——. (1994) 2005. *Wherever You Go There You Are: Mindfulness Meditations in Everyday Life.* New York: Hyperion.

——. 2003. "Mindfulness-Based Interventions in Context: Past, Present, and Future." *Clinical Psychology: Science and Practice* 10:144–56.

Kahneman, Daniel. 2011. *Thinking, Fast and Slow.* New York: Macmillan.

Kahneman, D., and A. Tversky. 1979. "Prospect Theory: An Analysis of Decision under Risk." *Econometrica* 47, no. 2: 263–91.

Kawanami, Hiroko. 2013. *Renunciation and Empowerment of Buddhist Nuns in Myanmar-Burma: Building a Community of Female Faithful*. Leiden: Brill.

Keane, Webb. 2015. *Ethical Life: Its Natural and Social Histories*. Princeton, NJ: Princeton University Press.

Kemper, Steven. 2015. "Bringing Vesak to the World: Anagarika Dharmapala's Contribution." 150th Birth Anniversary of Anagarika Dharmapala International Conference, September 21–22, 2015, Department of Mass Communication, University of Kelaniya and the Ministry of Buddhasasana, Sri Lanka.

Khoury, B., T. Lecomte, G. Fortin, M. Masse, P. Therien, V. Bouchard, M. A. Chapleau, K. Paquin, and S. G. Hofmann. 2013. "Mindfulness-Based Therapy: A Comprehensive Meta-analysis." *Clinical Psychology Review* 33, no. 6: 763–71.

Kirmayer, Laurence J. 2015. "Mindfulness in Cultural Context." *Transcultural Psychiatry* 52, no. 4: 447–69.

Kitiarsa, P. 2009. "Beyond the Weberian Trails: An Essay on the Anthropology of Theravāda Asian Buddhism." *Religion Compass* 3, no. 2: 200–224.

Kondo, Dorinne. 1990. *Crafting Selves: Power, Gender, and Discourses of Identity in a Japanese Workplace*. Chicago: University of Chicago Press.

Kornfield, J., ed. 1996. *Living Dharma: Teachings of Twelve Buddhist Masters*. Boulder, CO: Shambhala.

Kuan, Tse-fu. 2008. *Mindfulness in Early Buddhism: New Approaches through Psychology and Textual Analysis of Pali, Chinese, and Sanskrit Sources*. London: Routledge.

Kusumaratne, Sagara. 2011. *The Role of Bhikkhus in Sri Lanka: A Sociological Analysis*. Colombo, Sri Lanka: Godage International.

Laidlaw, James. 2002. "For an Anthropology of Ethics and Freedom." *Journal of the Royal Anthropological Institute* 8, no. 2: 311–32.

Lambek, Michael, ed. 2010. *Ordinary Ethics: Anthropology, Language, and Action*. New York: Fordham University Press.

Langer, Ellen. (1989) 2014. *Mindfulness*. Reading, MA: Da Capo.

Langer, Rita. 2007. *Buddhist Rituals of Death and Rebirth: Contemporary Sri Lankan Practice and Its Origins*. New York: Routledge.

Leksakun, Santi. 2014. "Puuraisiang nainatanakong gayatri chakravorty Spivak" [The subaltern in the perspective of Gayatri Chakravorty Spivak]. MA thesis, Chiang Mai University, Thailand.

Lindahl, Jared R., N. E. Fisher, D. J. Cooper, R. K. Rosen, and W. B. Britton. 2017. "The Varieties of Contemplative Experience: A Mixed-Methods Study of Meditation-Related Challenges in Western Buddhists." *PLOS ONE* 12, no. 5, e0176239.

Lindsay, Emily K., and J. David Creswell. 2015. "Back to the Basics: How Attention Monitoring and Acceptance Stimulate Positive Growth." *Psychological Inquiry* 26, no. 4: 343–48.

Li tamataro, Paw. n.d. *Anapan satpawonmai*. Wat Asokara. (In Thai.)

Long Paw Tian Jitisuko. 1984. *Detuapuurusuktua*. Bangkok: Jiaktannukunkanprim Press. (In Thai.)

Loos, Tamara. L. 2006. *Subject Siam: Family, Law, and Colonial Modernity in Thailand*. Ithaca, NY: Cornell University Press.

Lopez, Donald. S. 2012. *The Scientific Buddha: His Short and Happy Life*. New Haven, CT: Yale University Press.

Luhrmann, T. M. 2012. *When God Talks Back: Understanding the American Evangelical Relationship with God*. New York: Alfred A. Knopf.

———. Forthcoming. "Knowing God." *Cambridge Journal of Anthropology*.

Mageo, Jeannette. 2003. *Dreaming and the Self: New Perspectives on Subjectivity, Identity, and Emotion*. Albany: SUNY Press.

———. 2011. "Empathy and 'as-if' Attachment in Samoa." In *The Anthropology of Empathy: Experiencing the Lives of Others in Pacific Societies*, edited by Douglas Hollan and Jason Throop, 69–93. New York: Berghahn.

Mahāsī Sayādaw. 1955. "Lessons of Practical Basic Exercises in Satipaṭṭhāna Vipassanā Meditation" by Mahāsī Sayādaw, published at the request of the Lanka Vipassanā Society by the Lanka Bauddha Mendalaya.

———. 1958. *Discourse on the Basic Practice of the Satipaṭṭhāna Vipassanā*. Rangoon: Burma Art.

———. 1979. *Satipaṭṭhāna Vipassanā Meditation: Criticisms and Replies*. Rangoon: Buddha Sasana Nuggaha.

Mahawira, Phra Kawaro, trans. 1988 [2518]. *Mahasatipatitan Sii* [The four foundations of mindfulness]. Bangkok: Borisat yello gan pim. (In Thai.)

Mahmood, Saba. 2005. *Politics of Piety: The Islamic Revival and the Feminist Subject*. Princeton, NJ: Princeton University Press.

Mānop 'Uppasamō. 2010 [2553]. *Tang sati dai čhai phon thuk satipatthān 4*. [Breaking mindfulness will cause bad results: The four foundations of mindfulness]. Krung Thēp Mahā Nakhōn: Samnakphim 'Amarin Thamma. (In Thai.)

Marchland, William. 2012. "Mindfulness-Based Stress Reduction, Mindfulness-Based Cognitive Therapy, and Zen Meditation for Depression, Anxiety, Pain, and Psychological Distress." *Journal of Psychiatric Practice* 18, no. 4 (July): 233–52.

Mark, J., G. Williams, and J. Kabat-Zinn. 2011. "Mindfulness: Diverse Perspectives on Its Meaning, Origins, and Multiple Applications at the Intersection of Science and Dharma." *Contemporary Buddhism* 12, no. 1: 1–18.

Markus, Hazel, and Shinobu Kitayama. 1991. "Culture and the Self." *Psychological Review* 98, no. 2: 224.

Mauss, Marcel. 1934. "Les techniques du corps." *Journal de Psychologie*. Reprinted in *Sociologie et Anthropologie* 32, no. 1: 3–4.

McDaniel, Justin. 2006. "Buddhism in Thailand." In *Buddhism in World Cultures: Comparative Perspectives*, edited by Steven Berkwitz, 101–28. Santa Barbara, CA: ABC-CLIO.

———. 2008. *Gathering Leaves and Lifting Words: Histories of Buddhist Monastic Education in Laos and Thailand*. Seattle: University of Washington Press.

———. 2011. *The Lovelorn Ghost and the Magical Monk: Practicing Buddhism in Modern Thailand*. New York: Columbia University Press.

McMahan, David, and Erik Braun, eds. 2017. *Meditation, Buddhism, and Science*. New York: Oxford University Press.

Mendelson, E. Michael. 1975. *Sangha and State in Burma: A Study of Monastic Sectarianism and Leadership*. Ithaca, NY: Cornell University Press.

Michal, Matthias, Manfred E. Beutel, Jochen Jordan, Michael Zimmerman, Susanne Wolters, and Thomas Heidenreich. 2007. "Depersonalization, Mindfulness, and Childhood Trauma." *Journal of Nervous and Mental Disease* 195, no. 8 (August 2007): 693–96.

Ministry of Buddhist Affairs, Sri Lanka. *Breathing Meditation, Grade 7*. 2013.

Ministry of Education. 2003. *Nak Tham' Chan Tri: Nangsue Buranakan Phanmai* [New integrated book for level three]. Bangkok: Khanachan Samnak Phim Liangchiang. (In Thai.)

Mizuno, K. (1982) 1989. Buddhist Sutras: Origin, *Development*, Transmission. Tokyo: Kosei.

Modinos, G., J. Ormel, and A. Aleman. 2010. "Individual Differences in Dispositional Mindfulness and Brain Activity Involved in Reappraisal of Emotion." *Social Cognitive and Affective Neuroscience* 5:369–77.

Mon, Mehm Tin. 1995. *Buddha Abhidhamma: Ultimate Science*. Yangon, Myanmar: Mehm Tay Zar Mon.

Moore, A., T. Gruber, J. Derose, and P. Malinowski. 2012. "Regular, Brief Mindfulness Meditation Practice Improves Electrophysiological Markers of Attentional Control." *Frontiers in Human Neuroscience* 6:1–15.

Moore, Adam, and Peter Malinowski. 2009. "Meditation, Mindfulness and Cognitive Flexibility." *Consciousness and Cognition* 18:176–86.

Morris, Rosalind. 2000. *In the Place of Origins: Modernity and Its Mediums in Northern Thailand*. Durham, NC: Duke University Press.

Munn, Nancy. 1992. "The Cultural Anthropology of Time: A Critical Essay." *Annual Review of Anthropology* 21:93–123.

Murray, Greg. 2015. "Do I Have a Self? (and Other Useful Questions from Buddhist Mindfulness)." *Australian and New Zealand Journal of Psychiatry* 49, no. 7: 593–94.

Naiwichit mantaiwanji. 1958. *Wisutimonoknipanidanmahasatipatan*. The Sayings of Phra techita abitham Makati tham kathi dhammajeriya (a Burmese monk).

Ñāṇamoli, Bhikkhu. 1964. *Mindfulness of Breathing: Buddhist Texts from the Pali Canon and Commentaries*. Kandy, Sri Lanka: Buddhist Publication Society.

———. (1972) 2008. *A Thinker's Notebook: Posthumous Papers of a Buddhist Monk*. Compiled by Nyanaponika Thera. Kandy, Sri Lanka: Buddhist Publication Society.

———, trans. 1995. *The Middle Length Discourses of the Buddha: A Translation of the Majjhima Nikaya (Teachings of the Buddha)*. Somerville, MA: Wisdom Publications.

Nauriyal, D. K., Michael S. Drummond, and Y. B. Lal, eds. 2006. *Buddhist Thought and Applied Psychological Research: Transcending the Boundaries*. New York: Routledge.

Neff, Kristin D., and Christopher K. Germer. 2013. "A Pilot Study and Randomized Controlled Trial of the Mindful Self-Compassion Program." *Journal of Clinical Psychology* 69, no. 1: 28–44.

Neubert, Frank. 2014. "Goenka." *Oxford Bibliographies Online*. http://www. oxfordbibliographies.com/view/document/obo-9780195393521/obo-9780195393521-0200.xml.

Nyanaponika, N. T. 1962. *The Heart of Buddhist Meditation*. London: Rider.

———. 1998. *Abhidhamma Studies: Buddhist Explorations of Consciousness and Time*. 4th ed. Boston: Wisdom.

Obeyesekere, Gananath. 1985. "Depression and Buddhism and the Work of Culture in Sri Lanka." In *Culture and Depression: Studies in the Anthropology and Cross-Cultural Psychiatry of Affect and Disorder*, edited by Arthur Kleinman and Byron J. Good, 134–52. Berkeley: University of California Press.

———. 1990. *The Work of Culture: Symbolic Transformation in Psychoanalysis and Anthropology*. Chicago: University of Chicago Press.

———. 2014. *Medusa's Hair: An Essay on Personal Symbols and Religious Experience*. Chicago: University of Chicago Press.

Pagis, M. 2009. "Embodied Self-Reflexivity." *Social Psychology Quarterly* 72:265–83.

Pandian, Anand. 2012. "The Time of Anthropology: Notes from a Field of Contemporary Experience." *Cultural Anthropology* 27, no. 4: 547–71.

Panyavduddho, trans. 2011. "Four Foundations of Mindfulness: The Buddha's Discourse in Romanized Pāli with English Translation." Wat Rai-khing, Am. Samphran, Nakhonpathom 73210, Thailand.

Patton, Tom. 2012. "In Pursuit of the Sorcerer's Power: Sacred Diagrams as Technologies of Potency." *Contemporary Buddhism* 13:2.

———. 2015. "The Wizard King's Granddaughters: Burmese Buddhist Female Mediums, Healers, and Dreamers." *Journal of the American Academy of Religion* 84, no. 2: 430–65.

Payutto, Phra Prayudh. (1971) 1985. *Sammāsati*. Bangkok: Rongpim jakranakumpim. (In Thai.)

———. 1992. *Dependent Origination: The Buddhist Law of Conditionality*. Translated by Bruce Evans. Bangkok: Buddhadhamma Foundation.

Praissman, S. 2008. "Mindfulness-Based Stress Reduction: A Literature Review and Clinician's Guide." *Journal of the American Academy of Nurse Practitioners* 20:212–16.

Prawet wai. 1984. *Witigesengsansut* [Commentary on the teaching of Phra Ajarn Kamkien suwinno]. Bangkok: Klum Suksaleh Patipat Tham Press. (In Thai.)

Prem worapom (aka pasanajito), Phra. 1977. "Satipatan Sii" [The four foundations of mindfulness]. Chiang Rai, Thammthan. (In Thai.)

Punnaji Thero, Hingulwala. 2017. "A Study of the Practice of Recollections (Anussati) in Buddhist Meditation." PhD diss., Huafan University.

Rahula, Walpola. 1974. *What the Buddha Taught*. New York: Grove.

Reynolds, Craig. 1991. *National Identity and Its Defenders, Thailand, 1939–1989*. Melbourne: Center of Southeast Asian Studies, Monash University.

Rhys Davids, T. W. 1881. *Buddhist Suttas*. Oxford: Clarendon.

Ringel, Felix. 2016. "Beyond Temporality: Notes on the Anthropology of Time from a Shrinking Fieldsite." *Anthropological Theory* 16, no. 4: 390–412.

Robbins, Joel. 2004. "The Globalization of Pentecostal and Charismatic Christianity." *Annual Review of Anthropology* 33:117–43.

Robbins, Joel, Julia Cassaniti, and T. M. Luhrmann. 2011. "The Constitution of Mind: What's in a Mind? Interiority and Boundedness." *Suomen Antropologi: Journal of the Finnish Anthropological Society* 36, no. 4: 15–20.

Roccasalvo, J. 1981. "The Thai Practice of Psychiatry and the Doctrine of Anattā." *Review of Existential Psychology and Psychiatry* 18:168–215.

Rodin, Judith, and Ellen Langer. 1976. "The Effect of Choice and Enhanced Personal Responsibility for the Aged: A Field Experiment in an Institutional Setting." *Journal of Personality and Social Psychology* 34, no. 2: 191–98.

——. 1977. "Long-Term Effects of a Control-Relevant Intervention with the Institutionalized Aged." *Journal of Personality and Social Psychology* 35, no. 12: 897.

Roemer, L., S. M. Orsillo, and K. Salters-Pedneault. 2008. "Efficacy of an Acceptance-Based Behavior Therapy for Generalized Anxiety Disorder: Evaluation in a Randomized Controlled Trial." *Journal of Consulting and Clinical Psychology* 76:1083–89.

Ryan, Richard M., Veronika Huta, and Edward L. Deci. 2008. "Living Well: A Self-Determination Theory Perspective on Eudaimonia." *Journal of Happiness Studies* 9, no. 1: 139–70.

Salem-Gervais, Nicolas, and Rosalie Metro. 2012. "A Textbook Case of Nation-Building: The Evolution of History Curricula in Myanmar." *Journal of Burma Studies* 16, no. 1: 27–78.

Samaranayake, Sajeeva. 2010. "Realizing the True Self for Nation Building." In *Challenges for Nation Building: Priorities for Sustainability and Inclusivity*, edited by Gnana Moonesinghe, 321–35. Colombo, Sri Lanka: Shramaya.

Samuels, Jeffrey. 2010. *Attracting the Heart: Social Relations and the Aesthetics of Emotion in Sri Lankan Monastic Culture.* Honolulu: University of Hawai'i Press.

Sauer, Sebastian, Harald Walsch, Stefan Schmidt, Thilo Hinterberger, Siobhan Lynch, Arndt Büssing, and Niko Kohls. 2012. "Assessment of Mindfulness: Review on State of the Art." *Mindfulness* 4, no. 1: 3–17.

Schedneck, Brooke. 2015. *Thailand's International Meditation Centers: Tourism and the Global Commodification of Religious Practices.* New York: Routledge.

Sedgwick, Eve Kosofsky. 2003. *Touching Feeling: Affect, Pedagogy, Performativity.* Durham, NC: Duke University Press.

Seeger, Martin. 2006. "The Bhikkhuni-Ordination Controversy in Thailand." *Journal of the International Association of Buddhist Studies* 29, no. 1: 155–83.

——. Forthcoming. [About *bhikkhunī*]. Chiang Mai, Thailand: Silkworm.

Segal, Z., M. Williams, and J. Teasdale. 2001. *Mindfulness-Based Cognitive Therapy for Depression: A New Approach to Preventing Relapse.* New York: Guilford.

Seligman, Rebecca, and Laurence Kirmayer. 2008. "Dissociative Experience and Cultural Neuroscience: Narrative, Metaphor and Mechanism." *Culture, Medicine and Psychiatry* 32, no. 1: 31–64.

Shulman, E. 2010. "The Sati-paṭṭhāna-sutta on Mindfulness, Memory, and Liberation." *History of Religions* 49:393–420.

——. 2016. *Rethinking the Buddha: Early Buddhist Philosophy as Meditative Perception.* New York: Cambridge University Press.

Shweder, Richard. 1994. "'You're Not Sick, You're Just in Love': Emotion as an Interpretive System." In *The Nature of Emotion*, edited by P. Ekman and R. Davidson, 32–44. Oxford: Oxford University Press.

———. 1999. "Why Cultural Psychology?" *Ethos* 27, no. 1: 62–73.

———. 2003. *Why Do Men Barbecue? Recipes for Cultural Psychology*. Cambridge, MA: Harvard University Press.

———. 2014. "The Tower of Appraisals: Trying to Make Sense of the One Big Thing." *Emotion Review* 6, no. 4: 1–3.

Shweder, Richard A., and Edmund J. Bourne. 1984. "Does the Concept of the Person Vary Cross-Culturally?" In *Culture Theory: Essays on Mind, Self, and Emotion*, edited by R. A. Shweder and R. A. LeVine, 158–99. Cambridge: Cambridge University Press.

Silanandabhivumsa. 1982. *The Venerable Mahasi Sayadaw Biography*. Abridged ed. Part 1. Rangoon: Buddhasana Nuggaha.

Silpakit, Orawan, Chatchawan Silpakit, and Pattaraphorn Wisajun. 2011. "The Validity of Philadelphia Mindfulness Scale Thai Version." *Journal of Mental Health of Thailand* 19, no. 3: 140–47. (In Thai.)

Skilling, Peter, Jason Carbine, Claudio Ciuzza, and Santi Pakdeekham, eds. 2012. *How Theravāda Is Theravāda? Exploring Buddhist Identities*. Chiang Mai, Thailand: Silkworm.

Soma Thera. 1941. *Introduction to the Sati-paṭṭhāna-sutta*. Dodanduwa, Sri Lanka: Island Hermitage.

Stonington, Scott. Forthcoming. *Spirit Ambulance: End-of-Life Care in Thailand*. Ithaca, NY: Cornell University Press.

———. 2016. "Anti-mindfulness: Competing Figures of Lay and Ascetic Coping for Chronic Pain in Thailand." Thai Studies Seminar Series, Harvard University, Cambridge, MA, March 24.

Strauss, Claudia, and Naomi Quinn. 1997. *A Cognitive Theory of Cultural Meaning*. Cambridge: Cambridge University Press.

Strong, John. 2011. "When Are Miracles Okay? Buddhist Rules against Displays of Supernatural Powers." Talk given at the Ho Center for Buddhist Studies, Stanford University, February 17.

Stuart, Daniel. Forthcoming. "Insight Transformed: Coming to Terms with Mindfulness in South Asian and Global Frames." *Religions of South Asia*.

Sugiura, Y., A. Sato, Y. Ito, and H. Murakami. 2012. "Development and Validation of the Japanese Version of the Five Facet Mindfulness Questionnaire." *Mindfulness* 3, no. 2: 85–94.

Susati metajukuru, Phra. n.d. *Pua pijaranakhwamta* [Analysis for dying]. Bangkok: Sat tung pai jangwat chompong At thammasantaamkat Press. (In Thai.)

Swearer, Donald. 1989. *Me and Mine: Selected Essays of Bhikkhu Buddhadasa*. Albany: SUNY Press.

Tambiah, Stanley Jeyaraja. 1976. *World Conqueror and World Renouncer: A Study of Buddhism and Polity in Thailand against a Historical Background*. Cambridge: Cambridge University Press.

———. 1984. *The Buddhist Saints of the Forest and the Cult of Amulets: A Study in Charisma, Hagiography, Sectarianism, and Millennial Buddhism*. Cambridge: Cambridge University Press.

Tannenbaum, Nicola. 1995. *Who Can Compete against the World? Power-Protection and Buddhism in Shan Worldview.* Ann Arbor, MI: Association for Asian Studies.

Tayaluh, Bhikksu. 1985. *Satimakabsasatrakongchiwit* [Sati: The wisdom of life]. Jangwat panga, Bangkok: Songchai gan pim Press. (In Thai.)

Tenney, Matt, and Tim Gard. 2016. *The Mindfulness Edge: How to Rewire Your Brain for Leadership and Personal Excellence without Adding to Your Schedule.* Hoboken, NJ: Wiley.

Terweil, Jan. 1978. "The Tais and Their Belief in Khwans." *South East Asian Review* 5, no. 1: 1–16.

Thammaraksa, Phra. 1987 [2530]. *Sati.* Publ lungseng gan pim bangkok. Thammthan (published locally in Thailand, handed out for free). (In Thai.)

Thanissaro Bhikkhu, trans. 2010. "Satipatthana Sutta: Frames of Reference." MN10. http://www.accesstoinsight.org/tipitaka/mn/mn.010.than.html.

———. 2011a. "One Tool among Many: The Place of Vipassana in Buddhist Practice." In *Access to Insight.* Legacy ed. http://www.accesstoinsight.org/lib/authors/thanissaro/onetool.html.

———. 2011b "The Path of Concentration and Mindfulness." In *Access to Insight.* Legacy ed. http://www.accesstoinsight.org/lib/authors/thanissaro/concmind.html.

Tipiṭaka. Chulalongkon Rachawitthayalai edition. www.geocities.wsu/tmchote/tpd-mcu/).

Tiyavanich, Kamala. 1997. *Forest Recollections: Wandering Monks in Twentieth-Century Thailand.* Honolulu: University of Hawai'i Press.

Tsai, Jeanne L., B. Koopmann-Holm, C. Ochs, and M. Miyazaki. 2013. "The Religious Shaping of Emotion: Implications of Affect Valuation Theory." In Handbook of the Psychology of Religion and Spirituality, 2nd ed., edited by R. Paloutzian and C. Park, 274–91. New York: Guilford.

Tsai, Jeanne L., F. F. Miao, and E. Seppala. 2007. "Good Feelings in Christianity and Buddhism: Religious Differences in Ideal Affect." *Personality and Social Psychology Bulletin* 33:409–21.

Tversky, Amos, and Daniel Kahneman. 1974. "Judgment under Uncertainty: Heuristics and Biases." *Science* 185, no. 4157: 1124–31.

Ünaldi, S. 2016. *Working towards the Monarchy: The Politics of Space in Downtown Bangkok.* Honolulu: University of Hawai'i Press.

Veidlinger, Daniel. 2006. *Spreading the Dhamma: Writing, Orality, and Textual Transmission in Buddhist Northern Thailand.* Honolulu: University of Hawai'i Press. Theravāda Asian edition, 2007. Chiang Mai, Thailand: Silkworm.

Wallace, B. A., and S. L. Shapiro. 2006. "Mental Balance and Well-Being: Building Bridges between Buddhism and Western Psychology." *American Psychologist* 61:690–701.

Weber, Max. (1930) 2002. *The Protestant Ethic and the "Spirit" of Capitalism and Other Writings.* New York: Penguin.

Weiner, Eric. 2008. *The Geography of Bliss: One Grump's Search for the Happiest Places on Earth.* New York: Twelve Books.

Wickremeratne, Swarna. 2006. *Buddha in Sri Lanka: Remembered Yesterdays.* Albany: SUNY Press.

Wijeratne, R. P., and Rupert Gethin. 2002. *Summary of the Topics of Abhidhamma and Exposition of the Topics of Abhidhamma.* Oxford: Pāli Text Society.

Williams, John, and Lidia Zylowska. 2009. *Mindfulness Bibliography*. Mindful Awareness Research Center, UCLA Semel Institute. http://marc.ucla.edu/body.cfm?id=38&oTopID=38.

Wilson, Jeff. 2013. *Mindful America: Meditation and the Mutual Transformation of Buddhism and American Culture*. New York: Oxford University Press.

Winichakul, Thongchai. 1994. *Siam Mapped: A History of the Geo-body of a Nation*. Honolulu: University of Hawai'i Press.

Wyatt, David. K. 2003. *Thailand: A Short History*. New Haven, CT: Yale University Press.

Zeamer, Emily. 2008. "Buddhism 'Updated': Technology, Technique, and Moral Imagination in Urban Thailand." PhD diss., Harvard University.

Zigon, Jarrett. 2007. "Moral Breakdown and the Ethical Demand: A Theoretical Framework for an Anthropology of Moralities." *Anthropological Theory* 7, no. 131: 131–50.

INDEX

Page numbers followed by letters *f* and *t* refer to figures and tables, respectively.

on, 152–53, 158–63, 166–82; as
conventional vs. ultimate truth,
116–17; culture and, ix, 17, 18, 239,
246, 248–50; definitions of, vii, 16,
27–28, 45–46, 54, 208, 209, 219,
228, 234, 236, 254n2; in everyday
life in Theravāda Asia, 3, 7, 10, 53,
112–17, 120–24, 214–15, 220–21;
Four Foundations of, 39–40, 62, 102,
132, 166, 254n7; as global concept,
viii, 147, 218, 242, 247, 248; and
impermanence/change, recognition
of, 18*t*, 50, 76, 106, 107, 131–32,
183, 190, 192, 214, 245; inclusiveness
of, 231–32; loss of, Buddhadasa on,
85; mental illness in absence of, 2,
3–4, 114–15, 130, 143, 145, 181–87;
monastic precepts and, 29, 30; monks
and practice of, 32–33, 34, 35, 41–42,
53; in multireligious society, 226, 228,
229–31; *Navakovada* on, 38–43, 46;
pluralism in, 234, 246, 248; practical
benefits of, 214–15; right *(sammā sati)*,
30, 41, 102, 191, 207, 208, 209–10;
sati and, relationship of, 2, 233–34;
social quality of, 17*t*, 124; Sri Lankan
perspectives on, 196, 200, 206–15;
Thai laypeople on, viii, 5–6, 59–60,
62–63, 112–17, 122–24, 133–34,
141; Thai monks on, 25, 26, 27, 31,
32–33, 53–58, 101–3; as therapeutic
intervention, 2–3, 4, 145–48, 186,
247–48; Tipiṭaka on, 33–34; Western
vs. Theravāda Asian understanding
of, viii–x, 16–18, 17*t*–18*t*, 228,
232–33, 234, 235–50, 236–45, 261n3;
wrong *(micchā sati)*, 191, 206, 207.
See also education about mindfulness;
meditation, and mindfulness; TAPES
of mindfulness
Mindfulness-Based Stress Reduction,
vii; in Sri Lanka, 224, 227, 228; in
Thailand, 4
mindfulness scales, 51, 194, 256n16
Mogoke, 160, 162

Moh, xii, 165, 180
monasteries, Buddhist: in Burma,
160–61, 161*f*; choice of, "grocery
store" theory of, 44, 68, 103; gender
inequality in, 90–91, 98, 206; offerings
at, 30–31; power relations in, 149; in
Sri Lanka, 198, 201, 202–4, 203*f*, 205;
in Thailand, 27, 36, 43–44, 253n1;
white strings in, 135*f*. *See also specific
monasteries*
monastic ordination: motivation for, 26,
98–99; temporary, 26, 172; women
and, 253n1
Mongkut (Thai king), 255n15
monks, Buddhist: background of, 26,
99–100, 113; in Burma, 151, 165–66,
204; in Burma, perspectives on
mindfulness, 166–73; daily schedule of,
30–31; on ghosts, reluctance to discuss,
139–40; at large monasteries, 44–45;
on meditation and mindfulness, 25, 26,
31, 32–33, 35, 49, 51, 56–58, 66, 105;
meditation practiced by, 32–33, 34,
35, 57–58, 104; mindfulness education
for, 37–43; novice, 25, 29, 36–37, 52*f*;
precepts followed by, 28–30; rituals
performed in community, 36*f*; as source
of information on mindfulness, 9, 11,
12, 29–30, 35; in Sri Lanka, 196, 202,
204, 217; in Sri Lanka, perspectives
on mindfulness, 206–15; in Thailand,
23–24, 31, 32*f*, 98, 151, 204; in
Thailand, perspectives on mindfulness,
25, 26, 31, 32–33, 53–58, 101–3;
wandering (forest/*thudong*), 23–24,
31, 32*f*, 98, 151, 204. *See also* female
monastics; monastic ordination
Mon Winitkhanatorn, Phra, 44–51,
57–58, 63, 107, 108
Moon, 201
moral goodness, and mindfulness, 18*t*;
Burmese perspectives on, 167, 170,
179, 191–92; Sri Lankan perspectives
on, 206; Thai perspectives on, 56, 100,
108, 207

wisdom: in Eightfold Path of Buddhism, 30; monastic precepts and, 29; morality and, 56
women: in Burmese monasteries, 172; in Sri Lankan monasteries, 196, 204, 205–6, 253n1; in Thai monasteries, 87, 90–91, 95, 98–99, 103, 253n1
wrong mindfulness *(micchā sati)*, 191, 206, 207

Yangon (Rangoon), Burma, 160
Yekyi village, Burma, 12*t*
yoga: limitations in teaching mindfulness, 233; in meditation retreat, 82–83
yup no phong no (walking meditation), 6, 86, 88, 89

Zeamer, Emily, 253n1

www.ingramcontent.com/pod-product-compliance
Lightning Source LLC
Chambersburg PA
CBHW030642270326
41929CB00007B/165